Lecture Notes of the Institute
for Computer Sciences, Social Informatics
and Telecommunications Engineering   8

Matthew Sorell (Ed.)

Forensics in Telecommunications, Information and Multimedia

Second International Conference, e-Forensics 2009
Adelaide, Australia, January 19-21, 2009
Revised Selected Papers

 Springer

Volume Editor

Matthew Sorell
School of Electrical and Electronic Engineering
The University of Adelaide, SA 5005, Australia
E-mail: matthew.sorell@adelaide.edu.au

Library of Congress Control Number: Applied for

CR Subject Classification (1998): K.5, K.4, I.5, D.4.6, K.6.5

ISSN   1867-8211
ISBN-10   3-642-02311-8 Springer Berlin Heidelberg New York
ISBN-13   978-3-642-02311-8 Springer Berlin Heidelberg New York

springer.com

© Springer-Verlag Berlin Heidelberg 2009
Printed in Germany

Typesetting: Camera-ready by author, data conversion by Scientific Publishing Services, Chennai, India
Printed on acid-free paper   SPIN: 12682874   06/3180   5 4 3 2 1 0

Preface

The Second International Conference on Forensic Applications and Techniques in Telecommunications, Information and Multimedia (e-Forensics 2009) took place in Adelaide, South Australia during January 19-21, 2009, at the Australian National Wine Centre, University of Adelaide.

In addition to the peer-reviewed academic papers presented in this volume, the conference featured a significant number of plenary contributions from recognized national and international leaders in digital forensic investigation.

Keynote speaker Andy Jones, head of security research at British Telecom, outlined the emerging challenges of investigation as new devices enter the market. These include the impact of solid-state memory, ultra-portable devices, and distributed storage – also known as cloud computing.

The plenary session on Digital Forensics Practice included Troy O'Malley, Queensland Police Service, who outlined the paperless case file system now in use in Queensland, noting that efficiency and efficacy gains in using the system have now meant that police can arrive at a suspect's home before the suspect! Joseph Razik, representing Patrick Perrot of the Institut de Recherche Criminelle de la Gendarmerie Nationale, France, summarized research activities in speech, image, video and multimedia at the IRCGN.

The plenary session on The Interaction Between Technology and Law brought a legal perspective to the technological challenges of digital forensic investigation. Glenn Dardick put the case for anti-forensics training; Nigel Carson of Ferrier Hodgson presented the perspective of an experienced commercial investigator, and Anna Davey of Forensic Foundations provided a detailed understanding of the admissibility of digital evidence.

That the focus of this year's conference had shifted to the legal, rather than the deeply technical, perspective was clear, enhanced in no small part by the incorporation of the International Workshop on e-Forensics Law in the program. Hon Jon Mansfield of the Federal Court of Australia presided over the workshop, which featured both plenary and peer-reviewed papers. Joe Cannataci, one of the architects of the Cybercrime Convention, presented his views on the convention and the direction of international law concerning crime and evidence in the digital domain. Gary Edmond raised some critical questions concerning evidence obtained from and through emerging technologies, and Michael Davis and Alice Sedsman raised some legal concerns around cloud computing. Glenn Dardick, presenting his workshop paper out of session, noted the effect of privacy and privilege on e-Discovery. The workshop academic session featured papers on digital identity, surveillance and data protection in virtual environments, and international legal compliance.

The 21 technical papers in this volume were presented in six technical sessions, including one poster session, covering voice and telephony, image source identification and authentication, investigative practice, and applications including surveillance.

The Brian Playford Memorial Award for Best Paper was presented to Irene Amerini and co-authors for her paper, "Distinguishing Between Camera and Scanned Images by Means of Frequency Analyis," after consultation with the Technical Program Committee Chair, Chang-Tsun Li, and members of the conference Steering Committee. Brian was one of the quiet behind-the-scenes organizers of the conference in 2008 and 2009 who was killed under tragic circumstances while on holiday in October 2008 in Slovenia.

The conference closed with a lively panel discussion, chaired by Andy Jones, addressing strategic priorities in digital forensics research. From that discussion, it is clear that the increasing sophistication of technologies, and the users of those technologies, is leaving investigators, lawmakers and the legal system scrambling to keep up.

Matthew Sorell

Organization

Steering Committee Chair

Imrich Chlamtac (Chair)	CREATE-NET, Italy
Peter Ramsey	University of Adelaide, Australia
Jill Slay	University of South Australia
Richard Leary	Forensic Pathways Ltd, UK
Gale Spring	RMIT University, Australia

Conference General Chair

Matthew Sorell   University of Adelaide, Australia

Local Chair

Peter Ramsey   University of Adelaide, Australia

Publicity Chair

Gale Spring   RMIT University, Australia

Conference Coordinator

Tibor Kovacs   ICST

Technical Program Chair

Chang-Tsun Li   University of Warwick, UK

Technical Program Committee

Ahmed Bouridane	Queen's University Belfast, UK
Anthony TS Ho	University of Surrey, UK
Barry Blundell	South Australia Police, Australia
Carole Chaski	Institute for Linguistic Evidence, USA
Che-Yen Wen	Central Police University, Taiwan
Der-Chyuan Lou	National Defense University, Taiwan
Francois Cayre	GIPSA-Lab / INPG, Domaine Universitaire, France
Hae Yong Kim	Universidade de Sao Paulo, Brazil
Henrik Legind Larsen	Aalborg University, Denmark

Hongxia Jin	IBM Almaden Research Center, USA
Huidong Jin	Nationa ICT Australia
Javier Garcia Villalba	Complutense University of Madrid, Spain
Jianying Zhou	Institute of Infocomm Research, Singapore
Jordi Forne	Technical University of Catalonia, Spain
Kostas Anagnostakis	Institute for Infocomm Research, Singapore
M. L. Dennis Wong	Swinburne University of Technology, Malaysia
Pavel Gladyshev	University College Dublin, Ireland
Peter Stephenson	Norwich University, USA
Philip Turner	QinetiQ and Oxford Brookes University, UK
Raymond Hsieh	California University of Pennsylvania, USA
Richard Mislan	Purdue University, USA
Roberto Caldelli	Universita' degli Studi Firenze, Italy
Simson Garfingel	US Naval Postgraduate School and Harvard University, USA
Svein Yngvar Willassen	Norwegian University of Science and Technology
Weiqi Yan	Queen's University Belfast, UK
Xingming Sun	University of Warwick, Uk
Yongjian Hu	Korea Advanced Institute of Science and Technology, Korea
Zeno Geradts	The Netherlands Forensic Institute
Indrajit Ray	Colorado State University, USA
Damien Sauveron	Universite de Limoges, France
Michael Cohen	Australian Federal Police, Australia
Jeng-Shyang Pan	National Kaohsiung University of Applied Sciences, Taiwan
Lam-For Kwok	City University of Hong Kong, Hong Kong
Jung-Shian Li	National Cheng Kung University, Taiwan
Mark Pollitt	University of Central Florida, USA
Geyong Min	University of Bradford, UK
Theodore Tryfonas	University of Glamorgan, UK
Helen Trehame	University of Surrey, U
Andre Aarnes	Norwegian University of Science and Technology
Jessica Fridrich	SUNY Binghampton, USA

Workshop Chair

Nigel Wilson	Bar Chambers, Adelaide, South Australia, and Law School, University of Adelaide

Workshop Programme Committee

Robert Chalmers	Adelaide Research and Innovation Pty Ltd, Australia
Jean-Pierre du Plessis	Ferrier Hodgson, Australia

Table of Contents

International Workshop on e-Forensics Law

A Novel Handwritten Letter Recognizer Using Enhanced Evolutionary Neural Network

Fariborz Mahmoudi, Mohsen Mirzashaeri, Ehsan Shahamatnia, and Saed Faridnia

Electrical and Computer Engineering Department,
Islamic Azad University, Qazvin Branch, Iran
{Mahmoudi,Mirzashaeri,E.Shahamatnia,SFaridnia}@QazvinIAU.ac.ir

Abstract. This paper introduces a novel design for handwritten letter recognition by employing a hybrid back-propagation neural network with an enhanced evolutionary algorithm. Feeding the neural network consists of a new approach which is invariant to translation, rotation, and scaling of input letters. Evolutionary algorithm is used for the global search of the search space and the back-propagation algorithm is used for the local search. The results have been computed by implementing this approach for recognizing 26 English capital letters in the handwritings of different people. The computational results show that the neural network reaches very satisfying results with relatively scarce input data and a promising performance improvement in convergence of the hybrid evolutionary back-propagation algorithms is exhibited.

Keywords: Handwritten Character Recognition, Neural Network, Hybrid Evolutionary Algorithm, EANN.

1 Introduction

Neural networks are powerful tools in machine learning which have been widely used for soft computing. The very first artificial neuron was introduced in 1943 by Warren McCulloch, a neurophysiologist, and Walter Pits, a logician, but due to the technical barriers no further work was made then. Since that time this topic has been attracted numerous of researchers and enormous improvements have been made to the subject. Artificial neural networks, ANN in short, are data processing techniques inspired from biological neurotic systems ambitiously aiming to model the brain. ANNs are popular within artificial intelligence applications such as function approximation, regression analysis, time series prediction and modeling, data processing, filtering and clustering, classification, pattern and sequence recognition, medical diagnosis, financial applications, data mining and achieving fine tuning parameters e.g. in fault-tolerant stream processing where balancing the trade off between consistency and availability is crucial [1, 2, 3, 4].

Within machine vision and image processing field, ANNs have been mostly applied to classification and pattern recognition [5]. Their special characteristics in being highly adaptive and learning make them suitable for comparing data sets and extracting patterns. Pattern recognition with neural networks includes a wide range

M. Sorell (Ed.): e-Forensics 2009, LNICST 8, pp. 1 – 9, 2009.

from face identification to gesture recognition. This paper focuses on English handwritten recognition. The learning process is implemented using a hybrid back-propagation neural network with genetic algorithm in which the convergence is important in recognizing the pattern.

Genetic algorithms are founded on bases of biological evolution model suggested by Darwin in 1859 under the theory of evolution by natural selection. GA was first introduced by John Holland in 1975 but was not wide spread until the extensive studies of Goldberg in 1989 published. Now, GA is a popular techniques due to its unique properties for complex optimization problems where there is no, or very little, information on the search space [6, 7].

Evolutionary algorithms' key feature is to find near-optimal answers in a complex search spaces. As a general search method they have been applied to many problems including classifiers, training neural networks, training speech recognition systems [8, 9, 10], in all these cases by properly characterizing the problem GA has been successfully employed.

This paper takes advantage of genetic algorithms. First the weights of neural network is generated randomly for a fixed number which is called initial population then by running the algorithm the population will converge to the goal.

The other core of this implementation is a neural network. Feed-forward network has been used for simulation. A typical feed-forward network consists of one input layer, one or more intermediate layer(s) called hidden layer(s) and one output layer. Each node in this network passes its data to the next node by an activation function. Different architectures can be designed for hidden layers but designing a successful architecture is problem dependent. It is known that if a network with several hidden layers can learn some input data, it can also learn those data with a single hidden layer but the time taken may be increased [11]. Our proposed approach addresses this problem.

The next section explains the feature vector extraction from handwritten character images and suggests a novel approach for character input for the neural network feeding. Section 3 describes the architecture of the neural network used and section 4 explores the hybrid genetic algorithm. Computational results and comparison between the proposed approach and conventional neural networks is provided in section 5. Finally, section 6 concludes this paper.

2   Preparing Input Data for Neural Network

As the name suggests, back-propagation network training is based on the propagation of errors to the previous layer. In this method, as data feed in the network, the network weights are accumulated and as the error is back propagated they are updated. Another method in training the network is by using evolutionary algorithms and specifically genetic algorithm for its convenience and suitability. Either of these methods has its own drawbacks. An adeptly designed hybrid approach seems to overcome these limitations and meanwhile exploits the advantages of both methods. The simulation results in section 5 demonstrate the truth of this claim. The back-propagation algorithm, BP in short, is vulnerable to local minima. By using genetic algorithms we

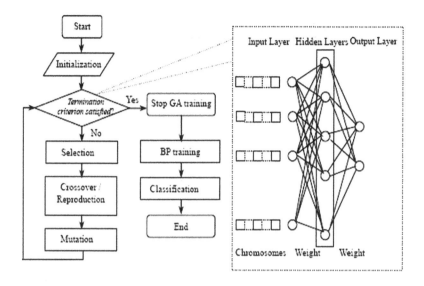

Fig. 1. General scheme of tuning neural network weights with GA

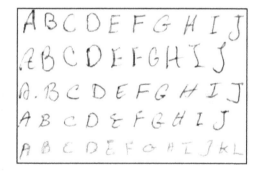

Fig. 2. Sample handwriting of 5 different persons

will overcome this issue; as the genetic algorithm searches fast the entire search space, the back-propagation algorithm is assigned to do the local search. Figure 1 illustrates the general concept of tuning neural network weight with genetic algorithms.

The input of the system is the scanned image of several different persons' handwriting of 26 English capital letters. Figure 2 represents sample different handwritten letters.

For preparing the input of the neural network, first the centroid of the scanned image of the letters is divided to four sections and the density of pixels in each section is calculated. The calculation of centroid and density is provided hereunder.

$$A = \sum_{i=1}^{n} \sum_{j=1}^{m} B[i, j] \tag{1}$$

$$\bar{x} \sum_{i=1}^{n} \sum_{j=1}^{m} B[i, j] = \sum_{i=1}^{n} \sum_{j=1}^{m} iB[i, j] \tag{2}$$

$$\bar{y} \sum_{i=1}^{n} \sum_{j=1}^{m} B[i, j] = \sum_{i=1}^{n} \sum_{j=1}^{m} jB[i, j] \tag{3}$$

$$\bar{x} = \sum_{i=1}^{n} \sum_{j=1}^{m} iB[i, j] / A \tag{4}$$

$$\bar{y} = \sum_{i=1}^{n} \sum_{j=1}^{m} jB[i, j] / A \tag{5}$$

$$COMPACTNESS \quad = \frac{p^2}{A} \geq 4\Pi \tag{6}$$

Where A denotes the area of the image and $B[i,j]$ denotes one pixel of the image. X and Y give the centroid of object. In the equation (6), p is the perimeter and A is the area of the image, thus the greater this measure is, more compact the object is. According to this equation maximum compactness stands for circle and objects with other shapes are less compact than circle.

3 Architecture of Neural Network Core

The neural network used in this paper is based on the fully connected feed-forward networks demonstrated in figure 3. The input layer consists of four nodes and the hidden layer is divided in two layers, each with ten nodes. The output layer has 26 nodes, each representing one English capital letter. With the provided settings only a single output node will be active in the network for each input.

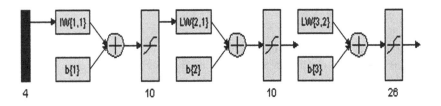

Fig. 3. Structure of artificial neural network core

The training algorithm of the network and weights update procedure and the error calculation is as below:

$$\Delta w_{ho}(s+1) = -\eta \sum_{i=1}^{H} \frac{\partial E}{\partial w_{ho}} + \alpha \Delta w_{ho}(s) + \frac{1}{1 - (\alpha \Delta w_{ho}(s))} \tag{7}$$

$$\Delta w_{ih}(s+1) = -\eta \sum_{i=1}^{N} \frac{\partial E}{\partial w_{ih}} + \alpha \Delta w_{ih} + \frac{1}{1 - (\alpha \Delta w_{ho}(s))} \tag{8}$$

Where, w_{ih} are the weights of input layer towards hidden layer and w_{ho} are the weights of hidden layer towards output layer. The constant parameter η determines the convergence ratio of the network and in our implementation is set to 0.1. By α parameter, momentum is incorporated into the network which helps the network to escape the local minima. In our implementation α is assigned the value 0.9. E stands for the error of the network and is calculated according to the equation below:

$$E = \frac{1}{2} \sum_{P=1}^{P} (O^o - T)^2 \tag{9}$$

In the equation (9), O is the output of the network and T is the real output expected. For all input values the square difference of these two parameters is calculated and the overall error of the network is determined.

4   Genetic Algorithm Core

The weights of the neural network core typically are produced by BP algorithm in the first place. But being trapped at local minima is a connate threat of this algorithm. To overcome this issue, in our approach the initial weights of the neural network is obtained by a genetic algorithm which can explore the entire search space fast and then the further improvements are made through BP algorithm.

The structure of genetic algorithm is depicted in figure 1. Individuals in the population of the GA are weights and bias values of the neural network. The initial population is generated under a uniform random distribution. By applying GA operators the population evolves to better fit the optimization criteria, which in our case is the better performance of the neural network. These operators need to be modified to be suitable for the ranges applicable to the ANN core as it is provided in the following parts. Selecting the best population of the weights is done in a way that the least discrepancy between the network output and the real output is resulted. A chromosome in this population is a square matrix of weights. If any element of this matrix is zero, two neurons of the corresponding indices are not connected; otherwise their connection weight is the real number of that gene.

4.1   Mutation

The mutation operator is implemented by randomly choosing a single chromosome and summing it with a uniformly generated random number. The mutation is preformed according to the equation (10).

$$C^{new} = C^{old} \bigcup_{i=1}^{n} \left[C_{j-\lambda} \bigcup \left(C_{\lambda}^{old} + \varepsilon \right) \right] \tag{10}$$

In the equation (10), C^{old} denotes the current chosen chromosome for mutation which has j genes. ε is a random number in the range [-1, 1]. λ represents a randomly selected gene from current chromosome that is to be modified. C^{new} represents the next generation of chromosome.

4.2 Recombination

The recombination operator is responsible for making diversity in the population of answers while keeping an eye on the better chances of suitability. This operator is applied by equation (11). In this recombination first a chromosome is selected, and then two random genes of this chromosome are swapped.

$$C^{next} = C^{sel} \bigcup_{i=1}^{n} \left[\left(C^{sel} - C^{sel}_{\alpha} - C^{sel}_{\beta} \right) \bigcup \left(C^{sel}_{\alpha} \longleftrightarrow C^{sel}_{\beta} \right) \right] \tag{11}$$

In the equation (11), α and β denotes the locus of the randomly selected genes in the chosen chromosome from the previous step.

4.3 Fitness Evaluation Function

Fitness function must be able to evaluate the suitability of the weights, individuals of population, for our neural network. To this end we calculate the total sum of network square errors. As the input data are fed to the network this measure is calculated and chromosome with the smallest total sum of square errors is appointed the maximum fitness. This leads the GA to find the most suitable set of weights and bias values for the neural network with least errors.

5 Simulation and Computational Results

The performance of the proposed approach has been evaluated by simulating with MATLAB. In [3] it is shown that training the neural network only by BP algorithm is very prone to be tangled in local minima. There have been several techniques suggested to overcome this drawback; one of the most successful ones is by using evolutionary algorithms. In this approach a customized genetic algorithm has been utilized in hybrid evolutionary feed-forward neural network which is responsible for searching entire search space while BP algorithms is responsible for local search.

The simulation results are obtained by feeding the neural network with the scanned image of 26 English capital letters in the handwritings of different people. Five different handwriting data sets have been used. The output of the system is the classification of letters independent of the specific writers' handwriting styles.

Further contribution is made in feeding the neural network with scanned character images input. For each letter the image centroid is calculated and accordingly the image is divided into four subsections, then these subsections are fed into the network.

Table 1. Numbers of Epochs Required for Network Convergence within Same Setting

Sample Letters:	A	I	E	O	U
Proposed Approach with Centroid:	2200	950	4600	-	-
Without Centroid:	2600	-	-	-	-

Table 2. Network Error Comparison for Some Sample Letters

Sample Letters:	A	I	E	O	U
Proposed Approach with Centroid:	0	0	0	0.19	0.2
Without Centroid:	0	0.4	0.19	0.2	0.2

Table 1 provides the comparison between the numbers of epochs required for convergence of the network in the proposed approach by computing the image centroid and in the case that image centroid is not taken into account, as in [3]. Table 2 represents the networks' errors. These tables are provided for sample letters. The simulation results showed that the proposed approach is promisingly successful in letter recognition. As shown in table 1 both algorithms are not converged with specified setting, but within the same settings the proposed approach converges with fewer epochs and according to table 2 with fewer errors. Finally, with 50000 epochs the algorithm is run for all alphabets.

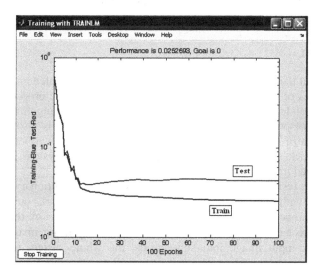

Fig. 4. Neural network output

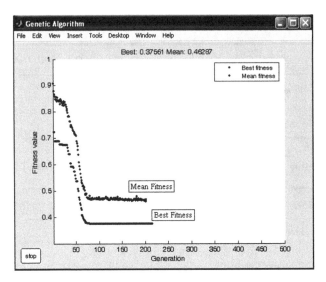

Fig. 5. Evolution of neural network weights

Figure 4 represents the proposed neural network output. As it is shown the network errors is reduced below 0.05 and hence the termination criteria is met and the algorithm stops. Figure 5 demonstrates the evolution of neural network weights with genetic algorithm.

There is a limitation of 50000 iterations on training phase. The network training is by entering all samples of one set handwritten letters in one step and the entire set in next steps. It should be noted that in training every step the order in which the letters are fed into the network must be different from the order of entered letters in the previous training step. Simulations are based on division of data set as 70% of all data used for training and the rest 30% is used for testing.

6 Conclusion

This paper aims at the problem of recognizing single alphabetical letters in the various handwriting styles of different people. We have opted to test the proposed algorithm on English capital letters due to their wide application in filling forms, and their intrinsic feature of preserving their block style. This approach is also applicable to learn and recognize the Farsi language alphabets written in various handwriting styles, but in block separate letters. The application of this system is in properly converting scanned images of official forms into text files.

The simulation results indicate that the proposed hybrid evolutionary feed-forward neural network with enhanced image feeding to the network outperforms the conventional approaches. The advantage is better performance of the network in training and correct classification of letters. Moreover, by using image centroid in dividing network input image into subsections, the whole system is invariant to translation, rotation, and scaling of input letters. Since these deformities are very common in handwritten texts, this approach demonstrates a promising property in real world applications.

References

1. Mahmoudi, F., Parviz, M.: Visual Hand Tracking Algorithms. In: IEEE Proc. Geometric Modeling and Imaging–New Trends, pp. 228–232 (July 2006)
2. Meinagh, M.A., Isazadeh, A., Ayar, M., Mahmoudi, F., Zareie, B.: Database Replication with Availability and Consistency Guarantees through Failure-Handling. In: IEEE Proc. International Multi-Conference on Computing in the Global Information Technology (ICCGI 2007), p. 14 (2007)
3. Mangal, M., Singh, M.P.: Handwritten English Vowels Recognition Using Hybrid Evolutionary Feed-Forward Neural Network. Malaysian Journal of Computer Science 19(2), 169–187 (2006)
4. Mangal, M., Singh, M.P.: Patterns Recalling Analysis of Hopfield Neural Network with Genetic Algorithms. International Journal of Innovative Computing, Information and Control (JAPAN) (2007) (accepted for publication)
5. Mahmoudi, F., Shanbehzadeh, J., Eftekhari, A., Soltanian-Zadeh, H.: Image retrieval based on shape similarity by edge orientation autocorrelogram. Journal of Pattern Recognition 36(8), 1725–1736 (2003)
6. Gao, W.: New Evolutionary Neural Networks. In: Proc. of International Conference on Neural Interface and Control, May 26-28 (2005)
7. Goldberg, D.: Genetic Algorithms. Addison-Wesley, Reading (1989)
8. Pal, S.K., Wang, P.P.: Genetic Algorithm for Pattern Recognition. CRC Press, Boca Raton (1996)
9. Gelsema, E.S.: Editorial Special Issue On Genetic Algorithms. Pattern Recognition Letters 16(8) (1995)
10. Auwatanamongkol, S.: Pattern recognition using genetic algorithm. In: IEEE Proc. of the 2000 Congress on Evolutionary Computation (2000)
11. Murthy, B.V.S.: Handwriting Recognition Using Supervised Neural Networks. In: Joint Conference on Neural network vol. 4 (1999)

Forensics for Detecting P2P Network Originated MP3 Files on the User Device

Heikki Kokkinen and Janne Nöyränen

Nokia Research Center,
Itämerenkatu 11-13, 00180 Helsinki, Finland
{heikki.kokkinen,janne.noyranen}@nokia.com

Abstract. This paper presents how to detect MP3 files that have been downloaded from peer-to-peer networks to a user hard disk. The technology can be used for forensics of copyright infringements related to peer-to-peer file sharing, and for copyright payment services. We selected 23 indicators, which show peer-to-peer history for a MP3 file. We developed software to record the indicator values. A group of selected examinees ran the software on their hard disks. We analyzed the experimental results, and evaluated the indicators. We found out that the performance of the indicators varies from user to user. We were able to find a few good indicators, for example related to the number of MP3 files in one directory.

Keywords: Peer-to-peer, P2P, MP3, forensics, binary classification, legal, copyright.

1 Introduction

This paper discusses technology to detect which Motion Picture Expert Group Audio layer 3 (MP3) files on the user device originate from peer-to-peer (P2P) networks. P2P file sharing applications and networks include for example Napster, Kazaa, Gnutella, eDonkey, and BitTorrent. P2P file sharing has created most of the traffic in the Internet in the past years. A significant amount of this traffic is copyright content with licenses, which do not allow sharing in the P2P networks. Though peer-to-peer networks are infamous for copyright infringements, there are also many legal ways to use P2P file sharing. Napster P2P application was enhanced with models to pay for the content [1]. The rights owners may allow the P2P file sharing with Creative Commons licenses [2] or in other ways. Increasing amount of companies use P2P file sharing to decrease their Content Distribution Network (CDN) costs, like Blizzard with World of Warcraft [3]. In a recently published post-payment copyright service the users are able to legalize their unauthorized media content by paying the copyright fees after downloading [4]. This paper describes the technology, which supports the post-payment copyright system by helping the user to select the files for which he wants to purchase the post-payment licenses. The technology suits also well for forensics purposes in finding evidence for copyright infringements. It is important to notice that post-payment copyright system and forensics are two different use cases for the technology, and they should not be mixed together.

M. Sorell (Ed.): e-Forensics 2009, LNICST 8, pp. 10–18, 2009.

The attempts to detect copyright content in the P2P networks have often been related to investigations of copyright infringements. Broucek et. al. describe general methodology for digital evidence acquisition for computer misuse and e-crime [5]. The ISPs have the best capabilities to collect information about the behavior of the investigated users. This kind of network collection is the most commonly used method for P2P copyright infringement forensics at the moment. Generic P2P traffic detection and prevention have been discussed in [6], and with emphasis on traffic mining in [7].

A commonly proposed method to detect copyright infringements in the user device is watermarking [8]. Koso et. al. apply Digital Signatures to watermarking [9]. The watermarking is a technology to embed information to content so that it does not alter the human perception of the content and so that the information is difficult to remove. The watermark is at investigation time used to track the source of the content. Digital Time Warping achieves independence from encoding and sampling [10]. An option to evaluate the source of a MP3 file is to carry out MP3 encoder analysis [11]. An application called Fake MP3 detector differentiates the files, which have different content as the name suggests [12]. The copyright infringement detecting and tracing are studied in [13].

In this paper we use an empirical method to detect which MP3 files on the user device originate from P2P networks. We identify 23 indicators, which show that a MP3 file has been downloaded from P2P network. We let six examinees to run the research software on their hard disks. All examinees have files originating from P2P network, and most of them have self-ripped files, as well.

After running the software the users manually classify which files are originated from P2P network. The research software records the values of all indicators for each MP3 file. We use the sensitivity and specificity performance metrics, which have commonly been used in binary classification context. The results show that the most suitable indicators vary from person to person, but a few indicators reveal well the P2P download origin.

In addition to the forensics use, the main application of the results is to help a user to select, which MP3 files are authorized and to which ones the user should purchase the license using the post-payment copyright system or by other means. The studied method evaluates the indicators. The P2P origin is in many cases a rule of thumb differentiating the authorized and unauthorized files of a typical user in Finland. Nevertheless, not nearly all P2P files are illegal, neither nearly all MP3 files without P2P history are legal. Even if the indicators were able to differentiate the P2P originated files with 100% accuracy, the legal status of the studied MP3 files would remain inaccurate. On the other hand, if the user was expected to classify his files to legal and illegal fully manual, going through thousands of files would be tedious, and this technology provides for the user a great help for the selection.

2   Materials and Methods

In this study we selected 23 indicators, which potentially show that a MP3 file is originated from a P2P network. We had six examinees. We developed software, which can run on an examinee's PCs and recorded the results of the indicators for each MP3 file. The examinees ran the software and classified the origin of the files. We used three types of indicators: file specific indicators, directory specific indicators, and album specific indicators.

2.1 File Indicators

The file indicators try to classify the files, in this case MP3 tracks, individually.

1)   *The file name, file path or file contains a P2P sharing group name like "EiTheLMP3".*The list of names was collected from two sites: [14] and [15].
2)   *The file path contains 1337 speak like "m@ke".*
3)   *ID3 tag comment field has an URL address like" http://www.torrentreactor.net/".*
4)   *ID3 tag comment field contains 1337 speak.*
5)   *ID3 tag title or comment field has a tag of a ware group tag like "RAGEMP3".*
6)   *ID3 tag comment field is not empty.*

2.2 Directory Indicators

The directory indicators go through the files in a directory and compare them with each other.

7)   *The file path has any of the following words: download, or shared.*
8)   *A directory contains over 40 MP3 files.*
9)   *A directory contains over 25 MP3 files.*
10) *The music in the directory has a longer total duration than 80 min.*
11) *The MP3 directory contains more than 3 other than music files.*
12) *The directory contains a file with the following type .nfo.*
13) *The directory contains a file with a following type .url, .torrent or .info.*
14) *There is a .txt file the same directory*
15) *There are no other tracks from the same album according to the album ID3 tag.*

2.3 Album Indicators

The album indicators study the common characteristics of the files, which have the same album ID3 tag.

16) *The track number is filled in some, but not in all tracks of the album.*
17) *All tracks are not encoded the same way (VBR or CBR)*
18) *The album files have different bitrate, only used for CBR.*
19) *All tracks do not have the same sampling rate.*
20) *Tracks vary from mono to stereo.*
21) *Many file indicators are present for the tracks of the album.*
22) *The file names contain capital and non-capital letters in a varying way.*
23) *The file names contain symbol characters in a varying way.*

2.4 Examinees

The examinees were selected so that they had a large amount of files, which originated both from P2P networks and from personal ripping from Compact Discs

(CD). The table 1 describes the MP3 software of the examinees. For simplicity the source of the MP3 files was expected to be either P2P network or personal ripping of CDs. As background information about the source we collected the users' CD ripper and MP3 encoder, and P2P file sharing application. MP3 re-tagging alternates the possibility to carry out the detection with the selected indicators. In some cases the player may also change the files or directories.

Table 1. Examinees' MP3 related software

User	Ripper	Tagger	P2P	Player
1	EAC-LAME, iTunes	Tag-Scanner	Azureus, eDonkey	iTunes, WMP
2	Audio-grabber		Bittorrent, Limewire	WinAmp, Rythmbox
3	WMP		WinMX	WinAmp
4	WMP		WinAmp	-
5	Audio-grabber		DC++, Bittorrent	WinAmp
6				WinAmp

In the table 2 we characterize the users according to the number of studied MP3 tracks and the percentage of illegal files.

Table 2. The number of tracks and percentage of illegal files for a user

User	1	2	3	4	5	6
Tracks	3394	1511	1946	905	2017	811
Illegal%	16.8	93.1	99.2	12.3	82.2	100

2.5 Metrics for Indicator Characterization

The commonly used performance metrics for binary classification are sensitivity and specificity. The typical application of the binary classification is to use medical examinations to find out if the patient has a certain disease or not. The examination results are divided to true positives (*TP*), true negatives (*TN*), false positives (*FP*), and false negatives (*FN*).

The sensitivity is defined

$$Sensitivity = \frac{TP}{TP + FN}. \tag{1}$$

The sensitivity describes which portion of the illegal files the indicator was able to find. The specificity is defined

$$Specificity = \frac{TN}{TN + FP}. \tag{2}$$

The specificity characterizes which part of the files, which were classified as legal, were really legal. When other than binary indicators are used or several binary indicators are combined together, it is possible to adjust the decision limit. If we want to change the decision limit so that our sensitivity increases, we lose in specificity and vice versa.

3 Results

We calculate the sensitivity and specificity values for each examinee per indicator. The summary of the sensitivity and specificity analysis can be found in the figure 1. The indicators are sorted according to the sensitivity average, the best indicator is on the left and the worse on the right. The standard deviation error bars show that there is a large variation in the capability to indicate P2P history for a MP3 file in the indicators. In most use cases the specificity value should stay close to 100%. The average specificity of indicator 6 is below 40%, but as we can see later in this section, it works well with the data of a few examinees.

The best average indicator for this group of examinees was *10) The music in the directory has a longer total duration than 80 min*. It has close to 100% specificity and the highest sensitivity (around 30%). The following indicators have also a reasonable sensitivity and close to 100% specificity: *9) A directory contains over 25 MP3 files, 8) A directory contains over 40 MP3 files, 16) The track number is filled in some, but not in all tracks of the album, 3) ID3 tag comment field has a URL, 17) All tracks are not encoded the same way (VBR or CBR), and 19) All tracks do not have the same sampling rate*. In the Figures 2, 3 and 4 we show the specificity and sensitivity of three individual examinees' data.

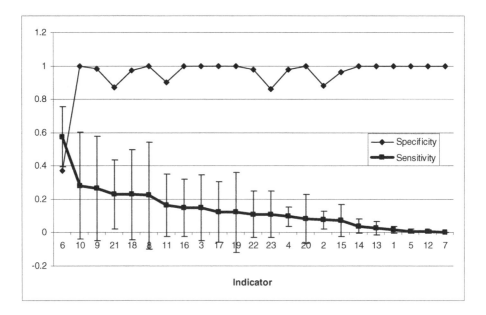

Fig. 1. Sensitivity average with standard deviation error bars and Specificity average

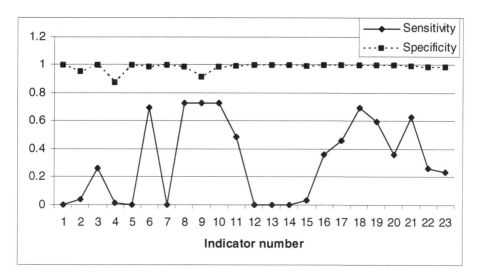

Fig. 2. Example of quite high sensitivity specificity (dashed)

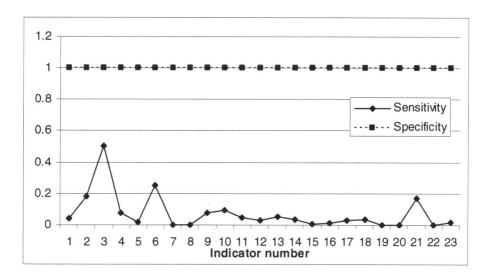

Fig. 3. Example of very high specificity (dashed) and low sensitivity

The figure 2 is a case where many indicators show that a file has been downloaded from P2P network and the specificity remains under control. Especially indicators *8) A directory contains over 40 MP3 files, 9) A directory contains over 25 MP3 files,* and *10) The music in the directory has a longer total duration than 80 min* perform well. These three indicators are related to each other and this examinee has downloaded many files one by one rather than as a whole album from P2P networks.

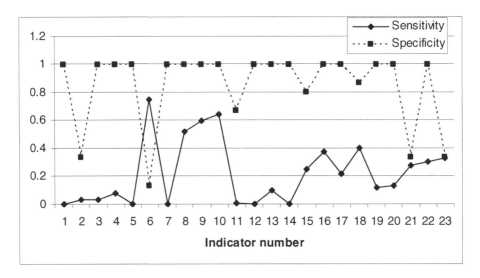

Fig. 4. Example of low specificity (dashed) and quite high sensitivity

The tracks are stored in one directory. Also indicators *18) The album files have different bit rate*, and *21) Many file indicators are present for the tracks of the album* have high sensitivity. The indicator *6) ID3 tag comment field is not empty* can keep the high specificity in this case.

In the figure 3 the specificity is constantly 100%. The best indicators are *3) ID3 tag comment field has a URL address, 6) ID3 tag comment field is not empty* and *21) Many file indicators are present for the tracks of the album*. The high specificity value is obvious result in this case, because this examinee had 100% of the files from P2P networks.

In the figure 4 the challenge are the low specificity values with many indicators. Especially, the indicator 6 shows very low specificity. The generally best performing indicators are the group of 8, 9 and 10, which indicate a large number of MP3 files in one directory. Also indicator *16) The track number is filled in some, but not in all tracks of the album* has high sensitivity and close to 100% specificity.

4 Discussion

In this paper we studied the performance of 23 indicators, which show that a MP3 file is potentially from a P2P network. We evaluated the indicators with binary classification performance metrics: sensitivity and specificity. The best indicator was *10) The music in the directory has a longer total duration than 80 min achieved* close to 30% average sensitivity and practically 100% specificity. Generally the related indicators 8, 9 and 10 which indicate a large number of MP3 files in the same directory performed well. The number of files in a directory does not principally have anything to do with P2P networks. It is just a way how users organize their MP3 files in the directories. By using the number of files, we take a bold assumption that there are only two main sources of MP3s, either ripping the CDs or downloading files from P2P network. P2P file sharing is so huge phenomenon that this assumption works especially with the people who either are investigated in the forensics methods or who are interested to use post-payment copyright type of services.

The obvious high specificity indicators *1) The file name, file path or file contains a P2P sharing group name like " EiTheLMP3", 2) The directory contains a file with the following type .nfo, .url, .torrent or .info, 3) ID3 tag comment field has a URL address like http://www.torrentreactor.net/", 4) The file path or file contains 1337 speak like "m@ke" or 5) ID3 tag title or comment field has a tag of a ware group like "RAGEMP3"* were not strongly visible in this group of examinees. The most common indicator of these was *3* showing URL address existence in the ID3 tag. It achieved an average of 15% sensitivity and practically 100% specificity. The related indicator *6* revealing any text in the comment had the highest sensitivity of all indicators, but due to very low specificity with a few users its accuracy was dropped significantly.

The specificity of the indicators varied from user to user significantly. One clear reason for very good specificity values was that a couple of examinees had practically all files from P2P networks. The number of examinees was rather small (6), and a few users did not have many files without P2P origin, making the specificity analysis less meaningful.

The results of this research can be used for forensics purposes to find out the P2P network origin of files on the device of the examined user. They can also be applied for post-payment copyright system to help the user to select the unauthorized MP3 files for license purchase. The examinees did not try to cover the origin of the P2P networks in their files. If one would systematically try to cover the traces by renaming, retagging and rearranging the files, these indicators may lose their effectiveness.

It would be interesting to research methods and algorithms, which could achieve the combinatory performance of all used indicators, and to study the performance of the methods by comparing to the performance of individual indicators. The studied indicators can individually be used to reveal the P2P origin of the MP3 files, if the examinees have not tried to remove the traces beforehand.

References

1. Alves, K., Michael, K.: The Rise and Fall of Digital Music Distribution Services: a Cross-Case Comparison of MP3.com, Napster and Kazaa. In: Cerpa, N., Bro, P. (eds.) Building Society Through E-Commerce, 1st edn., University of Talca, Talca (2005)
2. Creative Commons licenses, http://creativecommons.org/licenses/
3. World of Warcraft – Frequently Asked Questions,
   `http://www.blizzard.co.uk/wow/faq/bittorrent.shtml`
4. Kokkinen, H., Ekberg, J.E.: Post-payment copyright for digital content. In: 5th Consumer Communications and Networking Conference, CCNC, pp. 1278–1283. IEEE, Las Vegas (2008)
5. Broucek, V., Turner, P.: Computer Incident Investigations: e-forensic Insights on Evidence Acquisition. In: 13th Annual EICAR Conference, Grand-Duche du Luxembourg (2004)

6. Ho, G.L., Taek, Y.N., Jong S.J.: The method of P2P traffic detecting for P2P harmful contents prevention. In: 7th International Conference on Advanced Communication Technology, vol. 2, pp. 777–780 (2005)
7. Togawa, S., Kanenishi, K., Yano, Y.: Peer-to-Peer File Sharing Communication Detection System Using Network Traffic Mining. HCI (8), 769–778 (2007)
8. Nikolaidis, N., Giannoula, A.: Robust Zero-Bit and Multi-Bit Audio Watermarking Using Correlation Detection and Chaotic. In: Digital Audio Watermarking Techniques and Technologies: Applications and Benchmarks. Idea Group Inc. (IGI) (2007)
9. Koso, A., Turi, A., Obimbo, C.: Embedding Digital Signatures in MP3s. IMSA. pp. 271–274 (2005)
10. Sung, B., Jung, M., Ham, J., Kim, J., Ko, I.: Feature Based Same Audio Perception method for Filtering of Illegal Music Contents. In: 10th Int. conference on Advanced Communication Technology, ICACT, pp. 2194–2198 (2008)
11. Böhme, R., Westfeld, A.: Statistical characterisation of MP3 encoders for steganalysis. In: International Multimedia conference, workshop on Multimedia and security, pp. 25–34. Magdeburg, Germany (2004)
12. Fake MP3 detector,
    http://www.sharewareconnection.com/fake-MP3-detector.htm
13. Mee, J., Watters, P.A.: Detecting and Tracing Copyright Infringements in P2P Networks. In: International Conference on Networking, International Conference on Systems and International Conference on Mobile Communications and Learning Technologies (ICNICONSMCL 2006), p. 60 (2006)
14. MP3 Kingz, http://www.mp3kingz.org/
15. NfoDB.com, http://www.nfodb.com/section_4_mp3_nfo.html

Image Encryption Using Chaotic Signal and Max–Heap Tree

Fariborz Mahmoudi[1], Rasul Enayatifar[2], and Mohsen Mirzashaeri[1]

[1] Electrical and Computer Engineering Department,
Islamic Azad University, Qazvin Branch, Iran
{Mahmoudi,Mirzashaeri}@QazvinIAU.ac.ir
[2] Department of Electrical and Computer Engineering,
Islamic Azad University, Firoozkooh Branch, Iran
r.enayatifar@iaufb.ac.ir

Abstract. In this paper, a new method is proposed for image encryption using chaotic signals and Max-Heap tree. In this method, Max-Heap tree is utilized for further complexity of the encryption algorithm, higher security and changing the amount of gray scale of each pixel of the original image. Studying the obtained results of the performed experiments, high resistance of the proposed method against brute-force and statistical invasions is obviously illustrated. Also, the obtained entropy of the method which is about 7.9931 is very close to the ideal amount of 8.

Keywords: Image Encryption, Max-Heap Tree, Chaotic Signal.

1 Introduction

Together with the rapid rate of multimedia products and vast distribution of digital products on internet, protection of digital information from being copied, illegal distribution is of great importance each day. To reach this goal, various algorithms have been proposed for image encryption [1-4]. Recently, due to the widespread use of chaotic signals in different areas, a considerable number of researchers have focused on these signals for image encryption [5-9]. One of the most important advantages of chaotic signals is their sensitivity to the initial conditions and also their noise-like behavior while being certain. In [5], the method of moving pixels is proposed for image encryption. In [6], an algorithm is proposed which is based on a key for the encryption of the image (CKBA[2]). In this method a chaotic signal is utilized to determine the amount of gray scale of the pixels. Later researches have shown that the aforesaid method is not secure enough [7].

In this paper, a new method is proposed for image encryption using chaotic signals and Max-Heap tree to make the encryption algorithm more complex and secure, in which the implementation of Max-Heap tree has caused that, even when the initial value of the chaotic function is revealed, the real amount of gray scale of each pixel cannot be accessed. In the following section, Max-Heap trees are primarily introduced in brief, and then the proposed method is analyzed. In the experimental results

M. Sorell (Ed.): e-Forensics 2009, LNICST 8, pp. 19 – 28, 2009.
© ICST Institute for Computer Sciences, Social Informatics and Telecommunications Engineering 2009

section, the functionality of this method is studied through some experiments. The reversibility of the method is studied in the next section and finally the conclusions are drawn.

2 Max-Heap Tree

One of the special trees which is widely applied in computer sciences is Max-Heap tree. This tree is a complete binary tree in which the initial value of each node is larger than or equal to the keys of its children.

Insertion of information in this tree is done as: the tree is always filled from left to right in the last line and then the next line. While inserting a new node, it is inserted in the far left empty space of the last line (not filled yet), so that the tree is always complete. Then the heapification is done, in which a node in the lowest point might be replaced by its parent as many times as it takes to be heapified. For instance, in case the insertion of 9 digits is as 5, 8, 2, 3, 4, 7, 9, 20, 14, the resulting Max-Heap tree is as follows:

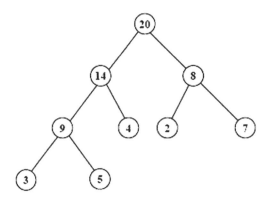

Fig. 1. Max-Heap Tree

3 Chaotic Signal

Chaos is a phenomenon that occurs in definable nonlinear systems which are highly sensitive to initial values, and trend to show random-like behavior. If such systems satisfy the conditions of Liapanov exponential equation, will continue to be in the chaotic mode. The main reason why these signals are utilized in image encryption is the definability of the system while being random-like; this caused the output of the system seem random to the invaders. Since it is definable by the encrypter, it is decodable. The advantages of these functions are studied in two parts:

a) Sensitivity to the initial value
This means that minor variation of the initial values can cause considerable differences in the next value of the function, that is when the initial signals varies a little, the resulting signal will differ significantly.

b) Random-like behavior

In comparison with the generators of ordinary random numbers, in which the series of generated random numbers are capable of regeneration, the random-number-generation methods utilized in chaotic function algorithms are able to regenerate the same random numbers, having the initial value and the transform function.

Eq. (1) is one of the most well-known signals to have random-like behavior and is known as Logistic Map Signal.

$$X_{n+1} = rX_n\left(1 - X_n\right) \tag{1}$$

The Logistic Map signal will have a chaotic behavior in case the initial value is $X_0 \in (0,1)$ and $r = 3.9999$ In fig. 2, the signal behavior with initial value is $X_0 = 0.5$ and $r = 3.9999$ can be seen.

The input of the system is the scanned image of several different persons' handwriting of 26 English capital letters. Figure 2 represents sample different handwritten letters.

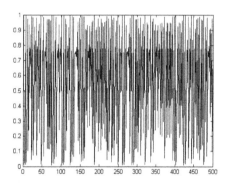

Fig. 2. The chaotic behavior of signal (1) in its 500 iterations

4 The Proposed Method

In this method, a binary Max-Heap tree is made by non-repetitive random numbers from 0 to 255, with random order, generated by the chaotic function of Logistic Map. This function needs an initial value to start out. To increase the level security, an 80-bit key is used to generate the initial value of the signal (Eq. (1)). This key can be defined as an ASCII character of the form:

$$K_0, K_1, ..., K_9 (ASCII) \tag{2}$$

In this key, K_i determines an 8-bit block of the key. The binary form of the mentioned key is as follows:

$$K = \begin{pmatrix} K_{01}, K_{02}, K_{03}, K_{04}, K_{05}, K_{06}, K_{07} \\ K_{08}, ..., K_{91}, K_{92}, K_{93} \\ K_{94}, K_{95}, K_{96}, K_{97}, K_{98}, (Binary) \end{pmatrix} \tag{3}$$

The initial value is resulted by Eq. (4).

$$X_0 = \begin{pmatrix} K_{01} \times 2^{79} + K_{02} \times 2^{78} + \\ K_{11} \times 2^{71} + K_{12} \times 2^{70} + \\ .... \\ K_{n7} \times 2^{1} + K_{n8} \times 2^{0} \end{pmatrix} / 2^{80} \tag{4}$$

On the other hand and as seen in fig. 2, the variation range of the signal is [0,1].This range is divide into P parts whose size is determines by:

$$\varepsilon = 1/P \tag{5}$$

Based on this segmentation, the range of the ith part is determined by:

$$\left((i-1)\varepsilon, i\varepsilon\right) \tag{6}$$

In this method, P is 256 (the number of gray scales). In the following part, the range in which X_1 that is generated by Eq. (1) and the initial value of X_0, will be determined. The number of this range is chosen as the first order, provided that this amount was not previously located in the range; this will continue as long as the signal magnitude is located in all P parts. Finally, non-repetitive random order will be generated in the range of (0,255) as:

$$Iteration = \left(it_1, it_2, ..., it_r\right) \tag{7}$$

Now, the first value of the iteration will be put into the root and the second one (based on the Max-Heap tree structure) in the tree; this will continue as long as all the numbers have filled the tree. Finally, a binary Max-Heap tree of 256 nodes will be generated in each node of which there is a unique number from 0 to 255. This tree is used to change the gray scale of the image pixels.

In the nest stage, 50 percent of the pixels of the first row of the image are selected by the use of Eq. (1), Eq. (2) (p=the image width) and the initial value of X_r (the last number generated by the chaotic signal in the last stage). The root of the tree generated in the previous stage replaces the first pixel of the next line. Knowing the tree structure, the children of the each node of the tree are put in a separate pixel of the image. Then, the value of each node is xored with the value of the pixel it is in. This will continue up to the last line. In this stage, three points are of great importance:

a) The position of the children of a node on the pixel is this way: if the node is in the position (x,y) of the image, the left-hand-side child is at (x+1,y-1) and the right-hand-side child is at (x+1,y+1).

b) In a pixel which contains more than one node, the value of all nodes and the value of the pixel are xored with each other (together) (nodes 15 and 10 in figs. 3a and 3b).

c) The image is assumed to be a node. Figs. 3a and 3b are examples of the proposed method, in which a 4×4 image and a Max-Heap tree of 6 nodes are considered.

In fig. 3b, by inserting the root on pixel 2 and assuming the image to be spherical, node 3 will be placed on pixel 12.

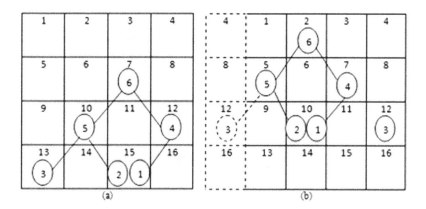

Fig. 3. (a) The root is located in pixel 7. (b) The root is located in pixel 2.

5   Experimental Result

A proper encryption method must be resistance and secure to various types of invasion, such as cryptanalytic invasions, statistical invasions and brute-force invasions. In this section, besides the efficiency of the proposed method, it is studied in terms of statistical and sensitivity analyses, in case of key changes. The results show that the method stands a high security level against various types of invasions.

5.1   Histogram Analysis

Histogram shows the numbers of pixels in each gray scale of an image. In fig. 4, the original image is seen in frame (a) and the histogram of the image in red, green and blue scales are seen in frames (b), (c) and (d), respectively. Also, in frame (e), the encrypted image (using key ABCDEF0123456789ABCD in a 16-scale) can be seen. In frames (f), (g) and (h), the histogram of the encrypted image in red, green and blue scales can be seen, respectively. As seen in fig. 4, the histogram of the encrypted image is totally different from that of the original one, which restricts the possibility of statistical invasions.

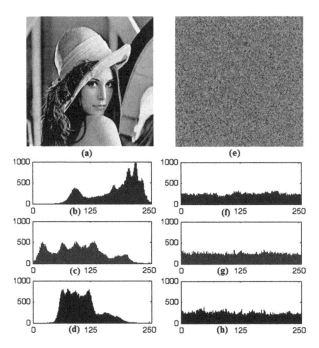

Fig. 4. (a) the main image, and (b), (c) and (d) respectively show the histogram of the lena image of size 256×256 in red, green and blue scales, and (e) shows the encrypted image using the key, ABCDEF0123456789ABCD in a 16-scale. (f), (g) and (h) show the histogram of the encrypted image in red, green and blue scales.

5.2 Correlation Coefficient Analysis

Statistical analysis has been performed on the proposed image encryption algorithm. This is shown by a test of the correlation between two adjacent pixels in plain image and ciphered image. We randomly select 1000 pairs of two-adjacent pixels (in vertical, horizontal, and diagonal direction) from plain images and ciphered images, and calculate the correlation coefficients, respectively by using the following two formulas (see table1 and Fig. 5(a) and (b)):

$$\text{cov}(x, y) = \frac{1}{N} \sum_{i=1}^{N} (x_i - E(x_i))(y_i - E(y_i))$$

$$r_{xy} = \frac{\text{cov}(x, y)}{\sqrt{D(x)}\sqrt{D(y)}} \tag{8}$$

where,

$$E(x) = \frac{1}{N} \sum_{i=1}^{N} x_i, \quad D(x) = \frac{1}{N} \sum_{i=1}^{N} (x_i - E(x_i))^2.$$

Here, $E(x)$ is the estimation of mathematical expectations of x, $D(x)$ is the estimation of variance of x, and $cov(x, y)$ is the estimation of covariance between x and y, where x and y are grey-scale values of two adjacent pixels in the image.

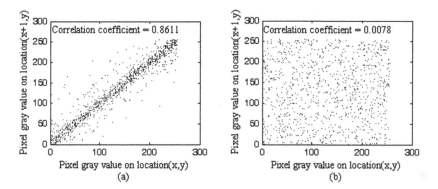

Fig. 5. (a) Correlation analysis of plain image; (b) Correlation analysis of ciphered image

Table 1. Correlation coefficient of two adjacent pixels in two images Plain Ciphered

	Plain	Ciphered
Horizontal	0.9412	-0.0165
Vertical	0.8611	0.0078
Diagonal	0.8878	-0.0089

5.3 Information Entropy Analysis

The entropy is the most outstanding feature of the randomness [13]. Information theory is a mathematical theory of data communication and storage founded by Claude E. Shannon in 1949 [14]. There is a well-known formula for calculating this entropy:

$$H(S) = \sum_{i=0}^{2N-1} P(s_i) \log\left(\frac{1}{P(s_i)}\right) \tag{9}$$

where $P_{(si)}$ represents the probability of symbol si and the entropy is expressed in bits. Actually, given that a real information source seldom transmits random messages, in general, the entropy value of the source is smaller than the ideal one. However, when these messages are encrypted, their ideal entropy should be 8. If the output of such a cipher emits symbols with an entropy of less than 8, then, there would be a possibility of predictability which threatens its security. The value obtained is very close to the theoretical value 8. This means that information leakage in the encryption process is negligible and the encryption system is secure against the entropy attack. Using the above-mentioned formula, we have got the entropy H(S) = 7.9931, for the source s= 256.

5.4 Key Space Analysis

In a proper method, key should have enough space so that the method is resistant against brute-force invasions. In the proposed method, there can be 2^{80} ($\approx 1.20893 \times 10^{24}$) different combinations of keys. Scientific results have shown that this number of key combinations is sufficient for a proper resistance against brute-force invasions.

5.5 Key Sensitivity Analysis

In fig. 6b, the encryption of the image for fig. 6a, using the encryption key of ABCDEF0123456789ABCD is seen. The encryption of the same image is also done using the keys BBCDEF0123456789ABCD and ABCDEF0123456789ABCE, respectively seen in figs. 6c and 6d.

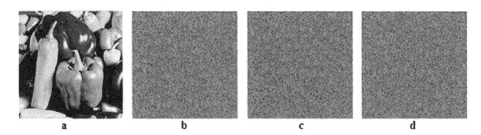

a   b   c   d

Fig. 6. The result of image encryption for an image (fig. 6a): using the encryption key of ABCDEF0123456789ABCD in 7b, the encryption keys BBCDEF0123456789ABCD and ABCDEF0123456789ABCE, respectively seen in 7c and 7d

In order to compare the obtained results, the average of correlation coefficient (horizontal, vertical and diagonal) of some specific points is calculated for each pair of encrypted images (table 2). The obtained results show that this method is sensitive to even small changes of the key.

For instance, the effect of the change in a pixel of the original image on the encrypted image was measured using two standards of NPCR and UACI [10,11]; NPCR is defined as the variance rate of pixels in the encrypted image caused by the change of a single pixel in the original image. UACI is also defined as the average of these changes. These two standards are as follows:

$$NPCR = \frac{\sum_{ij} D(i, j)}{W \times H} \times 100\% \tag{10}$$

$$UACI = \frac{1}{W \times H} \left[\sum_{i,j} \frac{|C_1(i, j) - C_2(i, j)|}{255} \right] \times 100\%$$

where H and W are respectively the length and width of the images, and C_1 and C_2 are two encrypted images of two images which are different in one pixel. D is defined as:

$$D(i, j) = \begin{cases} 1 & if \quad C_1(i, j) = C_2(i, j) \\ 0 & otherwise \end{cases}$$

The obtained values of an image with the size 256×265 are as follows: NPCR=0.9952%, UACI=0.339%

The value obtained in table 2 clearly shows that this method is resistant to differential attacks.

Table 2. The average of correlation coefficient (horizontal, vertical and diagonal) of some specific points for each pair of the images

encrypted image-Fig	6b and 6c	6c and 6d	6b and 6d
correlation coefficient	-0.0113	0.0125	-0.0074

6 Decoding an Encrypted Image

One of the vitalities of an image encryption method is its reversibility of the encrypted image to the original one. Using the proposed method, decoding an encrypted image takes place as follows: As mentioned in section 3, one of the significant properties of chaotic functions is that, having the initial value and the transform function, the series of the numbers generated by the function can be regenerated. In this paper, having the key, the initial value of the chaotic function can be generated; therefore, the required series of numbers for the generation of Max-Heap tree is provided. Then, the last generated value by the chaotic function of the previous stage is used to choose the first pixel of the first line. Unlike the encryption method, the tree is not transformed on the chosen pixel; instead, the position of the pixel is saved in the *PosPixel* series. Then the position of the second pixel of the first line is determined by the chaotic function. Thereby, the position of half of the pixels of the first line is saved in *PosPixel*. This will continue through the last line, where the following series is produced:

$$PosPixel = \begin{pmatrix} (1,1), (1,2), ..., \left(1, \dfrac{n}{2}\right) \\ (2,1), (2,2), ..., \left(2, \dfrac{n}{2}\right) \\ .... \\ (n,1), (n,2), ..., \left(n, \dfrac{n}{2}\right) \end{pmatrix}_{n \times \frac{n}{2}}$$

In PosPixel, in each element of ij, I determines the row number and j the normalized form of the first generated number by the Logistic Map in the range of [0,n].

In the next step, the pixel in the position of the last value of *PosPixel*, (n, n/2), is used as the first pixel to be transformed and gone under Xor operation (as explained in section 4). This will continue up to the first value of the PosPixel series, (1, 1). And finally, the decoded image is regenerated.

7 Conclusion

In this paper, a new method of image encryption has been proposed, which utilizes chaotic signals and the Max-Heap tree for higher complexity. As seen in the experimental results, this method shows a very proper stability against different types of invasions such as decoding invasions, statistical invasions and brute-force ones. The high entropy of the method (7.9931) shows the capabilities of the proposed method.

References

1. Mitra, A., Subba Rao, Y.V., Prasanna, S.R.M.: A New Image Encryption Approach using Combinational Permutation Techniques. International Journal of Computer Science, 1306–4428 (2006)
2. Chang, C.-C., Yu, T.-X.: Cryptanalysis of an encryption scheme for binary images. Pattern Recognition Letters, 1847–1852 (2002)
3. Joshi, M., Chandrashaker, Singh, K.: Color image encryption and decryption using fractional Fourier transform. Optics Communications, 811–819 (2007)
4. Roterman, Y., Porat, M.: Color image coding using regional correlation of primary colors. Image and Vision Computing, 637–651 (2007)
5. Alsultanny, Y.A.: Random-bit sequence generation from image data. Image and Vision Computing, 1178–1189 (2007)
6. Yen, J.-C., Guo, J.-I.: A New Chaotic Key-Based Design for Image Encryption and Decryption. In: Proceedings IEEE International Conference on Circuits and Systems, vol. 4, pp. 49–52 (2000)
7. Li, S., Zheng, X.: Cryptanalysis of a Chaotic Image Encryption Method. In: Proceedings IEEE International Symposium on Circuits and Systems, Scottsdale, AZ, USA, vol. 2, pp. 708–711 (2002)
8. Kwok, H.S., Tang, W.K.S.: A fast image encryption system based on chaotic maps with finite precision representation. In: Chaos, Solitons and Fractals, pp. 1518–1529 (2007)
9. Behnia, S., Akhshani, A., Ahadpour, S., Mahmodi, H., Akhavan, A.: A fast chaotic encryption scheme based on piecewise nonlinear chaotic maps. Physics Letters A, 391–396 (2007)
10. Chen, G., Mao, Y.B., Chui, C.K.: A symmetric image encryption scheme based on 3D chaotic cat maps. In: Chaos, Solitons & Fractals, pp. 74–82 (2004)
11. Mao, Y.B., Chen, G., Lian, S.G.: A novel fast image encryption scheme based on the 3D chaotic baker map. In: Int. Bifurcat Chaos, pp. 544–560 (2004)
12. Pareek, N.K., Patidar, V., Sud, K.K.: Image encryption using chaotic logistic map. Image and Vision Computing, 926–934 (2006)
13. Young, L.-S.: In: Branner, B., Hjorth, P. (eds.): NATO ASI Series, p. 293. Kluwer Academic Publishers, Dordrecht (1995)
14. Shannon, C.E.: Bell Syst. Tech. J. 28, 656 (1949)

Investigating Encrypted Material

Niall McGrath, Pavel Gladyshev, Tahar Kechadi, and Joe Carthy

University College Dublin, Dublin, Ireland

Abstract. When encrypted material is discovered during a digital investigation and the investigator cannot decrypt the material then s/he is faced with the problem of how to determine the evidential value of the material. This research is proposing a methodology of extracting probative value from the encrypted file of a hybrid cryptosystem. The methodology also incorporates a technique for locating the original plaintext file. Since child pornography (KP) images and terrorist related information (TI) are transmitted in encrypted format the digital investigator must ask the question *Cui Bono?* – who benefits or who is the recipient? By doing this the scope of the digital investigation can be extended to reveal the intended recipient.

Keywords: Encryption, Ciphertext, OpenPGP, RSA, Public & Private Keys.

1 Introduction

Law enforcement agencies (LEA) encounter encryption in relation to the distribution of KP [1] and of TI [2] offences. For example a KP distributor encrypts the KP material with PGP and posts it into a newsgroup or interest group via anonymous re-mailer or via an instant messenger system. The accomplice who is subscribed to that group receives encrypted material and can decrypt it. The anonymity of all involved parties is preserved and the content cannot be decrypted by bystanders. The use of PGP encryption in general has been cited [3] as a major hurdle in these investigations. In addition, during digital investigations evidence is often discovered which extends the scope of the investigation. These are compelling reasons for the computer forensic investigator to be able to identify encrypted material, examine it and finally extract evidential value from it. This paper presents a methodology that was formulated from experiments and it facilitates the identification of the recipient of PGP encrypted material. As an adjunct to this a technique that identifies the plaintext file that was encrypted is presented. Subsequently a technical evaluation was carried out in a case study to validate the methodology.

2 Problem Description

The investigation of subject A is initiated and a forensic image of the hard disk drive (HDD) is taken. Analysis is carried out and it is found that there is a significant amount of ciphertext files and plaintext files containing evidence. Subject A is a suspected distributor/seller of KP and subject B whose identity is unknown is the recipient of the encrypted material. The objective of this research is to establish an evidential link

M. Sorell (Ed.): e-Forensics 2009, LNICST 8, pp. 29–35, 2009.

between the encryptor and the recipient of PGP encrypted material and subsequently identify the plaintext file that was encrypted. In this scenario subject A must have had subject B's public key and PGP encrypted the plaintext material to form the ciphertext. Subject B can decrypt the ciphertext with his private key when he receives it. PGP is a hybrid cryptosystem where the ciphertext created by it follows the OpenPGP message format specified in [4]. A hybrid cryptosystem is a combination of symmetric and asymmetric encryption. A symmetric key is session generated and then this is used to encrypt data. The symmetric key is then encrypted using the recipient's public key. The public key can be stored and distributed by a key server. The symmetrically encrypted data and the asymmetrically encrypted symmetric key are the major components of a PGP ciphertext data-packet. PGP also compresses data before encryption for added security because this helps remove redundancies and patterns that might facilitate cryptanalysis, compression is only applied to the symmetrically encrypted data-packet. PGP typically uses the *Deflater* (zip) algorithm for compression.

2.1 Methodology

The methodology which facilitates the investigation of PGP encryption is outlined in Fig 1 and consists of a number of steps that are described in the following sections.

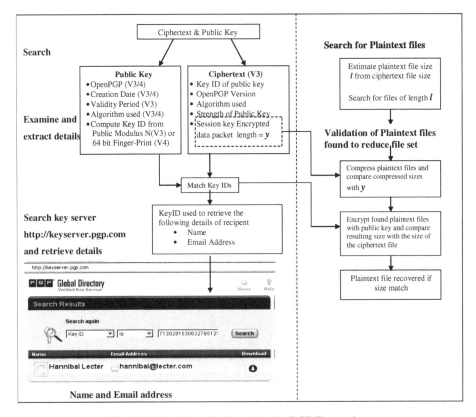

Fig. 1. Methodology for investigating PGP Encryption

In order to validate this research a framework of Java classes was created to generate OpenPGP encryption keys and data, a file parser to extract and analyse information from data, a test harness and a compression engine that examined ZIP compression.

2.1.1 Searching for Public Key and Ciphertext Artefacts

The first step of the methodology is to search for OpenPGP artefacts on the subject's HDD i.e. public keys and ciphertext files. Certain hexadecimal values can be used as signatures when searching for OpenPGP artefacts. These values have been determined experimentally and are shown in Fig 2. and Fig 3.

OpenPGP-PublicKey (V4)	Search Signature
512 Bit Key	\x98\x4d\x04
1024 Bit Key	\x98\x8d\x04
2048 Bit Key	\x99\x01\x0d\x04

Fig. 2. OpenPGP version 4 Public Key Search Criteria

OpenPGP-Ciphertext (V3)	Search Signature
512 Bit Key	\x84\x4c\x03
1024 Bit Key	\x84\x8c\x03
2048 Bit Key	\x85\x01\x0c\x03

Fig. 3. OpenPGP version 3 Ciphertext Search Criteria

When searching for public keys the linear relationship in equation 1, which has been determined experimentally, can be used to estimate the public key file size from the key strength. Key strength can be determined from section 2.1.3 below.

$$y = 3.9802x - 184 .$$
(1)

where x=key size in bytes and y = key strength in bits.

(1) was observed from the data of 300 generated RSA asymmetric keypairs i.e. 100 keypairs each of 512, 1024 & 2048 bit strengths.

2.1.2 Analysis of Public Key Artefacts-Examine and Extract Details

For each found public key file the next step of the methodology is to determine the following components of the OpenPGP public key: *Version* number, *Creation Date*, *Validity Period* (only for V3), *Algorithm* type and the *Public Modulus* (N). The low order 64 bits of N is the *Key ID* for a V3 key. The *Key ID* for a V4 key is the lower order 64 bits of the key finger print. This has to be computed because it is not an element of the OpenPGP specification however the method of computation is specified in the OpenPGP standard [4]. *Creation Date* and *Validity Period* are used to search for the corresponding ciphertext file because the timestamp of the ciphertext file will obviously be greater or equal to *Creation Date* of public key and less than or equal to *Validity Period* (if V3). The location of these items in the public key is specified in [4].

2.1.3 Analysis of Ciphertext Artefacts-Examine and Extract Details
For each ciphertext file found the following components of the OpenPGP ciphertext are determined: *Version* number, *Key ID* and *Key strength* of the public key used to create the ciphertext and *length* of *Symmetric Key Encrypted Data Packet*. The location of these items in the ciphertext is specified in the OpenPGP standard [4].

2.1.4 Matching the Key ID from Public Key and Ciphertext
In the next step the *Key ID* retrieved from ciphertext has to be compared with the computed *Key ID* from the public key. When a match occurs then it can be concluded that the public key was used to create the ciphertext under analysis.

2.1.5 Search Key Server – http://keyserver.pgp.com
Subsequently, the *Key Id* of public key is used to search a designated keyserver for *name* and *email address* of the owner of the public key i.e. the recipient of the encrypted material. These details are easily retrieved by inputting the *Key ID* into the website.

2.1.6 Approximating the Size of Plaintext File from ciphertext File
This is the initial step to searching for the original plaintext file. From the experiments carried out it was determined that there is a linear relationship between ciphertext file size and plaintext file size of JPG files, please see equation 2 below. Once l is evaluated then plaintext files of length l bytes can be used to reduce the size of the candidate file set.

$$y = 1.0019 \, l - 8249.9 .$$

(2)

where y=length of encrypted JPG file and l = length plaintext JPG file

(2) was derived from the generated data of encrypting a number of JPG files with a 100 RSA keys each of 1024 bit strength; using AES 256 bit symmetric encryption with ZIP compression.

2.1.7 Validation
The final step is to validate the candidate plaintext file(s) that are identified by the approximating process above. This is done by passing the plaintext files through the *Deflater Engine*, which compresses the files. The *number* of compressed bytes that the plaintext file deflates to closely approximates the *length* of the data packet to be session key (symmetrically) encrypted. This size is the *length* of data packet after compression has taken place. Finally each plaintext file (in the reduced file set) is encrypted. This will definitively determine the original plaintext file that was encrypted and exchanged.

2.2 Case Study

This case study is modelled on the described problem above and the methodology is applied practically to reveal the recipient of the exchanged encrypted material and to search for the original plaintext file. Techniques for investigating recently run programs, the registry and *NTUSER.dat* file and internet search history are outlined in [5]. In addition there are specialised techniques listed in [6] for investigating AIM related incidents. An investigation was carried out based on these techniques and it was established that an incident where America Online Instant Messenger (AIM) is used in conjunction with PGP encryption took place. An encrypted file that was transferred to subject B using AIM was located. AIM provides real-time one-to-one messaging between computers and attachments can be encrypted with the recipient's PGP public key.

2.2.1 Search and Analysis of Artefacts – Extraction of Significant Information

An Encase® search was executed with the criteria in Fig 2 and Fig 3. Then the parser was run to carry out the automated analysis and matching of the public key and corresponding ciphertext *Key ID*s. When a match is detected between the two *Key IDs* output is generated, please see parser output in Fig 4.

Output from Parser
Analysis of PGP Public Key Artefact
Version 4. Computed *key ID* value is *71302815306327851 29.* *Key Created Sat Jun 14 13:04:46 2008.* Validity Period: N/A because key is Version 4. *Value = 1, RSA -> Encryption* key strength is 1024.
Analysis of PGP Ciphertext Artefact
Version 3. *key ID retrieved from ciphertext is 7130281530632785129* *Key Strength is 1024 bit* *Value = 1, RSA -> Encryption* *Length of compressed data packet to be session key encrypted is 3729810.*
Match of Key IDs from Public Key & Ciphertext Files
Key ID from Public Key and Key ID from Ciphertext match -> Public Key was used to encrypt the Ciphertext.

Fig. 4. Output from Parser

2.2.2 Approximating the Size of Plaintext File from ciphertext File

Since the size of the ciphertext file identified by the parser is 3,729,956 bytes, then using equation 2, *l* evaluates to 3,731,116.8. Then a search for plaintext files of length 3,731,116.8 bytes is carried out. This search yielded 7 candidate files. In order to further reduce this file set a validation process was carried out, which is explained below.

2.2.3 Validation

The *Deflator* engine was then used to determine what size the 7 plaintext files, short listed in the previous steps, will compress to. Using the ciphertext file from the parser output; the length of data packet to be session key encrypted is 3729810. This is the size that the original plaintext data compresses to before encryption takes place. Therefore the number of compressed bytes, that the plaintext files *deflates* to, will closely approximate to a size of 3729810 bytes. This process reduces the file set down to 2 candidate files.

Finally these 2 plaintext files were encrypted giving 2 new ciphertext files of definitive sizes. These sizes were compared with the original ciphertext file size. Hence the original plaintext file that was encrypted and exchanged with AIM was conclusively determined. This was the designated file that contained evidence. Incidentally, 3729810 is the size of the file after compression takes place and then after encryption this becomes 3729824. This is due to the fact that OpenPGP uses CFB mode encryption and this mode operates on blocks of fixed length i.e. 16 bytes. This will give rise to the "stair casing effect" in terms of size of the encrypted file. The encrypted block size will be padded out to fit the block size.

3 Conclusion

The proposed methodology encompasses the searching for PGP public keys and encrypted material, the analysis of these and subsequently the extraction of the *Key Id* of the key used to encrypt the plaintext file. This enables the identification of the intended recipient (owner of public key) of the encrypted material by searching a global directory service like PGP key server. The integrated search technique facilitates the identification of the original plaintext file. Then by viewing the contents of the plaintext it can be determined if it is evidence or not. (We are assuming that the participation of subjects A and B in the exchange of encrypted material was wilful and knowing.) If the contents hold evidence the LEA can now serve a search warrant on subject B to seize his HDD. The methodology adheres to computer forensic standards of evidence *Search & Seizure, Acquisition and Retrieval*. In addition the methodology which was carried out in the Irish jurisdiction does not violate any civil liberties and the subjects' right to privacy is upheld. Irish law operates exclusionary rules in respect of evidence which has been gathered illegally or in breach of constitutional rights. However, *Section 8* of the *Data Protection Law* in Ireland provides an investigative clause i.e. disclosure of personal data in certain cases. There is also the *Anton Piller Order* which deals with special investigative circumstances like serious crime which provides for the right to search premises and seize evidence without prior warning.

4 Research Contribution

A methodology for the investigation of encrypted material has been formulated. This methodology facilitates the extraction of evidential value from the encrypted material to enable the identification of the recipient of the encrypted material. The incorporated search technique correlates the ciphertext file under investigation with the original plaintext file. This reduces the investigation time by carving the data under investigation into a significantly reduced file set. This is an entirely novel approach to investigating encrypted material and it is fully automated.

References

1. Carter, H.: Paedophiles jailed for hatching plot on internet (2007)
2. Joseh, S.: Hamas Terror Chat Rooms, December 11 (2007)
3. Siegfried, J., et al.: Examining the Encryption Threat, Computer Forensic Research and Development Center. International Journal of Digital Evidence (2004)
4. Callas, J., et al.: PGP Corporation OpenPGP Message Format (November 2007)
5. Bunting, S.: The Official EnCase Certified Examiner Guide. Wiley, Chichester (2008)
6. Dickson, M.: An Examination into AOL Instant Messenger 5.5. Elsevier Ltd., Amsterdam (2006) (Digital Investigation 3)

Legal and Technical Implications of Collecting Wireless Data as an Evidence Source

Benjamin Turnbull, Grant Osborne, and Matthew Simon

Defence and Systems Institute, University of South Australia
Mawson Lakes Campus, Mawson Lakes, South Australia 5095
Benjamin.Turnbull@unisa.edu.au, Grant.Osborne@unisa.edu.au,
Matthew.Simon@unisa.edu.au

Abstract. The collection of digital devices for forensic analysis is an area that requires constant revision. New technologies and connectivity options change what devices are able to hold electronic evidence and also the methods needed to secure it. This work focuses on the development of an 802.11-based wireless networking (Wi-Fi) forensic analysis tool that can aid in the identification and collection of evidence by identifying the presence of wireless networks and the devices to which they are attached. Specifically, this paper seeks to discuss the potential legal and technical challenges faced in the development of a wireless forensic tool.

1 Introduction

It has been hypothesized that the collection and analysis of wireless signals is of potential benefit to investigators. Specifically, investigators may wish to know of wireless networks within an area and the topography of each when identifying and collecting physical evidence. This may be for both proactive and reactive investigations.

There are several forms of misuse and crime that current investigative processes are unlikely to detect and identify, with the result that such devices may not be seized as sources of evidence, despite potentially having potential value (Turnbull & Slay 2005). Several cases exist in the public domain to substantiate this claim. There are also a number of potential, but unsubstantiated methods that wireless devices can be misused that may remain undetected by investigating bodies.

The electronic analysis of computers and devices would be incomplete if devices are undetected when collection occurs as they will not be present for later analysis. This is especially possible for wireless devices and systems that may be active but not physically accessible. Additionally, within a computer forensic examination, there is no published process for extracting the number and details of wireless networks that a device has connected to.

There have been several academic sources calling for the need for further investigation into the forensic collection and analysis of wireless devices noting several potential issues that may result from its use. Mike Schiffman, formerly of *@Stake*, was the first to discuss the need for a forensically sound 802.11 tool or series of tools at the 2002 Blackhat computer security conference (Schiffman 2002).

However, the potential contents and uses of this toolkit were never discussed and the project remained incomplete. From an academic perspective, Casey and Ferraro stated in the text *Investigating Child Exploitation and Pornography; the internet, law and forensic science* that:

"Wireless access to the Internet will undoubtably create new challenges for law enforcement. Wireless computing devices are by nature highly mobile, and wireless Internet access is more difficult to track than hard-wired systems. Security weaknesses also can wreak havoc because attributing criminal activity to an individual can become difficult"(Casey & Ferraro 2005). D'Ovidioa (2007) has also acknowledged the growing potential for wireless devices to be misused which he states as a factor in the growth of computer-based crime.

Schiffman (2002), Casey and Ferraro (2005) and D'Ovidioa (2007) have identified a research need. Wei (2004) has taken this further and discussed possible means of countering the issues raised and introduces the idea of wireless forensics as a possible extension to network forensics. Wei introduced several possible locations of evidence in a wireless network and made a distinction between the possible sources: evidence from the network and evidence via the network. However, this work gives no further details or discussion on wireless forensics either as a form of network forensics or with wireless devices potentially being a form of evidence.

This work seeks to explore the Australian context for the development of wireless networking analysis as a forensic tool, specifically on the effectiveness, forensic soundness and legality. Specifically, it is the authors assertion that a wireless network forensic tool, as with any other computer forensic program, should comply with fundamental forensic principles. Specifically the system should have the following features:

- Minimal interaction - minimal interaction with potential sources of evidence, and where such interaction is required, the interaction and effects understood and justifiable.
- Accuracy and repeatability – the use of the system in the same environment will provide the same result. Also, that the system operates accurately, and the technical limitations (if any) are known.
- Operation in accordance with all legal requirements.

These three features represent forensic minimums for software that potentially has a legal outcome. The first feature can be related to work from McKemmish (1999) or Pollitt (2007) and is linked with forensic process. The second feature required in a forensic application is an extension on scientific principle ensuring repeatability in experimentation. The final feature stated is of importance in all areas of computing, but requires in-depth consideration in the development of forensic and analysis tools where the product may have legal outcomes.

2 Existing Wireless Network Scanning Software

There are several products, designed for both consumers and for network administrators, which perform wireless site surveys and monitor network traffic. Beyond the systems provided by Operating Systems, the most applicable examples of wireless network monitors are the applications *NetStumbler* (Milner 2004) and *Kismet* (Kershaw 2007).Prior to developing an application to search for wireless networks for forensic investigators, it is wise to analyse similar existing applications that perform similar functions.. Whilst there are several other applications, both open-source and commercial, these are two that encompass a large cross-section of the community. Both have a standard feature-set and implement known methods.

The major difference between NetStumbler and Kismet is their mode of operation. NetStumbler is active while Kismet is passive in nature (Vladimirov, Gavrilenko, et al 2004). Active wireless network scanners actively probe networks by sending out *probe request* packets, to which wireless Access Points respond with *probe responses*. Passive network scanners do not actively probe networks in the area. The card enters a mode of operation called *monitor mode*, which allows it to receive all network traffic on a given channel without having to join a specific network.

From a forensic perspective, there are several issues with active network scanners:

- Information gathered relates only to wireless Access Points and Peer-to-peer networks, rather than other clients and devices which a wireless card cannot immediate connect to.
- There is a reliance on wireless Access Points to be self-identifying.
- Active wireless scanners are interacting with the wireless networks for which they are gathering information. Any such interaction will alter the environment and is detectable.

The designed use of active network discovery is for users to locate wireless networks. It is understandable that the most immediate limitation in its use is that it will only detect wireless Access Points or Peer-to-Peer wireless networks. It will not provide an outline of all devices on a network.

Whilst the use of the probe request and probe response frames are part of the IEEE 802.11b/a/g wireless specifications (Institute of Electrical and Electronic Engineers 1999), there are several vendors that deviate from the specification by allowing wireless Access Points to ignore probe requests. This practice is called 'cloaking' and will effectively hide wireless Access Points from active network scanning used by Operating Systems and active network scanners such as NetStumbler. Whilst this presents a limitation, it does not invalidate any findings from such systems but may mean that the findings are incomplete. Networks found would not be incorrect, but more networks may exist than discovered.

It is for three reasons that active network scanners are less than ideal for forensic purposes: they rely on Access Points being self identifying, limited information is obtainable (only wireless Access Points, rather than all networked devices) and interaction is required..

By contrast to active network scanners, applications such as Kismet are passive. They operate by placing the wireless card into monitor mode, which allows the receipt of all wireless data on a specific channel without any interaction. Analysis of this data may allow all wireless network Access Points and clients to be discovered, regardless of their cloaked status. In principle, the use of passive network scanning is more suitable for forensic purposes. No interaction is required to collect information, as no packets are sent. Additionally, all network devices can be identified rather than just Access Points. The issue that makes existing implementations of passive wireless network scanners less than suitable for forensic purposes relates to the potential legal issues with current implementations. This is introduced as follows.

3 Legality of Wireless Network Interception

The Australian Telecommunications Act (1997) and Telecommunications (Interception and Access) Act (1979) has equivalent legislation in many western countries. These define the law for private individuals, companies and law enforcement, to intercept different forms of telecommunications.

The definition of a telecommunications network is equally applicable to wired and wireless computer networking. However, the definition of a telecommunications network within the Telecommunications Act (1997) and the Telecommunications (Interception and Access) Act differ. The Telecommunications Act is much broader in its definition, stating that a *"a "telecommunications network" means a system, or series of systems, that carries, or is capable of carrying, communications by means of guided and/or unguided electromagnetic energy"* whereas the Telecommunications (Interception and Access) Act (1979) appends *"...or both, but does not include a system, or series of systems, for carrying communications solely by means of radiocommunication"*.

From respective definitions, it can be interpreted that whilst the Telecommunications Act does consider purely wireless networks as telecommunications networks (as does the Radiocommunications Act), the Telecommunications (Interception and Access) Act does not. The additional wording in the definition for a telecommunications network explicitly excludes networks that are solely radiocommunication-based.

Although the Radiocommunications Act (1992) may be applicable in some circumstances, a wireless network may or may not be entirely wireless – it may or may not have wired components. Any non-wireless component makes such a network a telecommunications network. It cannot be easily determined whether a wireless network operates purely by radio-frequency or is connected to a wired network.

To fully examine all legal issues, both forms of wireless network must be examined – the legalities for purely radio-based communication and a wireless network that has a wired component. To ensure legal compliance, both acts of legislation must be followed, so that regardless of network topology is, the interception of data is legal.

In the event that a network topology has both a wired and wireless component, the most appropriate legislation regarding network data interception is the Telecommunications (Interception and Access) Act (1979). Of note is that this legislation specifically prohibits the capture and storage of network data without a warrant. There are several exceptions such as being an intended recipient, or as required for finding faults in service by authorised individuals. This is relevant to this work, given that the purpose of the intended application relates directly to the capture and analysis of wireless network traffic. However, the term "data" within this legislation is interesting, as it does not include metadata, but relates directly to the payload of a packet or frame.

In all IP-based networks, headers of data-packets in transit may be examined by either intermediate nodes or by nodes in a shared broadcast medium (Zalewski 2005).

This information is analogous to the address on an envelope and the frame's payload being the private contents. Network-level protocols are defined such that intermediate nodes need only examine headers rather than the payload. Relating this information to legislation documenting telecommunications interception, there are obvious issues should that header-information interception be included in such legislation. Principally, interception of packet header-data is intrinsic to the operation of such networks. It is therefore not surprising that the Telecommunications (Interception and Access) Act (1979) does not legislate conditions for intercepting header information, or metadata regarding communication. There is therefore no legal impediment outlined in the Telecommunications (Interception and Access) Act that prevents the collection of such data. The frame and packet payloads themselves may be considered communication; however headers may be defined as a form of metadata. Relating this legislation to existing wireless applications in existence, it can be inferred that passive network discovery applications may be illegal by virtue of the fact that they record raw frames – both headers and payloads - from wireless networks. This is against legislation within the Telecommunications (Interception and Access) Act (1979) and cannot legally be performed without a warrant. However, Kismet, in its fundamental operation, operates similarly to all 802.11 network devices. In a shared collision domain, all network data must be collected by every client. Through header analysis, clients can discard packets if they are not the intended recipient. Therefore, if the proposed system was to only analyse and store frame headers, there would not be a requirement under the Telecommunications (Interception and Access) Act (1979) to obtain a warrant.

At this stage, the options for developing a wireless forensic tool are to either adapt an existing open-source passive wireless network scanner, or to develop an equivalent from the ground-up. There are advantages and disadvantages to each of these two methods. Whilst it is beneficial to leverage on existing, operational systems, it has been discussed that the end-user operational requirements and legal strictures for systems such as Kismet are very different to that required for forensic investigators. Kismet is designed to locate wireless networks, perform network-based testing and alerts. It does not discuss any legal issues associated with its use. A tool designed for investigators will require some overlap in functionality with a network administration utility, but will require differences in collection, logging and in the interface.

Adapting existing source code is a potential disadvantage in the development of a forensic wireless network scanning application. Large-scale modifications would be required to ensure that legal requirements are met. Specifically, before existing passive network capture software is used, payloads would need to be stripped from the captured data. This would require substantial sections of the code to be rewritten. For this reason, the decision was made to develop the proposed system without any reliance on existing passive scanning software products. This allowed the software development team to ensure that legal constraints were maintained in all sections of the code.

4   Conclusion and Outcomes

Whilst development of this tool is ongoing, its creation can now be validated as conforming to network and computer forensic science principles. Without such in-depth analysis, it is possible that application outcomes would have been legally unusable or technically less than adequate. This work highlights the potential pitfalls that may occur in the use of non-forensic software for forensic purposes; there are constraints required for forensic outcomes and software used. There are several areas of future work that this research has highlighted, and the most obvious is the development of the tool discussed. Similarly, this work has highlighted that the use of non-forensic tools for forensic purposes is not always appropriate, legal or technically sound.

References

Australian Legislation - Radiocommunications Act (1992)

Australian Legislation - Telecommunications Act (1997)

Australian Legislation - Telecommunications (Interception and Access) Act (1979)

Casey, E., Ferraro, M.: Investigating Child Exploitation and Pornography; the internet, law and forensic science. Elsevier Academic Press, Massachusetts (2005)

D'Ovidioa, R.: The evolution of computers and crime: complicating security practice. Security Journal (2007)

Institute of Electrical and Electronic Engineers. 802.11b Standard (1999), http://www.standards.ieee.org/ (retrieved May 24, 2003)

Kershaw, M.: Kismet Readme - Kismet 2007-01-R1 (2007), http://www.kismetwireless.net/documentation.shtml (retrieved January 12, 2007)

McKemmish, R.: What is forensic computing? Australian Institute of Criminology (1999), http://www.aic.gov.au/ (retrieved March 12, 2003)

Milner, M.: NetStumbler v0.4.0 Release Notes (2004), http://www.netstumbler.com/downloads/netstumbler_v0.4.0_release_notes.pdf (retrieved November 13, 2006)

Pollitt: An Ad Hoc Review of Digital Forensic Models. In: Second International Workshop on Systematic Approaches to Digital Forensic Engineering (SADFE 2007) (2007)

Schiffman, M.: The need for an 802.11 Wireless Toolkit. Paper presented at the Proc. BlackHat Security Conference, Las Vegas, United States of America, July 31 (2002)

Turnbull, B., Slay, J.: The 802.11 Technology Gap Case Studies in Crime. In: Tencon 2005 - IEEE Region 10 Conference, Melbourne, November 21 (2005)

Vladimirov, A.A., Gavrilenko, K.V., et al.: Wi-Foo: The Secrets of Wireless Hacking. Pearson / Addison Wesley, Boston, Massachusetts (2004)

Wei, R.: On A Conceptual Model of Network Forensics System for Information Security. In: The Proceeding of The Third International Conference of Information Systems Technology and its Applications STA 2004, Salt Lake City, Utah, United States of America (2004)

Zalewski, M.: Silence on the Wire: A field guide to passive reconnaissance and indirect attacks. No Starch Press Inc., San Francisco (2005)

Medical Image Authentication Using DPT Watermarking: A Preliminary Attempt

M.L. Dennis Wong, Antionette W.-T. Goh, and Hong Siang Chua

Information and Security Research Laboratory,
Swinburne University of Technology, Sarawak Campus, Malaysia
{dwong,agoh,hschua}@swinburne.edu.my
http://www.swinburne.edu.my

Abstract. Secure authentication of digital medical image content provides great value to the e-Health community and medical insurance industries. Fragile Watermarking has been proposed to provide the mechanism to authenticate digital medical image securely. Transform Domain based Watermarking are typically slower than spatial domain watermarking owing to the overhead in calculation of coefficients. In this paper, we propose a new Discrete Pascal Transform based watermarking technique. Preliminary experiment result shows authentication capability. Possible improvements on the proposed scheme are also presented before conclusions.

Keywords: Biomedical Image, Discrete Pascal Transform, Fragile Watermarking, Content Authentication.

1 Introduction

The progression of information technology in the past decade has resulted in proliferation in the field of health care information management. One fine example of this successful coupling of information technology and biomedicine is the move to store biomedical images in digital form. This move is well received by medical informatics practitioners as digital media can be easily archived, searched for and retrieved compared to its analog counterparts.

Despite the aforementioned feature of merits, there are arising concerns with regards to the security management of medical data which remain a critical bane to the practical implementation and deployment of Medical Information Systems (MIS). Among others, the major risk comes with the agility of medical media itself, as it is increasingly easier to manipulate digital images to one's content with digital image editing software readily installed in personal computers. Hence, any IT literate person with basic image editing knowledge could alter a biomedical image that leads to a different prognosis. With some level of persistence, the alteration may well be perceptually difficult to detect. In the scenario of medical insurance fraud, clusters of microcalcifications could be intentionally added to a healthy mammogram to indicate possible occurrence of breast cancer. Inversely, these regions could be removed intentionally from the mammogram,

M. Sorell (Ed.): e-Forensics 2009, LNICST 8, pp. 42–53, 2009.

resulting in an erroneous diagnosis that could lead to successful insurance policy approval or conversely claims.

Due to the strict nature of biomedical images, the research community readily adopted digital watermarking methods [1] as a viable solution to offer direly needed security to the digital biomedical images. Most watermarking schemes proposed for general image authentication are of the fragile type [2]. Fragile watermarking algorithms are usually strict tamper detection tools. They are built on the basis of inserting a watermark in such a way that any attempt to alter the host image will also result in destroying the watermark itself. As such, any manipulation of the image immediately causes the content itself to lose integrity. Another advantage of using fragile watermarking schemes is that one can locate the regions of distortions on the image that have been tampered with. Consequently, a medical expert can ascertain the level of trustworthiness of the image received to ensure accurate diagnosis.

Examples of biomedical image content authentication schemes work based on fragile watermarks can be found in [3,4] and [5].

In this paper, we report our preliminary attempt in designing a novel Transform Domain fragile watermarking method for biomedical image authentication, namely the Discrete Pascal Transform (DPT). Aburdene and Goodman first proposed the version of DPT studied herein based on a variation of the Pascal matrix [6]. To the best of our knowledge, this is the first biomedical image watermarking using DPT. The main motivation of choosing DPT as the transform domain is mainly owing two unique features of DPT. First, as it will be discussed later, the inverse transform of the DPT is equal to the forward transform itself. This specific property will eventually lead to a smaller footprint during VLSI implementation. Second, various multiplier-less implementation of DPT has been deviced [7,8]. This will lead to great speed in VLSI implementation.

Besides, DPT, when realized as a difference equation, leads to high pass filtering. Hence altering the DPT coefficients is the same as altering the high frequency components. The latter is a common idea available in other transform domain such as Discrete Cosine Transform and Discrete Wavelet Transform.

The outline of the paper is as follows. Section 2 discusses the role of watermarking with respect to the security of digital biomedical images. Section 3 describes the technicalities of the DPT in detail. An approach based on the DPT is demonstrated in Section 4 for digital biomedical image content authentication. Empirical results are presented in Section 5 with benchmarking results against potential attacks. Finally, some outstanding issues and future works are given before conclusions is drawn.

2   Biomedical Image Watermarking

2.1   Security of Medical Data

Coatrieux et al. [1] states the three mandatory components of security of medical data, namely, confidentiality, reliability and availability. They can be further explained as follows:

- **Confidentiality:** Only the entitled users have access to the medical information;
- **Availability:** This refers to the ability of a medical information system to be used by the entitled users in the stipulated conditions of access; and
- **Reliability:** This is tied to the aspects of integrity and authentication, where the integrity part checks that the information has not been altered by unauthorized persons and the authentication part checks that the information belongs to the entitled user and is issued from the right source.

2.2   Providing Security through Watermarking

In 1993, the Digital Imaging and Communications in Medicine (DICOM) standard [9] was developed to provide interoperability between all current and future medical systems from different manufacturers. This standard is now adopted by the medical community for the purpose of storing, transmitting and viewing medical images. It is also required by all Electronic Health Record (EHR) systems that include imaging information as an integral part of the patient record [9]. DICOM dependent medical specialties include radiology, cardiology, dentistry, surgery, neurology, breast imaging, and radiotherapy.

Conventionally, each DICOM medical image is associated with a patient's private data such as patient's name, age, results of examination/diagnosis, time taken, etc. All these private information are recorded into a meta data or header file, which is appended to the image. The DICOM standard stores the image data and the meta data separately. Clearly, this is dangerous as the link between the image and the textual information is practically non-existent. Using watermarking, it is possible to embed the meta data into the image data. This way, we introduce a situation where both pieces of information will depend on each other to provide the full information in a more secure manner. Not only does watermarking reduce the happenings of a mismatch between the image data and the patient's meta data, but it also prevents the loss of the header file when the image undergoes some intentional processing.

Watermarking has a very important role in medical image security in terms of confidentiality, integrity and authentication [1]. The three main objectives of applying watermarking in the medical domain according to [1] are:

- **data hiding** for the purpose of inserting meta data and other information so that the image is more useful or easier to use;
- **integrity control** which checks that the image has not been modified in an unauthorized manner; and
- **authenticity** which traces the origin of an image.

2.3   Watermarking Requirements for Biomedical Image Authentication

The criteria for generic watermarking authentication [10] can be applied to the medical domain. However, rigorous bindings in the medical domain due to strict ethics and legislative rules [1] require other authentication features to substitute those in generic data authentication which are insufficient and sometimes too rigid for use in biomedical image authentication.

Based on literature review, requirements specific to watermarking-based biomedical image authentication include:

Imperceptibility/Reversible Watermarking. It is desirable that any watermarking should not affect the quality of the biomedical image. No distortion introduced by watermarking or degradation of image quality should be tolerated as this could result in a fallacious diagnosis. Thus, the watermarking should be reversible, in the sense that the original pixel values must be recovered exactly [11], and therefore recovering the original image (without the embedded watermark).

Integrity Control. Biomedical images usually undergo some preprocessing such as enhancement and contrast stretching [1] while being interpreted by a radiologist. As such, it is important to define whether the originally obtained image or the image processed by the radiologist should be used as a reference for integrity control.

Besides unintentional modification such as the image processing activities mentioned above, we must also address the malicious act of intentionally tampering images for illegal purposes. As such, we can easily see two levels of integrity control [3], that is:

- **strict** integrity control, where the modification of even one bit is not allowed; and
- **content-based** integrity control, where pixels are allowed to differ to the extent that the semantics of the image remain preserved.

Authentication. Transmission of biomedical images over the Internet for the purpose of telediagnosis and widespread exchange of medical data by the medical community has made authentication of biomedical images an essential issue. Coatrieux et al. [1] states that a critical requirement is to authenticate different parts of an Electronic Patient Record (EPR), in particular, the images.

3   Discrete Pascal Transform

The Discrete Pascal Transform (DPT) was introduced by Aburdene and Goodman [6]. It is a member of the discrete polynomial transform family and is based on a variation of the Pascal matrix.

The DPT coefficients, as with the case of other linear transformations, can be calculated using a transformation matrix, P. In the case of DPT, P takes the form of a lower-triangular matrix whose elements, P_{ij}, are equal to:

$$P_{ij} = \begin{cases} (-1)^j \binom{i}{j} & i \leq j \\ 0 & \text{otherwise} \end{cases}$$

where $\binom{i}{j} = \dfrac{i!}{j!(i-j)!}$ with i, j as non-negative integers.

The discrete Pascal transform of a one-dimensional vector, x, can then be defined as:

$$X = Px \tag{1}$$

where x, X are N x 1 vectors and P is the N x N Pascal transform matrix. An example of the the Pascal matrix of dimension $N = 4$ is given below:

$$P_{4 \times 4} = \begin{bmatrix} 1 & \cdot & \cdot & \cdot \\ 1 & -1 & \cdot & \cdot \\ 1 & -2 & 1 & \cdot \\ 1 & -3 & 3 & -1 \end{bmatrix}$$

where zero entries are replaced with · for clarity.

As such, we can see that the matrix P can be obtained from left compacting the row elements of a Pascal's triangle into a zero matrix and then alternating the signs of the columns.

The basic properties of the P matrices are:

- All elements in the first column are equal to 1,
- All matrices are lower triangular,
- The sum of the elements in each row (except of the first one) are equal to 0, and
- All matrices are equal to their inverse.

As the elements of the Pascal transform matrix that are above the diagonal are equal to zero, we can derive the forward DPT as:

$$X_k = \sum_{n=0}^{k} (-1)^n \binom{k}{n} x_n \tag{2}$$

where x_n is the data sequence, X_k are the transform coefficients and $k = 0, 1, ..., N - 1$.

With the inverse of the Pascal matrix equal to the Pascal matrix itself, we can calculate the inverse DPT using the same equation as the forward transformation:

$$x = P^{-1}X = PX \tag{3}$$

In summation, it can be expressed as:

$$x_n = \sum_{n=0}^{k} (-1)^k \binom{n}{k} X_k \tag{4}$$

The matrix P can also be applied to a two-dimensional image, $\mathfrak{X}$, where the DPT coefficients can be obtained through:

$$X = P\mathfrak{X}P^T \tag{5}$$

where P^T is the transpose of matrix P
or equivalently:

$$X = (P(P\mathfrak{X})^T)^T \tag{6}$$

4   Proposed Method

4.1   Description of the Method

The proposed approach takes on the method of watermarking in a transform domain, namely the Discrete Pascal Transform (DPT) [6]. Recent research is mostly based on the frequency or transform domains as they offer better performance in terms of fidelity and detectability. The introduction of the DPT has brought about intensive study in applications such as signal processing and image processing, as well as communications and control systems [6].

In this work, we integrate a fragile watermarking approach that embeds the authentication information - in our case, we use a randomly generated secret - into the biomedical image itself. The authentication watermark is embedded in the transform coefficients of the entire image, thereby allowing strict integrity control on the overall image. In this way, regardless whether the region is of interest or non-interest, the quality of the image after watermarking will not be affected and the diagnostic value of the image is preserved. It is also possible to detect which portions of the image has been tampered with. This is known as the *localization* feature.

The proposed watermarking scheme attempts to address the three components of security of medical data and meets the requirements of watermarking-based biomedical image authentication mentioned in Section 2.

4.2   Algorithm

The embedding and authentication process of the proposed watermarking scheme is detailed here.

Selection of Embeddable Coefficients. We chose to implement the scheme on a 4 x 4 transform. Only six coefficients in a 4 x 4 transform block are used for embedding. The position of the six coefficients is shown in the matrix below:

$$\begin{bmatrix} 1 & n & n & n \\ n & 6 & 10 & 14 \\ n & 7 & 11 & 15 \\ n & 8 & 12 & 16 \end{bmatrix}$$

where n denotes the position of the chosen coefficients and the numbers indicate the remaining coefficients. It is noteworthy that the nature of the assignment of embedding in those particular coefficients (i.e. elements $2, 3, 4, 5, 9$, and 13) has been shown by a series of experiments to cause the least degradation to the image quality.

Generation of Quantization Codebook. Compared to cryptographic-based image authentication methods which authenticate binary representations of the image, watermark-based approaches adopts a tamper detection mechanism based on the fragility of the imperceptible watermark. One approach is the quantization -based watermarking [12,13] which is by oblivious by nature. However, conventional quantization-based watermarking methods are sensitive toward modification and cannot differentiate between incidental manipulations and malicious tampering. As such, there is a need to decrease the fragility of the embedded watermark to ensure that incidental manipulations are not treated as malicious tampering causing the occurrence of false errors. To increase the robustness of the embedded watermark, the quantization intervals can be widened.

By nature, all medical images are usually grayscale images. Hence, we can restrict ourselves to integer values between 0 and 255 for computation purposes when determining the quantization levels. Given the nature of the DPT itself, one would find that it is necessary to form the quantization codebook with each quantization function having three quantization steps.

Watermark Embedding Procedure. Given a host image, I, of dimension $M_I \times N_I$, and a binary watermark image, W, of dimension $M_W \times N_W$, we can then choose the block size, $B = \dfrac{M_I N_I}{M_W N_W}$. For practicality, we have chosen a randomly generated binary message in place of a binary image.

Existing literature review [14,15] discusses the possibility of using the DICOM header or important portions of it as the watermark. In reality, the textual data stored in the DICOM header which consists of sensitive data such as patient information can be used as the watermark as long as it does not exceed the size of $M_W N_W$.

The host image, I, is first divided into adjacent non-overlapping blocks, B. As mentioned earlier, B would consist of a 4 x 4 block. For each block, we perform the two-dimensional DPT on the block to obtain the block of DPT coefficients (B_p).

We embed a watermark value by modulating a selected transform coefficient into the quantized interval determined from the corresponding watermark value:

$$B'_p = Q_0(B_p) \quad \text{if} \quad W(i,j) == 0$$

or

$$B'_p = Q_1(B_p) \quad \text{if} \quad W(i,j) == 1$$

After which, we apply the two-dimensional DPT again on the encoded block to obtain the spatial domain image. (Note that the forward and inverse DPT is the same operation).

In an attempt to maintain a high fidelity on the watermarked image, we have chosen Q_0 and Q_1 to embed the watermark value of 0 and 1 respectively.

Authentication Procedure. During the authentication process, the watermarked image is again divided into non-overlapping blocks and for each block, the DPT coefficients are calculated by applying the DPT on the specific block. A simple majority vote scheme is then used to allow more robust decoding of the embedded check bits. If most of the coefficients are even, then the bit encoded is '0', otherwise the bit encoded is '1'.

The choice of a majority voting scheme would work well with end-users of a telediagnosis system who may have limited knowledge in the medical field, for example, administrative clerks. Hence, they may have trouble detecting modifications made to a digital x-ray if a reference image is unavailable. Thus, it is practical to use such a system which basically checks whether the image received is authentic or not and then, displays the results in a straightforward manner.

5   Experimental Results

The test set consisted of 512 x 512 grayscale single frame biomedical image samples provided by S. Barré [16]. The proposed scheme was implemented on Matlab R2006a with the aid of its Image Processing Toolbox (Version 5.2). For simplicity but without loss of generality, we demonstrate experimental results of the proposed watermarking scheme on three 512 x 512 grayscale images, namely OT-MONO2-8-hip, OT-MONO2-8-colon and OT-MONO2-8-a7. The watermark used was a randomly generated string of binary numbers of the matrix size 128 x 128.

Figs. 1 illustrates the original images and the corresponding watermarked images respectively. As it can be seen, the perceptual quality of the watermarked image is still preserved, hence, meeting the strict requirements of biomedical image watermarking.

To examine the quality of the watermarked image, we used the peak signal-to-noise ratio (PSNR) signal quality evaluation parameter. Even though the PSNR is normally not associated with perceptual quality, it can provide a measure of image distorsion in terms of numerical values.

We can see that the watermarked versions of the three biomedical images look identical to the original images. The perceptual difference is minimal as indicated by its recorded PSNRs shown in the following table:

Table 1. PSNR Recorded for the Proposed Watermarking Scheme

No.	Image Name	PSNR (dB)
1	OT-MONO2-8-hip	32
2	OT-MONO2-8-colon	33
3	OT-MONO2-8-a7	30

To test the authentication scheme, we modified the content of the OT-MONO2-8-hip image as shown in Fig. 2 (a) by adding a shaded region in the middle of the image. In a fragile watermarking scheme, any alteration to the watermarked image would result in an alteration in the watermark itself as well. The retrieved watermark from the modified watermark image is shown in Fig. 2(b).

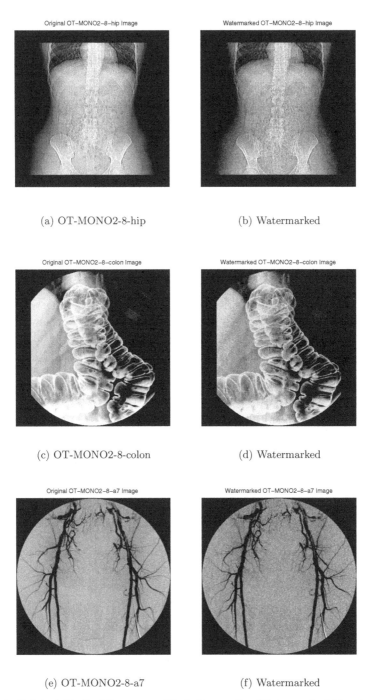

(a) OT-MONO2-8-hip   (b) Watermarked

(c) OT-MONO2-8-colon   (d) Watermarked

(e) OT-MONO2-8-a7   (f) Watermarked

Fig. 1. Original Medical Images vs Their Respective Watermarked Counterparts

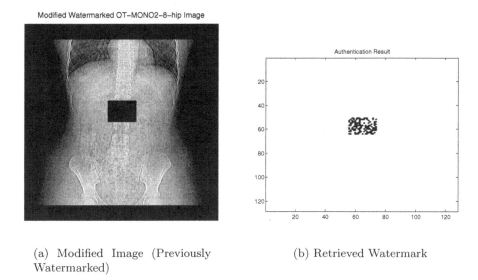

(a) Modified Image (Previously
Watermarked)

(b) Retrieved Watermark

Fig. 2. An Illustration of the Authentication Ability

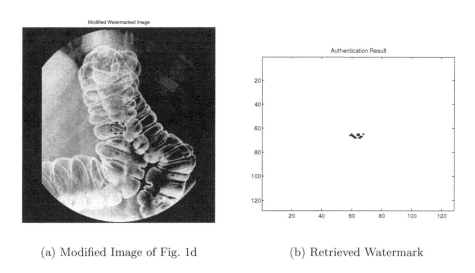

(a) Modified Image of Fig. 1d

(b) Retrieved Watermark

Fig. 3. A More Realistic Alteration Attempt

6   Conclusion and Future Works

While in general, we have shown that Watermarking in DPT domain is workable,
there exists issues that require further investigation. First, the PSNR obtained
from the existing scheme is not satisfactory for practical deployment. Depending on the image region, there exists visible artifacts in monotonous region. An

improved PSNR can be obtained by reducing the quantization steps but our experiments have shown that while achieving 10 dB increase in PSNR, the scheme will not withstand simple LSB erasure attack. An alternative might be selective watermarking where only certain segments of an image are watermarked. We await further results to confirm this intuition. Other perceptual metrics, e.g. Structural Similarity[17], should be taken in account as evaluation metrics.

Second, the security of the current scheme depends solely on the secrecy of the code book. In future version of the scheme, more effort should be put into code book design to prevent reverse engineering of the code book used. Selective watermarking will also increase the security of the current scheme.

From our experiments, it was shown that the current scheme withstands simple attacks such as the erasure of the LSB. As most medical images will be stored in their compressed form, it would be worthwhile to investigate methods of allowing the current scheme to withstand acceptable compression ratio.

In conclusion, an experimental scheme based on DPT for fragile watermarking was proposed and presented in this paper. The scheme is devised primarily with future real time VLSI implementation in mind. We envisage that, with careful revisions, the scheme is potentially useful for digital biomedical media authentication applications.

Acknowledgement

The authors would like to expressed their gratitudes to Swinburne University of Technology (Sarawak Campus) for the support of this work through the Swinburne Sarawak Seed Grant Scheme.

The authors would also like to thank Raphael C.-W. Phan, Loughborough University for his useful discussion in relation to this work.

References

1. Coatrieux, G., Maitre, H., Sankur, B., Rolland, Y., Collorec, R.: Relevance of watermarking in medical imaging. In: Proc. 3rd IEEE EMBS Int. Conf. Inform. Technology Applicat. in Biomedicine. 3rd Workshop Int. Telemedical Inform. Soc., Arlington, USA, pp. 250–255 (November 2000)
2. Walton, S.: Information authentification for a slippery new age. Dr. Dobbs Journal 20(4), 18–26 (1995)
3. Coatrieux, G., Maitre, H., Sankur, B.: Strict integrity control of biomedical images. In: Proc. SPIE: Security and Watermarking of Multimedia Contents III, vol. 4314 (2001)
4. Acharya, R., Niranjan, U.C., Lyengar, S.S., Kannathal, N., Lim, C.M.: Simultaneous storage of patient information with medical images in the frequency domain. Comput. Methods and Programs in Biomedicine 76, 13–19 (2004)
5. Ho, A.T.S., Zhu, X., Shen, J.: Authentication of biomedical images based on zero location watermarking. In: Proc. 8th Int. Conf. Control, Autom., Robot., and Vision (2004)

6. Aburdene, M.F., Goodman, T.J.: The discrete pascal transform. IEEE Signal Processing Letters 12(7), 493–495 (2005)
7. Skodras, A.N.: Fast discrete pascal transform. Electronics Letters 23, 17367–17368 (2006)
8. Zhong, Q.-C., Nandi, A.K., Aburdene, M.F.: Efficient implementation of discrete pascal transform using difference operators. Electronics Letters 43, 1367–1368 (2007)
9. DICOM Standard
10. Rey, C., Dugelay, J.-L.: A survey of watermarking algorithms for image authentication. EURASIP J. on Appl. Signal Processing 2002(6), 613–621 (2002) (special issue on image analysis for multimedia interactive services)
11. Macq, B., Dewey, F.: Trusted headers for medical images. In: Proc. DFG VIII-DII Watermarking Workshop (1999)
12. Chen, B., Wornell, G.W.: Quantization index modulation methods for digital watermarking and information embedding of multimedia. Journal of VLSI Signal Processing 27, 7–33 (2001)
13. Eggers, J.J., Bauml, R., Tzschoppe, R., Girod, B.: Scalar costa scheme for information embedding. IEEE Trans. Signal Processing 51(4), 1003–1019 (2003)
14. Coatrieux, G., Lecornu, L., Roux, C., Sankur, B.: A review of image watermarking applications in healthcare. In: Proc. 28th Annu. Int. Conf. of the IEEE EMBS, pp. 4691–4694 (2006)
15. Coatrieux, G., Quantin, C., Montagner, J., Fassa, M., Allaert, F.A., Roux, C.: Watermarking medical images with anonymous patient identification to verify authenticity. In: Proc. 21st Int. Congress of the European Federation for Medical Informatics MIE 2008, pp. 667–672 (2008)
16. Barré, S.: Medical imaging: Samples (2003)
17. Wang, Z., Bovik, A.C., Sheikh, H.R., Simoncelli, E.P.: Image quality assessment: From error visibility to structural similarity. IEEE Transactions On Image Processing 13(4), 600–612 (2004)

Robust Correctness Testing for Digital Forensic Tools

Lei Pan and Lynn M. Batten

School of EIT, Deakin University, Burwood, Victoria 3125, Australia
{l.pan,lmbatten}@deakin.edu.au

Abstract. In previous work, the authors presented a theoretical lower bound on the required number of testing runs for performance testing of digital forensic tools. We also demonstrated a practical method of testing showing how to tolerate both measurement and random errors in order to achieve results close to this bound. In this paper, we extend the previous work to the situation of correctness testing.

The contribution of this methodology enables the tester to achieve correctness testing results of high quality from a manageable number of observations and in a dynamic but controllable way. This is of particular interest to forensic testers who do not have access to sophisticated equipment and who can allocate only a small amount of time to testing.

Keywords: digital forensics, correctness testing, data carving tools.

1 Introduction

Working from a legal perspective, digital forensics is one of the most potent deterrents to digital crime. Within the last ten years, more than a dozen definitions of digital forensics have been proposed; however, the one common element in all these definitions is the preparation of evidence for presentation in a court of law. In courtrooms, witnesses present the facts of a case as perceived by them. But a witness sometimes serves as an "expert" in giving personal opinions about what has been found or observed during a digital investigation. Such opinions are formed on the basis of professional experience and deductive reasoning.

A digital forensic expert must be familiar with many forensic tools, but no expert can know or use all of the forensic tools available. Questions regarding digital forensic software tools used in an investigation are often asked in the courtroom. Such questions may be phrased as: "have you personally used tool A?"; "did you use tool B because it is faster than tool A?"; "among tools A, B and C, which tool performs better in assisting this case?"; and so on. The judge, as well as lawyers on opposing sides, may be very interested in the answers to these questions in order to find possible flaws or errors in the reasoning.

Where can the forensic expert obtain information about the effectiveness of the tools he chooses to use? Current testing work is led by a few official organizations [2,3,4] often government supported, with many results unavailable to the

M. Sorell (Ed.): e-Forensics 2009, LNICST 8, pp. 54–64, 2009.

general public, or only published for tools which have become commonly used. Mohay [9] has argued that the increasing time gap between available testing results and the release of testing results of new tools is a major reason why newly developed tools are rarely accepted into general digital forensic practice.

The focus of this paper is on developing a simple way of helping an expert witness in digital forensics to implement some standard software tests in order to be ready with answers for questions such as those above. Because the quality of software tools depend on many parameters, testing paradigms vary on the basis of the tester's intention; thus a test may be aimed at performance, correctness, reliability or security.

In previous work [10] the authors focused on testing the performance of tools. In this paper, we focus on correctness testing in the context of the forensic tool testing discussed in [1,15]. A correctness test evaluates how much the functionality of a tool differs from the user's expectations. The definition of correctness and the results of any test for correctness must both be measurable. In this paper, we define 'correctness' as both *accuracy* and *precision* of the tool.

We phrase our problem as: how can an expert witness without any specialized equipment quickly and correctly gain knowledge of the capacity for correctness of a given set of digital forensic tools? We propose an effective and efficient correctness testing framework. Our framework regulates what digital forensic tools should be compared in one experiment and it determines a testing plan prior to the experiment so that the tester can balance the test effort against the accuracy of the test results Moreover, the framework interprets the test results and includes necessary conditions for their reproducibility. The key contributions of this work are two-fold: (a) the development of a correctness testing methodology for digital forensic tools achieving effectiveness and efficiency simultaneously, and (b) theoretical and practical contributions for forensic expert witnesses from the findings of a case study.

Our methodology on executing testing plans is described in Section 2. Section 3 provides an example to illustrate our methodology. The paper is summarized in Section 4.

2 Our Approach

In previous work [10,11], the authors described the background of forensic tool testing as a scientific method and introduced orthogonal arrays [7] as an approach to organizing testing runs. We shall use the same terminology as in that paper. In this section, we demonstrate how the use of orthogonal arrays gives us a flexible methodology for testing correctness of forensic tools. The approach is dynamic and improves the quality of testing results during the execution. Our methodology reduces the impact of inaccurate observations with large values by using Taguchi's logarithmic function [14]; it detects outliers by engaging paired Student t-tests [16]; and it determines the number of necessary observations by applying recent statistical findings.

In an array, each parameter corresponds to a column and each test performed corresponds to a row. The entries in the array are the values taken on by the parameters. These entries are placed according to constraints set by the testing requirements. In general, we wish only that the constraints are those of fairness (each value of every parameter of the system should be tested an equal number of times) and blindness (no conclusions are drawn until the entire test is ended). These conditions are the primary focus of special types of arrays known as 'orthogonal arrays' or OAs. In what follows, N will refer to the number of rows and k to the number of columns of the array. The entries in the array can be taken from any set S of size s. In the general case, there is an additional parameter t known as the *strength*, but it is sufficient for our purposes to always use $t = 2$. We can now give the definition due to [7]: An $OA(N, k, s, 2)$ is an $N \times k$ array with entries from S such that

F every $N \times 2$ sub-array contains each pair of elements of S the same number of times as a row.

In other words, any row of the array restricted to any two columns appears the same number of times in the restriction. An OA allows us to test the performance of a tool against itself, or to test it against other tools on the same parameter set.

We lay out two key strategies to tackle the testing error issue. First, we set a simple criterion to identify the potentially contaminated observations, referred to as *suspicious samples*. The negative effect caused by suspicious samples will be mitigated by introducing additional observations with fewer contaminated ones. We increase the robustness of testing results by using the logarithmic function in the Taguchi method [14], and predict the total number of testing observations by using Zhou and Zhu's result in [17]. Second, we alter the standard execution order of a testing array from row-wise to column-wise. This technique enables additional observations to be introduced on demand and so a tester can improve the quality of testing results without interrupting the experiment.

2.1   Reducing the Impact of Errors

In any experiment, errors are inevitable. Generally, errors are of two types — measurement error and random error. A measurement error is any bias caused by the observation methods or instrument used. A random error is caused by the variation of the experimental environment. The first type of error can be dealt with by good calibration, while the second is more difficult to handle. In either case, data outliers will occur once the error has accumulated to a certain level. An outlier is "an observation that lies an abnormal distance from other values" [8]. The effect of outliers is to distort the results of the test, and so their impact must be reduced. There are several ways to effective reduction of outlier impact, but we choose that of Taguchi et al. in [13,14].

Taguchi proposed the use of the logarithmic function $f(x) = -10 \log(x^2)$ [13], which has the effect of reducing the impact of error for real input values of $x > 1$, but increasing the impact for $0 < x < 1$. Thus, use of the logarithmic scale makes it increasingly important to obtain accurate results with small values. When less precise measuring devices are used to obtain observation results, a measuring error may introduce an outlier which strongly degrades the quality of the results.

In order to identify suspicious data, we therefore propose the following algorithm which is applied to the logarithmic version of the data.

Algorithm input: a set of test output observations in real numbers and a known (or estimated) margin of error caused by measuring errors.
Algorithm output: a set of suspicious data in real numbers.
Begin Algorithm

Step 1. Subtract the margin of error from each value in the set of observations to obtain a second set of data.
Step 2. Apply the paired Student t-test on the two data sets.
Step 3. If the two data sets are not significantly different according to the t-test, then output an empty set and terminate the algorithm; otherwise, proceed to *Step 4*.
Step 4. Output a set containing the smallest observation from the first set, repeated as many times as it occurs. Then go back to *Step 1* using an input the difference between the first set and the output set.

This algorithm will eventually terminate and output a set of real numbers or an empty set. If the output set is nonempty, we define the elements in the set as *suspicious samples*. If suspicious samples are detected, then we will need to improve the quality of testing results by ensuring enough instances of observations.

The next subsection will discuss how to obtain an adequate number of observations.

2.2 Determining the Number of Tests to Run

To reduce the impact of outliers, merely applying Taguchi's logarithmic function is insufficient because observations with small values have to be accurate. To improve the quality of these observations, more test runs will reduce the impact caused by any random error, and an appropriate statistical analysis reduces the impact caused by any measurement error.

Zhou and Zhu in [17] determined the relationship between the number of suspicious samples and the number of observations. Their Theorem 1 is restated in the following theorem in order to fit our situation.

Theorem 1. *Suppose that an experimental design has N rows. Then for any integer $R \geq 1$, in order for $N \times R$ observations to withstand the impact caused by the measure error and the random error, the number of suspicious samples should not exceed*

$$N_c = \min \left\{ \left\lfloor \frac{N-1}{2} \right\rfloor + \left\lfloor \frac{N+1}{2} \right\rfloor \cdot \left\lfloor \frac{R-1}{2} \right\rfloor, \ N \cdot \left\lfloor \frac{R-1}{2} \right\rfloor \right\},$$

where $\lfloor x \rfloor$ denotes the largest integer less than or equal to x.

Specifically, there are $\left\lfloor \frac{N-1}{2} \right\rfloor + \left\lfloor \frac{N+1}{2} \right\rfloor \cdot \left\lfloor \frac{R-1}{2} \right\rfloor$ outliers caused by the measurement error and $N \cdot \left\lfloor \frac{R-1}{2} \right\rfloor$ outliers caused by the random error.

Theorem 1 indicates that increasing the number of observations increases the overall credibility of the results. This theorem also indicates that a large product of the N value (the row size of the testing array) and the R value (the replication number) is crucial for tolerating experimental errors. This theorem implies that the R value must be equal or larger than 2 to tolerate outliers caused by the measurement error, and must be equal or larger than 3 to tolerate outliers caused by the random error.

We use the results of this theorem to determine the necessary number of observations for an experiment so that the impact of outliers will be negligible. The next subsection presents our new adaptive procedure for executing an experiment.

2.3   Our Adaptive Procedure

Consolidating the above ideas and results, we present an adaptive procedure for conducting tests. The procedure helps the tester to obtain high-quality testing results based on a given testing array. Our procedure ensures that the overall quality of the results is good enough for deriving reliable and trustworthy conclusions, because this procedure reduces the impact of outliers caused by experimental errors to a negligible level.

Procedure input: an $N \times k$ orthogonal array associated with the experiment.
Procedure output: $N \times R$ observations.
Begin Procedure

Step 1. Execute the array once so that each row will be tested. After this step, the tester should have conducted N observations associated to every row of the array.

Step 2. Transform the results by using Taguchi's logarithmic function and check for suspicious samples in accordance with Section 2.1. If there are no suspicious samples, go to *Step 6*; otherwise, letting m be the number of suspicious samples, proceed to the next step.

Step 3. Compare m with the value of N_c in Theorem 1, and increase R to the smallest value of R such that $m \leq N_c$.

Step 4. Let R' be the number of observations which have already been made. Retest using the array $R-(R'+1)$ times. The execution order is column-wise. (Input may be changed at this stage; see the example of Section 3.)

Step 5. Transform the new results using the logarithmic function and search for suspicious samples again. Newly identified suspicious samples should be counted before proceeding to the next step.

Step 6. Test each row of the array for the last time, transform the results and do a final check for suspicious samples. If the number of suspicious samples exceeds the number identified in Theorem 1, then go back to *Step 3*; otherwise, the experiment is completed.

End Procedure

Our methodology provides a cure for the error-handling problem suffered by the Taguchi method. It has the following advantages over these two methods:

- Our method fulfills the blindness requirement. That is, no conclusions are drawn before a test is completed.
- Our method does not waste testing effort. That is, every observation is kept, so that the tester knows the exact testing effort and the complete set of results.
- Our method is more automated than Taguchi model. Our method does not require the tester to determine the replication number before the start of a test, and does not pause the test before an adequate number of observations are obtained.

3 Correctness Testing of Data Carving Tools

To illustrate the procedure of obtaining good-quality results from a comparative experiment, we conducted a correctness test on data carving tools. We chose the number of false positives as the only metric on which to compare the correctness across the tool set. If a tester wishes to test additional items, these must be dealt with one at a time. In particular, we evaluated the correctness of these tools by the number of unsuccessfully recovered files. In this experiment, a data carving tool is a tool whose input data format is the raw image of a disk partition and whose output data format is that of the recovered file.

We chose five data carving tools. The choice of tools is represented as sequential integers. In this experiment, we included 5 scenarios:

0 *Foremost*
1 *FTK*
2 *Magicrescue*
3 *Scalpel*
4 *X-Way Forensics*

An OA whose total number of rows is divisible by 5 was required if each of these five scenarios was tested once; accordingly, if three scenarios were tested twice and two scenarios were tested once, then the number of rows should be divisible by 8.

We considered recovering 3 common types of files — MS word documents, jpeg files and MS xls files. By excluding (labeled as "0") or including (labeled as "1") these types of files in the testing input image, we had a total of 3 binary parameters in the experiment, and so needed an OA with at least 3 columns and 6 rows.

We iterated through the online OA library [12,10]. No 5×4 or 6×4 OA was available. We found several options with 16 rows satisfying the **F** condition, and we did not choose any OA with more rows to save the overall testing effort. The closest fit is the 16×9 array listed below. It has one column with 8 variables which we list first and use to allocate tools to be tested, and 8 columns with binary variables. The OA is indexed as

$$16 \quad 4(*) \quad 2^8 \quad 8^1$$

in table 1 on the page http://www.research.att.com/~njas/doc/cent4.html.

$$
\begin{array}{l}
0\ 0\ 0\ 0\ 0\ 0\ 0\ 0\ 0 \\
0\ 1\ 1\ 1\ 1\ 1\ 1\ 1\ 1 \\
1\ 0\ 0\ 0\ 0\ 1\ 1\ 1\ 1 \\
1\ 1\ 1\ 1\ 1\ 0\ 0\ 0\ 0 \\
2\ 0\ 0\ 1\ 1\ 0\ 0\ 1\ 1 \\
2\ 1\ 1\ 0\ 0\ 1\ 0\ 0\ 0 \\
3\ 0\ 0\ 1\ 1\ 1\ 1\ 0\ 0 \\
3\ 1\ 1\ 0\ 0\ 0\ 0\ 1\ 1 \\
4\ 0\ 1\ 0\ 1\ 0\ 1\ 0\ 1 \\
4\ 1\ 0\ 1\ 0\ 1\ 0\ 1\ 0 \\
5\ 0\ 1\ 0\ 1\ 1\ 0\ 1\ 0 \\
5\ 1\ 0\ 1\ 0\ 0\ 1\ 0\ 1 \\
6\ 0\ 1\ 1\ 0\ 0\ 1\ 1\ 0 \\
6\ 1\ 0\ 0\ 1\ 1\ 0\ 0\ 1 \\
7\ 0\ 1\ 1\ 0\ 1\ 0\ 0\ 1 \\
7\ 1\ 0\ 0\ 1\ 0\ 1\ 1\ 0
\end{array}
$$

We arbitrarily related each of the columns (other than the first) to one of the 3 binary parameters and deleted the last 5 columns. In terms of redundant symbols ("5", "6" and "7") in the first column, we substituted them with the first three scenarios ("0", "1" and "2") respectively.

We compared the MD5 hash values of the recovered files and those of the original files. The possible MD5 collision indicated that we should employ 1 miscounted file per 1,000 files as margin of error. Moreover, we assume a base false positive rate is 0.002. Then we followed the procedure in Section 2.3 step by step:

Step 1. By following the array instructions using the DFTT testing image #11 [6], we obtained 16 observations (one for each row). In order from the first row to the last row, the false negatives were:

$$0.002, 1.002, 0.002, 0.002, 0.002, 1.002, 0.002, 1.002,$$

$$1.002, 0.002, 1.002, 0.002, 0.002, 0.002, 1.002, 0.002.$$

Step 2. These 16 numbers were transformed by using Taguchi's logarithmic function to obtain the sequence:

$$53.979, -0.017, 53.979, 53.979, 53.979, -0.017, 53.979, -0.017,$$

$$-0.017, 53.979, -0.017, 53.979, 53.979, 53.979, -0.017, 53.979.$$

Subtracting the margin of error 0.0005 from the results in *Step 1*, we obtain possibly contaminated observations as:

$$0.001, 1.001, 0.001, 0.001, 0.001, 1.001, 0.001, 1.001,$$

$$1.001, 0.001, 1.001, 0.001, 0.001, 0.001, 1.001, 0.001.$$

By applying Taguchi's function to the second set of observations adjusted for error, we then obtained a second transformed sequence:

$$60.000, -0.009, 60.000, 60.000, 60.000, -0.009, 60.000, -0.009,$$

$$-0.009, 60.000, -0.009, 60.000, 60.000, 60.000, -0.009, 60.000.$$

A paired t-test indicated a significant difference between these two sequences (t = -5.0106, df = 15 with p-value = 0.0001551). By following the outlier detection algorithm mentioned in Section 2.1, we removed the observations of the least value from the original observation set and identified ten potential outliers which are equal to 0.002 in *Step 1*.

So we proceed to *Step 3*.

Step 3. To tolerate 10 potential outliers, Theorem 1 requires 16×3 observations. And the number of actual outliers which can be handled by these observations is

$$\min\left\{\left\lfloor\frac{16-1}{2}\right\rfloor + \left\lfloor\frac{16+1}{2}\right\rfloor \cdot \left\lfloor\frac{3-1}{2}\right\rfloor, 16 \cdot \left\lfloor\frac{3-1}{2}\right\rfloor\right\} = \min\{7+8\cdot1, 16\cdot1\} = 15.$$

Step 4. By using the DFRWS-06 challenge image file [5], we ran the test array once more and obtained 16 new observations. From the first row to the last, the false positives were:

$$0.002, 13.002, 0.002, 8.002, 1.002, 10.002, 1.002, 5.002,$$

$$6.002, 3.002, 10.002, 3.002, 4.002, 4.002, 9.002, 2.002.$$

Step 5. We found no more suspicious samples in the available 32 observations other than the ten observations identified in *Step 2*.

Step 6. By running the test array for the last time and using the DFTT testing image #12 [6], we obtained another 16 observations (one for each row). From the first row to the last, the false positives were:

$$0.002, 0.002, 0.002, 3.002, 1.002, 2.002, 1.002, 1.002,$$

$$2.002, 2.002, 0.002, 0.002, 2.002, 1.002, 2.000, 1.002.$$

There are five suspicious samples in this set of observations: the five smallest values equal to 0.002. Therefore, we have in total 15 potential outliers in this experiment. Our 48 observations are obtained in 3 group tests, so our experimental results can tolerate these 15 outliers as calculated in *Step 3* according to Theorem 1. So we completed the experiment with this set of 48 observations shown in Table 1.

The average execution times in each testing run varied in a relatively wide range from zero to 5, as shown in Figure 1. Variations in false positives between different runs were evident — the three largest values were 4.669, 4.335 and

Table 1. The Experimental Results of the 16-Run Correctness Test for the Data Carving Tools

Row	Group 1	Group 2	Group 3
1	0.002	0.002	0.002
2	1.002	13.002	0.002
3	0.002	0.002	0.002
4	0.002	8.002	3.002
5	0.002	1.002	1.002
6	1.002	10.002	2.002
7	0.002	1.002	1.002
8	1.002	5.002	1.002
9	1.002	6.002	2.002
10	0.002	3.002	2.002
11	1.002	10.002	0.002
12	0.002	3.002	0.002
13	0.002	4.002	2.002
14	0.002	4.002	1.002
15	1.002	9.002	2.002
16	0.002	2.002	1.002

4.002 observed respectively in run 2, run 4 and run 15; the three smallest values were 0.002, 0.002 and 0.669 observed respectively in run 1, run 3 and run 5.

The observed values in runs 1 and 2, runs 10 and 11, and runs 7 and 8 were consistently small. This corresponded to the two most efficient carving tools — *Foremost* and *Scalpel*. In fact, *Scalpel* was developed based on *Foremost*. Besides the choice of tools, the inclusion of jpeg files also had significant impact on the false positives.

In this test, the first group of observations provided much inaccurate information as the DFTT testing image has a broad mixture of files; however, we managed to achieve the correct results by introducing extra observations with

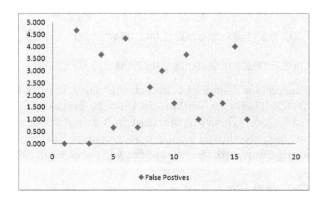

Fig. 1. Average False Positives of Data Carving Tools Observed in the 16 Testing Runs

better quality. Therefore, the overall quality of testing data was good enough to reveal accurate information about the correctness of the tools.

4   Conclusions and Future Work

A robust correctness testing method for digital forensic tools was presented in this paper. In order to deliver the most accurate result, we demonstrated that multiple observations are necessary. Moreover, we have shown that the choice of OA determines the testing pattern and provides the number of testing cases; our adaptive experimental approach guarantees that testers achieve testing results of good quality through a limited number of observations.

Our approach enables general testers to compare the performance of digital forensic tools without using sophisticated equipment or spending a large amount of time. The testing results have proved the validity and the effectiveness of our methodology. Most importantly, our methodology can be fully automated so that a computerized tester may be developed to replace human testers in the future.

Acknowledgment

The authors would like to acknowledge the constructive comments made by the anonymous referees and the help from the conference organizers.

References

1. Beckett, J., Slay, J.: Digital Forensics: Validation and Verification in a Dynamic Work Environment. In: Proceedings of the 40th Annual Hawaii International Conference on System Sciences (HICSS 2007), p. 266a (2007)
2. CFTT group from NIST. Disk Imaging Specifications. NIST technial report (2001)
3. CFTT group from NIST. Digital Data Acquisition Tool Specification. NIST technial report (2004)
4. CFTT group from NIST. Digital Data Acquisition Tool Test Assertions and Test Plan. NIST technial report (2005)
5. Digital Forensics Research Workshop. DFRWS06 Forensic Challenge, http://www.dfrws.org/2006/challenge/index.shtml
6. Brian Carrier. Digital Forensics Tool Testing Images, http://dftt.sourceforge.net/
7. Hedayat, A.S., Sloane, N.J.A., Stufken, J.: Orthogonal Arrays: Theory and Applications. Springer, Heidelberg (1999)
8. NIST/SEMATECH. e-Handbook of Statistical Methods, http://www.itl.nist.gov/div898/handbook/
9. Mohay, G.: Technical Challenges and Directions for Digital Forensics. In: Proceedings of the 1st International Workshop on Systematic Approaches to Digital Forensic Engineering (SADFE 2005), pp. 155–161 (2005)
10. Pan, L., Batten, L.M.: A Lower Bound on Effective Performance Testing for Digital Forensic Tools. In: Proceedings of the 2nd International Workshop on Systematic Approaches to Digital Forensic Engineering (SADFE 2007), pp. 117–130 (2007)

11. Pan, L.: A Performance Testing Framework for Digital Forensic Tools. PhD thesis Deakin University (2007)
12. Sloane, N.J.A.: A Library of Orthogonal Arrays,
    `http://www.research.att.com/~njas/oadir/index.html`
13. Taguchi, G.: Introduction to Quality Engineering: Designing Quality Into Produces and Processes. White Plains (1986)
14. Taguchi, G., Chowdhury, S., Wu, Y.: Taguchi's Quality Engineering Handbook. Wiley, Chichester (2004)
15. Wilsdon, T., Slay, J.: Digital Forensics: Exploring Validation, Verification and Certification. In: Proceedings of the 1st International Workshop on Systematic Approaches to Digital Forensic Engineering (SADFE 2005), pp. 48–55 (2005)
16. Youden, W.J.: Statistical techniques for collaborative tests. In: Statistical Manual of the Association of Official Analytical Chemists, p. v–63 (1975)
17. Zhou, J., Zhu, H.: Robust Estimation and Design Procedures for the Random Effects Model. The Canadian Journal of Statistics 31(1), 99–110 (2003)

Surveillance Applications of Biologically-Inspired Smart Cameras

Kosta Haltis[1], Lee Andersson[1], Matthew Sorell[1], and Russell Brinkworth[2]

[1] School of Electrical and Electronic Engineering,
[2] School of Molecular and Biomedical Science
University of Adelaide SA 5005, Australia
russell.brinkworth@adelaide.edu.au

Abstract. Biological vision systems are capable of discerning detail and detecting motion in a wide range of highly variable lighting conditions. We describe the real-time implementation of a biological vision model using a high dynamic range video camera and a General Purpose Graphics Processing Unit (GPGPU) and demonstrate the effectiveness of the implementation in two surveillance applications: dynamic equalization of contrast for improved recognition of scene detail; and the use of biologically-inspired motion processing for the detection of small or distant moving objects in a complex scene.

Keywords: Surveillance, digital video processing, biological vision, motion detection, image enhancement.

1 Introduction

Flying insects have extraordinary visual capabilities that allow them to navigate in cluttered environments without collisions, perform spectacular aerobatic manoeuvres [1] and discriminate the motion of visual targets camouflaged within complex background textures (*visual clutter*). These are all challenging tasks for artificial vision systems that have attracted substantial attention from scientists and engineers.

One such challenge is discerning detail in high dynamic range images, given that typically only 8-bit (256 level) luminance is usually available in digital imaging. This presents itself as a limitation on the information content, by which we mean, specifically, the distinguishability of objects within an image, available for capture from a scene under difficult lighting conditions. High dynamic range (HDR) imaging processes allow capture over a much larger luminance range, however such images are not supported by the majority of image display and storage media. While there are conventional engineering solutions, such as gamma correction and tone mapping, we consider a biologically-inspired approach based on photoreceptor cells, whose purpose is precisely luminance range compression [2]. A model for this process has been developed, and allows the operation to be carried out on HDR images in software.

The photoreceptor model is well suited to parallel computation but is computation-ally expensive in a conventional serial computing environment. The model has therefore been implemented on a General Purpose computing Programmable Graphic

M. Sorell (Ed.): e-Forensics 2009, LNICST 8, pp. 65 – 76, 2009.

Unit (GPGPU). This allows the model to be applied to HDR images and the resulting images to be displayed in real time.

A user study has been performed to explore the performance of the photoreceptor HDR compression technique against typical linear scaling of the luminance range and subsequent gamma adjustment for display. This study concluded that the photoreceptor model is consistently able to retain equal or greater information content of scene through the biologically inspired range compression technique, particularly under complex lighting conditions.

This system has the potential for application within military and consumer imaging systems including surveillance, target detection, security monitoring, and face and text recognition software.

2 Biologically-Inspired Vision Model

Many conventional camera systems tend to have poor performance when capturing images of scenes with complex lighting conditions. They tend to either struggle to capture details in the darkest or brightest parts of the scene, and occasionally in both.

Fig. 1. Images captured with a conventional camera with different exposure settings and global gain adjustments

The reason for this is that these conventional cameras generally use a relatively simple global adjustment to the luminance on each frame as a whole, in an attempt to improve the final image output quality. However, in many cases the resulting image quality is poor. Conventional cameras usually can only capture an 8-bit range of luminance levels (256 possible values) despite the huge range of possible luminance levels that natural lighting conditions provide (in the order of 10^8 possible values) [3]. This is evident in Figure 1. Overall, the processing that is performed on each image is approximately linear across all the pixels within the image.

2.1 Spatial and Temporal Image Processing

Spatial image processing is a form of processing performed on each pixel based on surrounding pixels of the same image. For HDR images, some spatial processing techniques that are used include tone mapping and gamma correction.

"Tone mapping" is a technique that is used to map a set of colours to another set. This is useful when attempting to perform dynamic range compression [4].

"Gamma Correction" is a nonlinear operation used to increase the dynamic range of the luminance of pixels within an image [5]. A simple format of a gamma correction encoding is power encoding, which takes the form shown in Equation 1. This function is generally used with a gamma value 0.45-0.50 for gamma correction prior to displaying images on a computer monitor.

$$V_{out} = V_{in}^{\gamma} \tag{1}$$

The results of post captured image stitching with spatial processing applied on a couple of image can be seen in Figure 2.

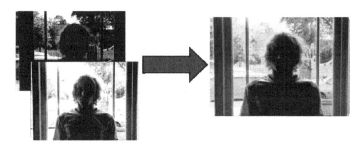

Fig. 2. High Dynamic Range image created by stitching spatially processed images

In terms of image quality, spatial image processing performs very well for images with both moving and stationary scenes. However, it requires largely iterative, and sometimes complex, calculations that depend on all surrounding pixels within the frame. This would make it difficult to perform real-time image processing on video footage using these techniques, especially if the frame resolution is large.

Temporal processing is the action of processing a pixel's new data value based on its previous states in time (that is, previous frames of a video sequence). Pure temporal image processing requires no knowledge of the surrounding pixels, and utilises the temporal characteristics for moving images for the processing.

The issue with temporal systems is that if there is no movement of an object within an image, the object will slowly fade to become less distinguishable from surrounding objects. Hence, the only way to constantly see detail in stationary objects is to continuously move the camera. This can be seen in the images in Figure 3.

The middle image is a snapshot in time after the camera had been stationary for several seconds. The right image is a snapshot in time during slow movement of the camera. It can be seen here that while the camera is moving, the markings on the cards and the card edges are much more defined.

In a system that performs spatial processing, the markings and card edges would be very visible, even in the stationary images. The reason that we can see stationary objects with our eyes is because our eyes are constantly jittering in fast but small amplitude motion known as *saccades*.

Fig. 3. Image Comparison between Raw (left), Temporal processing on stationary images (middle), Temporal processing on moving images (right). The left image has saturated luminance and the detail has faded and in the centre image. Constant small-scale motion in the right image refreshes the detail.

2.2 Photoreceptor Model

While biological vision systems vary in complexity and capability, our interest is in insect vision which incorporates temporal, but not spatial, processing in the photoreceptors [6, 7]. Insect motion vision can be modelled in three primary stages - Photoreceptors, Lamina Monopolar Cells, and Motion Processing.

Photoreceptors receive light through the optical system of the eye, applying non-linear dynamic range compression to achieve a high dynamic range of optical luminance. Photoreceptors are equivalent to pixels and act on a pixel-by-pixel basis and are discussed in more detail below.

Lamina Monopolar Cells in flies remove redundancy in both space and time in an optimal way based on the local light level [8]. Processing steps include variable and relaxed high-pass filtering in both space and time depending on light levels [9], signal amplification and a saturating non-linearity. The end result, as seen in Figure 4, highlights edges and areas of relative movement.

Motion Processing is used to calculate the motion of every pixel relative to the camera. This is modelled by the so-called Reichardt Correlator [10], which compares a pixel with a delayed signal from other surrounding pixels. This is done via a non-linear multiplicative interaction between the two channels. This motion calculation

Fig. 4. Lamina Monopolar Cells in flies remove redundancy in both space and time, highlighting edges and areas of relative movement. The image on the left is a single frame after simulated photoreceptor processing; on the right is the output of the simulated LMC stage in which motion detail is retained.

relative to the visual system can then be used to perform velocity estimation of object within the field of view.

Photoreceptors

The photoreceptors provide the first stage of processing for the Biological Visual system. They are responsible for Dynamic Range Reduction of the input images. The biological eye is able to see a much larger dynamic range than can be linearly encoded by the photoreceptors [11].

Biological Visual Systems use complex Non-Linear Dynamic Range Reduction at the pixel level in an attempt to improve the final image output. This system dynamically adjusts the dark and bright areas of the images independently through temporal pixel-wise operations.

The dark pixels are brightened and the bright pixels are darkened to equalize the luminance throughout the whole image, hence reducing the dynamic range of the image.

A model for the Biological Photoreceptors, which can be seen in Figure 5, was proposed by Mah et al in [11] as an extended version of the model by Van Hateren and Snippe [12]. This photoreceptor model has been shown to closely resemble the system response of the fly's visual system and has good results on improving the image output. The model can be broken down into 4 individual stages:

- Stage 1 is a Low Pass Filter (LPF) with variable gain and corner frequency, to model varying adaptation speeds in different lighting conditions, acting to increase the information captured over a wide range of light intensities by reducing gain as intensity increases.
- Stage 2 is a Non-linear Divisive feedback via LPF, providing rapid short term adaptation of the photoreceptor response to rapid large variations in light intensity through logarithmic compression of the input.
- Stage 3 is an Exponential Divisive feedback loop via a LPF. This stage is responsible for shifting the operating range of the model. The LPF in this stage provides slow adaptation, to provide the longer term adaptation of the system to variations in light intensities.
- Stage 4 is Naka-Rushton transformation, where a constant is added to the input and the result used in a divisive feed forward operation. This stage provides a final global gain control for further amplification to the darker parts of the image.

The result of the full photoreceptor system is to compress the image from high dynamic range to a low dynamic range, by way of independent pixel gain control. This compression system also enhances the useful information capture in the process.

The full system effectively provides an approximate form of high pass filtering (HPF). Hence, the system is effective in scenes of temporal variations such as local or object movement, or through the use of saccadic like local motion of the image capture device.

The effect is that areas of change are emphasised with greater detail, while temporally stationary objects, such as background regions, fade to a common gain value as the variable gain of the system reaches steady state.

This temporal system has useful advantages over spatial based processing (which occurs primarily in the laminar monopolar cells) since the photoreceptor makes use of frame history to further improve images. Some improvements include reducing noise and filling in data that may be missing in any one frame of the image stream. An example of the output of the photoreceptor model can be seen in Figure 6.

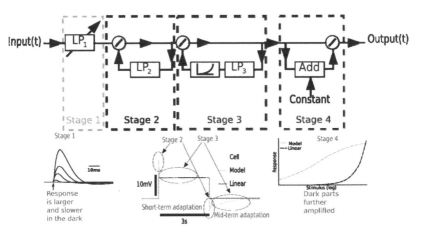

Fig. 5. Photoreceptor model block diagram and typical step responses of the model [3]

Fig. 6. Raw image (left) and improved detail after photoreceptor processing (right)

3   Implementation

The key opportunity for implementation of the proposed biologically-inspired vision system was the recognition that pixel-wise image processing could be computed in parallel using a parallel processing system designed for such graphics applications. The objective was to achieve real-time processing at the full image resolution (640 by 480 pixels) at full frame rate (25 or 30 full frames per second).

3.1 High Dynamic Range Camera

HDR images can be created using a technique called "image stitching" or through Analogue-to-Digital Conversion (ADC) techniques. State-of-the-art High Dynamic Range cameras incorporate an ADC up to 14 bits, providing a dynamic range of 16000:1 (84dB).

Image Stitching involves using multiple images of ideally the same frame at different exposure settings to generate a higher dynamic range for all pixels within the image. This technique uses these multiple images to generate HDR layers. Image stitching may be performed on within software after transferring the image layers, or in some cases within the camera's firmware.

The camera used in this work was the Basler A601f-HDR. This camera performs the image stitching on-chip post capture and delivers the 16-bit HDR image by firewire (IEEE1394) for software capture and processing.

3.2 General Purpose Graphics Processing Unit

A General Purpose computing Graphics Processing Unit (GPGPU) is a multi-processing core unit which is designed for computing many parallel, pipelined and often identical processes on very large segmented data sets. As the photoreceptor model fits this description precisely, it is an obvious candidate for GPGPU implementation, especially as software-only implementation on a dual-core Pentium processor only achieved frame rates in the order of 10 frames per second after significant code optimisation.

An NVIDIA GeForce 8800 GT processor was used for all GPU related processing requirements in our work, although any compatible GPGPU could be substituted. These processing cards are now quite cheap and are widely used for graphics-intensive applications such as video game play.

The GPGPU supports 14 multiprocessor blocks, each with 8 cores, representing a total of 112 processing cores. Each core is clocked at 600MHz, has local access to

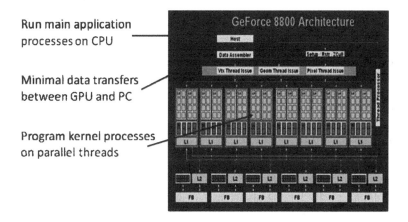

Fig. 7. The photoreceptor model was implemented on an NVIDIA GeForce 8800 GT General Purpose Graphics Processing Unit (adapted from [13])

cache memory and registers and global access to 512MB of memory. The global memory is accessible by the host CPU and has a transfer bandwidth of 57.6Gbit/s, more than sufficient to hold temporary frame data for real-time processing. The GPGPU operates as a co-processor, allowing parallel CPU management of data processing while the GPGPU implements the photoreceptor model in parallel. The architecture of the GPGPU implementation is shown in Figure 7.

3.3 Processing Bottlenecks

There are two threads running on the main CPU, in this case an Intel C2Duo dual-core processor at 2.8GHz. One thread handles image acquisition from the camera or hard drive, requiring 21.5ms. The second thread handles the complete image processing, including image scaling, gamma correction and display (19.5ms), and the photoreceptor model.

Implementing the photoreceptor model on the CPU requires 75ms, resulting in a frame period of 94.5ms, approximately 10 frames per second. Using the GPGPU requires just 8.5ms per frame, reducing the frame processing time to 28ms with a frame rate of 36 frames per second. It is therefore possible to process pre-recorded video faster than real time, and also meet the real-time requirements for direct processing from the camera. Further optimization, by scheduling the GPGPU to process in parallel with the CPU thread, could potentially increase the processing speed to 50 frames per second.

4   Applications and Performance Evaluation

Although there are many metrics of the efficacy of a surveillance camera, system or network, the ability to recognize objects and detail, and the ability to automatically detect motion are of particular interest and relevance in the case of surveillance applications of the described visual processing system. We therefore conducted an objective test to demonstrate the effectiveness of the photoreceptor-based processing for detail recognition, and a demonstration of the full model for motion detection of small objects in the field of view.

The former demonstration has direct applications in such areas as number plate pre-processing for automatic or manual character recognition and the identification of other objects under complex lighting conditions; the latter demonstrates the ability to pick out moving objects such as aircraft in the sky or people walking across a cluttered background.

4.1 Object and Detail Recognition

A test was conceived to compare the effectiveness of an 8-bit representation of an unprocessed video stream (except for global brightness control) with the photoreceptor based processing model for the application of detail recognition through the use of playing cards. Under complex lighting conditions of bright and dark areas with various levels of reflection, it is often difficult to determine the suit and the number of objects on a card, making cards a suitable basis for testing.

Five image streams that were captured using these playing cards. Each contained a different setup in terms of lighting conditions, the types of cards used, and the way in which they were displayed. The true configuration of the experiment was noted separately for comparison purposes.

Both the conventionally processed and the photoreceptor-processed image streams were saved as 8-bit JPG images and compiled into 10 individual tests (5 for each processing method). These images were then shown to a variety of people on different days, where they were asked to write down the card numbers and suits in the order that they were displayed in the images. These results were quantified to provide a measure of the efficacy of the processing for detail recognition.

Of the five sets, two resulted in 100% recognition under both unprocessed and processed conditions, and so were discarded. The fifth test included cards which were too far away to clearly identify the faces even under optimal lighting conditions due to the low resolution of the card features, and so are also not considered here. Of the two tests with meaningful results, Test 1 consisted of 20 tests and Test 2 of 40 tests, namely the identification of the correct suit and number of 20 cards as in Figure 8.

As the images were available as a sequence of frames, subjects were permitted to work back and forth through the frame set to find the best possible representation of each card. It can be seen from the test results in Figure 9 that the amount of useful information that was obtained by the test participants varies depending on the lighting situation. If users were unable to identify the card they were to leave the answer blank.

Fig. 8. Test configurations for visual comparison. Test 2 is above, Test 1 below. To the left are the unprocessed frames; to the right are frames after photoreceptor processing. Note that if global gain control were used, either the central cards would be in saturated luminance as shown, or the end cards would be too dark.

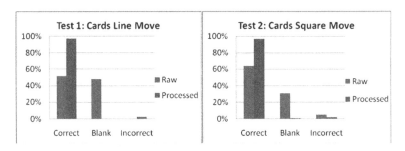

Fig. 9. Quality performance test results for both subjective recognition tests. In the raw images the no-response (blank) rate is high but drops to near zero after processing. The correct response rate after processing exceeds 95% (that is one or two errors) in each case.

Tests 1 and 2 consisted of a bright beam on the cards, causing luminance saturation on the faces of the cards. It appears as if the bio-inspired processing model has performed very well with a dramatic improvement in the number of correct readings. We conclude that under the appropriate resolution conditions, photoreceptor processing can lead to improved visibility of object artefacts in surveillance vision.

4.2 Motion Detection

Security surveillance relies on seeing as much information as possible within the cameras' fields of view. These camera systems would reduce issues with seeing details in shadowed or excessively bright areas within the fields of view at various times of the day; especially if the area under surveillance is exposed to direct sunlight.

Security surveillance could also benefit significantly from the additional stages of the Biological Vision Model (the LMC and Motion detection stages). Figure 10 shows

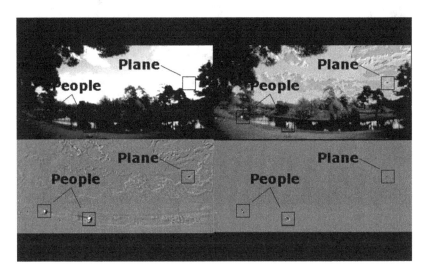

Fig. 10. Direct comparison of motion processing from each stage of a Bio-Inspired Camera System

a side-by-side comparison of the outputs of the Bio-inspired camera system prototypes at each of the Biological vision model. This image demonstrates how small objects relative to a scene can be monitored with ease. After photoreceptor luminance normalization (top right), it is possible to see objects both in the sky and on the ground simultaneously. The bottom left image shows highlighting of edges of objects with some movement within a scene. The bottom right corner shows motion detection within the scene. The intensity of these pixels represents the speed of the moving objects relative to the image capture device.

Second (LMC) and third (Motion Detection) level processing would still be useful on images retrieved from standard camera systems, however, for best results a HDR camera with the First level processing (Photoreceptor stage) will be needed as it is impossible to recover information lost when a linear global gain-controlled system is used. The complete system will ensure that useful information is maximised and the most accurate target detection and tracking will be possible. In the example images below, if the first level processing was skipped, the objects may not have been detected due to them travelling in either the darkest or brightest areas of the image. These areas are where the conventional camera system is more likely to fail in this application.

5 Future Work and Conclusions

We have demonstrated that it is possible to implement the photoreceptor stage of the biologically-inspired vision processing system using inexpensive off-the-shelf consumer graphics processing hardware, and provided some details of the surveillance applications of the proposed approach.

There are several areas of future work. High dynamic range cameras are not currently used in surveillance applications due to their relatively high cost, although there are emerging double-photodiode pixel based imaging sensors being developed according to Yamada [14] which would see a reduction in cost due to economies of scale. There is sufficient processing capability in the GPGPU in the developed system for implementation of Stage 2 and Stage 3 processing within the GPGPU environment, completing the implementation using commercially-available hardware.

Acknowledgements

This work was supported by a research grant from the Australian Research Council (LP0667744).

References

1. Land, M.F., Collett, T.S.: Chasing behavior of houseflies. J. Comp. Physiology A 89, 525–538 (1974)
2. Laughlin, S.B., Weckström, M.: Fast and slow photoreceptors — a comparative study of the functional diversity of coding and conductances in the Diptera. J. Comp. Physiology A 172, 593–609 (1993)

3. Brinkworth, R.S.A., Mah, E.L., O'Carroll, D.C.: Bioinspired Pixel-Wise Adaptive Imaging. In: Proc. SPIE, vol. 6414, pp. 641416-1–641416-7 (2007)
4. Ashikhmin, M.: A tone mapping algorithm for high contrast images. In: Proc. 13th Eurographics workshop on Rendering, pp. 145–156 (2002)
5. Sato, K.: Image-Processing Algorithms. In: Nakamura, J. (ed.) Image Sensors and Signal Processing for Digital Still Cameras, pp. 223–254. Taylor & Francis Group, Boca Raton (2006)
6. Payne, R., Howard, J.: Response of an insect photoreceptor: a simple log-normal model. Nature 290, 415–416 (1981)
7. Matić, T., Laughlin, S.B.: Changes in the intensity-response function of an insect's photoreceptors due to light adaptation. J. Comp. Physiology A 145, 169–177 (1981)
8. van Hateren, J.H.: A theory of maximizing sensory information. Biological Cybernetics 68, 68–70 (1992)
9. Juusola, M., Uusitalo, R.O., Weckstrom, M.: Transfer of graded potentials at the photoreceptor interneuron synapse. J. General Physiology 105(1), 117–148 (1995)
10. Hassenstein, B., Reichardt, W.: Systemtheoretische Analyse der Zeit-, Reihenfolgen- und Vorzeichenauswertung bei der Bewegungsperzeption des Rüsselkäfers Chlorophanus. Z. Naturforsch 11b, 513–524 (1956)
11. Mah, E.-L., Brinkworth, R., O'Carroll, D.: Implementation of an elaborated neuromorphic model of a biological photoreceptor. Biological Cybernetics 98, 357–369 (2008)
12. van Hateren, H., Snippe, H.P.: Information Theoretical Evaluation of Parametric Models of Gain Control in Blowfly Photoreceptor Cells. Vision Research 41, 1851–1865 (2001)
13. NVIDIA Corp.: NVIDIA GeForce 8800 GPU Architecture Overview, http://www.nvidia.com/object/IO_37100.html
14. Yamada, T.: CCD Image Sensors. In: Nakamura, J. (ed.) Image Sensors and Signal Processing for Digital Still Cameras, pp. 95–142. CRC Press, Boca Raton (2006)

The Development of a Generic Framework for the Forensic Analysis of SCADA and Process Control Systems

Jill Slay and Elena Sitnikova

Defence and Systems Institute, University of South Australia
Mawson Lakes SA 5095 Australia
Jill.slay@unisa.edu.au

Abstract. There is continuing interest in researching generic security architectures and strategies for managing SCADA and process control systems. Documentation from various countries on IT security does now begin to recommendations for security controls for (federal) information systems which include connected process control systems. Little or no work exists in the public domain which takes a big picture approach to the issue of developing a generic or generalisable approach to SCADA and process control system forensics. The discussion raised in this paper is that before one can develop solutions to the problem of SCADA forensics, a good understanding of the forensic computing process, and the range of technical and procedural issues subsumed with in this process, need to be understood, and also agreed, by governments, industry and academia.

Keywords: SCADA, process control systems, security, forensics.

1 Introduction

A Supervisory Control and Data Acquisition (SCADA) system is used for gathering real time data, monitoring and controlling process equipment from automated systems in geographically distributed locations. They can be used to automate processes such as:

- Electricity power generation, transmission and distribution,
- Oil and gas refining and pipeline management,
- Water treatment and distribution,
- Chemical production and processing,
- Railroads and mass transit.

There is continuing and ongoing interest in researching generic security architectures and strategies for managing SCADA and process control systems. A major aspect of this type of approach [1] is the use of proprietary forensic computing tools [2] or specially developed network forensic architectures [1] to analyse network traffic at the packet level so as to be able to collect evidence after a potential event. Other researchers work at the junction of security and forensics examining intrusion detection and event logging in SCADA networks running specific protocols with the aim of providing

M. Sorell (Ed.): e-Forensics 2009, LNICST 8, pp. 77–82, 2009.

solutions that may reduce the risk of a catastrophic event should a system be breached and also providing electronic evidence that might eventually allow the perpetrator to be taken to court.

Documentation from various countries on IT security does now begin to recommendations for security controls for (federal) information systems which include connected process control systems. Thus we do recognise the maturity (even in our own work [3], [4]) of the development of general and generalisable security architectures and frameworks which then provide a foundation for the development of technical solutions and administrative processes around which sound SCADA and process control systems security can be built and assured. However, little or no work exists in the public domain that takes a big picture approach to the issue of developing a generic or generalisable approach to SCADA and process control system forensics.

The assertion in this paper is that before one can develop solutions to the problem of SCADA forensics, a good understanding of the forensic computing process, and the range of technical and procedural issues subsumed within this process, need to be understood, and also agreed, by governments, industry and academia. This paper then examines systematically:

- What is forensic computing?
- What evidence should be collected from SCADA and process control systems and where might this evidence be located?
- How can an enterprise be prepared for a possible forensic investigation?

2   What Is Forensic Computing in a Control System Context?

This question has been asked many times in academic literature but still needs to be considered in a SCADA and process control system context. We have asserted previously [5] that forensic computing (electronic evidence collection, digital evidence collection) has developed out of a demand for service from the law enforcement community and has typically developed in an ad hoc manner rather than a scientific one. It has since developed into a discipline that crosses the corporate, academic, legal, and scientific as well as the law enforcement domains and it is developing both as a discipline and as a forensic science.

If we take a holistic perspective we see that forensic (meaning 'for the court') computing is about collecting evidence that can be presented to a court after a crime has taken place. This means that we only need to be able to collect enough of the right kind of evidence to provide conclusive proof that a crime has been committed. In our definition, there is a distinct difference between the process of forensic computing investigation and that of incident recovery and response. Incident response and recovery is an essential feature of the security of SCADA and process control systems, and it would be hard to find a SCADA or control system that was part of the national critical infrastructure which did not have established procedures for response and recovery. These systems, as opposed to commercial or corporate information systems, are built with [6] redundancy and minimum mean time to repair with a primary focus on availability since they control the major national utilities, or major industries such as oil, mining, commodity production and transport.

Although there is no single accepted standard, there is a basic computer forensic methodology including rules and procedures forensic computing investigators should follow. McKemmish [7] has four rules for forensic computing investigations: *"minimal handling of the original, account for any changes, comply with the rules of evidence and do not exceed your knowledge"*. He also identifies and details the four stages of a forensic investigation: *"identification of digital evidence, preservation of digital evidence, analysis of digital evidence and presentation of digital evidence"*.

Chain of custody is another aspect that is integral to a computer forensic investigation. Chain of custody is the process of tracking evidence to ensure it is of the highest integrity when presented in court. Without a properly executed chain of custody, a defence lawyer could argue that the evidence may have been tampered with or not looked after properly. The chain of custody needs to record all persons who handled or had access to the evidence and what actions were performed on the evidence.

Forensic computing, if seen as a specialty within computer science, is different from other branches of computing as the output must be derived from a process that is legally acceptable [7]. Forensic computing is still a developing branch of IT, however, there are many practices and methods that have been developed and have been accepted by experts in the field. These methods are also accepted in a court of law because they have been shown to be reliable and produce accurate results. Using unknown or untested third party software for forensic analysis is not generally acceptable and could mean the conclusions drawn from analysis are regarded with low integrity or not admissible at all [7].

3 SCADA and Control Systems

The implementation of Control Systems up to 20 years ago gave no thought to the defence or security issues that could be faced in the operation of these systems. Aging systems with little processing power and network strength, bedded on adapted windows operating systems, have been connected to the internet for efficiency and cost effectiveness. These systems now face threats from an un-trusted network connection as well as the human errors in the control of these systems.

Systems consist of numerous technologies ranging from legacy to state of the art systems with the processing power to match. In his paper on Control Forensics, Fabro [8] makes a distinction between three possible system architectures. They are:

- Modern / Common Technologies – which have modern computing capabilities and are still sponsored by the vendor;
- Modern / Proprietary Technologies – which have been created in the last ten years and are fully supported and understood by the vendors and owners;
- Legacy / Proprietary Technologies – systems have been deployed further than ten years ago and have moderate capabilities.

Legacy systems are commonly PLC based systems with computers used to control the output and display to the HMI.

Modern systems have often been modified to suit operational requirements in other organisations. Modern control systems have more than enough processing power to monitor and process information as well as controlling the systems that they are designed for. The problem still remains that remote locations rely on sending information back to the control site. The networks that carry this information have increased in bandwidth, so the conjecture of slowing the network due to the transfer of more information is not warranted. However, an attack that controls the information that is transmitted across that medium could go unnoticed until it is detected further down the line by its effects.

4   Evidence from SCADA and Control Systems

Internationally, we discover the usage of legacy SCADA systems which were built on proprietary protocols and operating systems. These have over the years been interconnected using Ethernet- based protocols, and with the addition of COTS software too. More recently, remote control via various forms of communication link has allowed efficient monitoring of field devices over the public internet.

This means that we have complex SCADA systems and control Ethernet LANS, inter connected with utility corporate networks, regulator networks, vendor networks and often with essential employee mobile device and home computer network access. Thus we find that, while SCADA is often presented as a simple network of remote devices working on simple protocols in real-time, there is an intricate web of IP and Ethernet networks surrounding these devices.

In some regard, this understanding of the complexity surrounding SCADA systems is of help in establishing what evidence we might collect and how. We can leverage much of the more general research in forensic computing and electronic evidence collection, to gain an understanding of the type of electronic evidence we might be looking for in a SCADA or process control system. If we assume that there has been an attack on a SCADA or process system and we have to plan how to investigate, then we start with the knowledge that some device would have been used to access the system. This access might have been via a small mobile device, access through a wireless link, access through a Denial of Service attack on a wired network, an attack on a PC running an insecure application or an attack on a web cam monitoring a remote device on the SCADA network. So we would assert that SCADA and process control system forensics cannot exist in a vacuum but the application of digital forensic approaches to SCADA and Control Systems however is new and quite complex in its approach.

5   Forensic Challenges

Traditional forensic challenges consist of the retrieval of data from volatile memory and network devices as well as storage devices. It often relies on incident response after the event, observing the recorded data from the attack because of inadequate logging and inappropriate administrational processes. Control systems further hinders the collection and analysis of information due to the nature and environment of these systems.

Traditional retrieval consists of the removal of the device and imaging of the data source. This can not be done in a control environment due to the real time environment and the inability to shut down specific zones.

The intermingling of data due to control systems producing huge amounts of information that is used in the control of the system in the form of set points and monitoring alarms and sensors. This information is stored on control servers that could also be trusted to store any forensic information. The process of filtering any relevant information from these huge amounts of data is both time consuming and limiting.

The volatility of the data due to the fact that enormous amounts of data are being logged for the operation of the system, data is often overwritten on some devices, commonly remote terminal units and field devices.

Legacy systems have very little computational power available for the analysis or recording and sorting of data that is produced in conjunction with control data. Any network connections are for the monitoring of production and set points. The systems are backed up frequently, with all information stored on servers that contain information that dates back to the start of operation. This information is recorded for the operation of the systems and provides evidence of previous and current set points. Accessing back up tapes for information would not hinder the operation of the systems, and would provide a life time of operation records, but mingled control and forensic data would have to be filtered to get valuable information.

Law enforcement investigators who might be called upon in the case of a breach of a SCADA system have a very good understanding of the computer and network data which needs to be provided to them by an organisation in the case of forensic investigation. However, they are often hampered in this work because Australian enterprises are not aware that they should collect computer and network data, log files and records in a systematic manner. This means that when a system breach occurs, or computer crime is suspected, the potential evidence is not available for law enforcement investigators to analyse, and in some cases has never been collected. Currently the IT management, and particularly the security management, of Australian organisations is largely governed by a series of national and international standards which are based on process models created before the widespread growth of computer crime. These lack any real and explicit focus on Forensic Readiness or the potential need to work in such a way that systems are designed and built to collect evidence.

6 Conclusion

Just as there is a need to develop generic security models for SCADA and process control systems, so there is a parallel need for a generic forensic framework for the same kind of systems. This framework needs to provide for the development of Forensic Readiness in an organisation, particularly one that is part of the national critical infrastructure. It also needs to provide an environment where well-established Forensic Computing functions can be carried out by law enforcement.

References

1. Chandia, R., Gonzalez, J., Kilpatrick, T., Papa, M., Shenoi, S.: IFIP International Federation for Information Processing. In: Goetz, E., Shenoi, S. (eds.) Critical Infrastructure Protection, vol. 253, pp. 117–131. Springer, Boston (2008)

2. Cassidy, R.F., Chavez, A., Trent, J., Urrea, J.: IFIP International Federation for Information Processing. In: Goetz, E., Shenoi, S. (eds.) Critical Infrastructure Protection, vol. 253, pp. 223–235. Springer, Boston (2008)
3. Slay, J., Miller, M.: A Security Architecture for SCADA Networks. In: Proceedings of the17th Australasian Conference on Information Systems, Adelaide, December 5-6 (2006)
4. Slay, J., Miller, M.: The Maroochy Water SCADA Breach: Implications of Lessons Learned for Research. In: Advances in Critical Infrastructure Protection, pp. 73–82. Springer, Boston (2008)
5. Beckett, J.J., Slay, J.: Digital Forensics: Validation and Verification in a Dynamic Work Environment. In: HICSS-40, Hawaii, January 3 (2007)
6. Miller, A.: Trends in Process Control Systems Security. In: IEEE Security and Privacy, pp. 57–60 (September/October 2005)
7. McKemmish, R.: What is Forensic Computing, Australian Institute of Criminology (1999)
8. Corporate & Technology Group of Freehills 2001, Cybercrime Act 2001 (Cth), FindLaw.com, viewed 27/03 (2006),
   http://www.findlaw.com.au/article/1408.htm
9. Fabro, M.: Recommended Practice: Creating Cyber Forensics Plans for Control Systems, Department of Homeland Security (2008)

FIA: An Open Forensic Integration Architecture for Composing Digital Evidence

Sriram Raghavan, Andrew Clark, and George Mohay

Information Security Institute, Queensland University of Technology,
Brisbane 4001, Australia
{s.raghavan,a.clark,g.mohay}@qut.edu.au

Abstract. The analysis and value of digital evidence in an investigation has been the domain of discourse in the digital forensic community for several years. While many works have considered different approaches to model digital evidence, a comprehensive understanding of the process of merging different evidence items recovered during a forensic analysis is still a distant dream. With the advent of modern technologies, pro-active measures are integral to keeping abreast of all forms of cyber crimes and attacks. This paper motivates the need to formalize the process of analyzing digital evidence from multiple sources simultaneously. In this paper, we present the forensic integration architecture (*FIA*) which provides a framework for abstracting the evidence source and storage format information from digital evidence and explores the concept of *integrating* evidence information from multiple sources. The FIA architecture identifies evidence information from multiple sources that enables an investigator to build theories to reconstruct the past. FIA is hierarchically composed of multiple layers and adopts a technology independent approach. FIA is also open and extensible making it simple to adapt to technological changes. We present a case study using a hypothetical car theft case to demonstrate the concepts and illustrate the value it brings into the field.

1 Introduction

In a digital investigation, investigators deal with acquiring digital data for examination. Digital records can vary in forms and types. Documents on a computer, telephone contact list, list of all phone calls made, trace of signal strengths from base station of a mobile phone, recorded voice and video files, email conversations, network traffic patterns and virus intrusions and detections are all examples of different types of digital records. Digital investigations must also contend with new challenges introduced by electronic equipment such as different devices, processor types, operating systems, storage formats and processing mechanisms that are used to store records in numerous formats. For the sake of this discussion, we restrict the classification of digital evidence to its source, data semantics and storage formats. We classify digital evidence based on its source, such as hard disks, volatile memory, or network traffic, its logical representation that defines its storage format and the type of information

M. Sorell (Ed.): e-Forensics 2009, LNICST 8, pp. 83–94, 2009.
© ICST Institute for Computer Sciences, Social Informatics and Telecommunications Engineering 2009

that can be extracted from the source which determines the evidence semantics. No digital investigation is complete without an elaborate and systematic analysis along all three dimensions identified above.

A variety of new digital devices are being introduced with rapid advances in digital technology. Coping with such advances has become challenging owing to the use of proprietary data structures and protocols in most devices rendering them difficult for interpretation without relevant documentation, let alone, in a forensically sound manner. The large volumes of data collected in typical cases can be attributed to this variety and sifting through them can be enormously time consuming. Although digital forensics is in its early stages, there is a definite need to categorize digital evidence. This categorization is expected to limit the investigation space and minimize the effort spent on examining a variety of digital evidence.

From a forensic standpoint, there is too much entropy in the forensic examination process to capture all data and process it in one go. There is a need for capturing, understanding and analyzing information from disparate digital sources uniformly. Cohen [7] describes the PyFlag network forensic architecture, which is an open-source effort in providing a common framework for integrating forensic analysis from diverse digital sources. While PyFlag does support multiple image types and formats, it can only mount and examine one image at a time. PyFlag, thus, sorely lacks an architecture such as the one described in this paper to make the analysis more cohesive. As a first step to providing a common forensic analysis framework, this paper presents the architecture for integrating evidence information from different sources irrespective of the logical type of its contents.

Turner [19] states that as devices become more specialized, forensic examiners will require acquaintance with as many different processing tools to interpret the data they contain. This is attributed to the fact that forensic tools can only process digital devices as independent monolithic entities. The problem that this paper addresses is the multifarious interpretation and analysis of such evidentiary data in a uniform manner independent of origination source and storage formats. A preliminary validation of the concepts has been carried out on a hypothetical case involving a single disk image. The development of a prototype is planned as the next logical step to carry out a more comprehensive examination. This paper presents a conceptualization to how evidence integration can be achieved using content information from diverse evidence sources.

To illustrate the significance of evidence integration, consider a hypothetical case where investigators seize a personal computer and a mobile phone from a suspect. In the context of the investigation, it is essential to analyze the data contained in these sources uniformly, irrespective of semantics and storage formats. It is imperative that such a forensic framework be developed to support data interpretation from multiple sources.

Assume that on initial examination, investigators recover a set of suspicious documents which leads to the extraction of email messages exchanged between the suspect and suspect's contacts. Irrespective of the location and type of storage (either on mail servers or on a personal hard drive as user client profile), the data derived reinforces support to existing evidence and hence must be added to the framework under the same case.

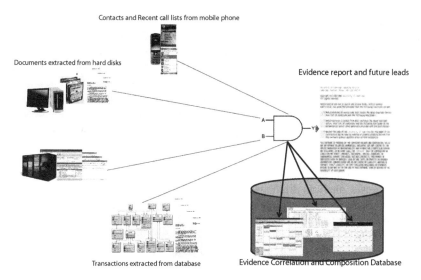

Fig. 1. An evidence composition example

The examination of email messages is expected to reveal some contact information and certain dates and times that might then be correlated with the current case to develop a *social calendar* of events and timelines. In addition, if the framework sources criminal records from a pre-existing repository that is indexed, then the correlation of extracted evidence with the repository can potentially reveal the underlying theme for the case, names and details of individuals involved, dates and times of activities reported or discussed relevant to the case. Such an extensive examination framework is illustrated in Figure 1. The framework aims to correlate (and hence compose) all reported information with the extracted evidence in an attempt to reconstruct the past. The rest of the paper is organized as follows. In Section 2, we review recent work in digital forensics and motivate the need for a common framework. In Section 3, we introduce the *forensic integration architecture*. In Section 4, we present a sample case study using a hypothetical case to demonstrate how FIA will operate. We conclude in Section 5 with a brief summary of the work reported and provide scope for future work.

2   State of the Art in Digital Investigations

Turner introduced the *digital evidence bags* (DEB) model [19] aimed at simplifying human interpretation. However, it is not intended to provide a methodology for combining different sources of evidence acquired at the various stages of an investigation process. Further, the model provides no scope for collecting and collating evidence from multiple digital sources which forms the crux of our work.

Schatz and Clark proposed a representation model to integrate metadata with evidence information in the sealed digital evidence bags (SDEB) [16]. The SDEB assumes the pre-existence of a forensic domain ontology model to support the representation of digital evidence. Such a model is yet to be developed.

Case et al. [6] introduce the FACE evidence correlation engine that parses data from different sources and correlates them. However, FACE assumes availability of all evidence sources at the start of analysis and the presence of known correlation in data. Besides, the engine does not integrate semantic information from evidence sources or provide for developing and validating assertions based on evidence analysis.

Alink et al. describe the XIRAF architecture [1] for indexing and retrieving stored digital evidence. The architecture indexes raw disk images and stores the content as annotated XML. However, XIRAF lays emphasis on feature extraction (indexing) and retrieval of digital evidence rather than on integrating evidence information that enables comprehensive forensic examination.

There are several other works in the literature that have reiterated the need for a common forensic analysis framework. Garfinkel highlights the problems associated with forensic analysis of raw computer disk images [9] and calls for the need to maintain an open and extendable standard for forensic analysis. Garfinkel introduced the Advanced Forensic Format (AFF) which is a two-layered forensic file system providing abstraction and extended functionality. However, the AFF is tailored to suit hard disk images and doesn't provide mechanisms to integrate evidence from multiple sources.

The Common Digital Evidence Storage Format Working Group has re-iterated the drawbacks with current forensic analysis tools [8] in terms of not being able to cope with multiple proprietary image formats. The authors emphasize the need for introducing a common digital evidence storage format that is common to a variety of evidence sources.

Beebe and Clark [2] argue the need for an objective based framework for digital forensics owing to the uniqueness of every forensic investigation. They divide the investigation process into 7 stages and propose a 2-tier hierarchical objectives framework. However, the focus of this framework is to maintain evidence integrity at all stages of an investigation which merely complements our focus in integrating evidence information and enabling further investigative leads.

Hosmer calls for the need to standardize the concept of digital evidence [11] to provide a common platform for investigators to perform forensic analysis. Since digital evidences can be altered, copied or erased, he proposed the 4-point principles of authentication, integrity, access control and non-repudiation for handing digital evidence.

Besides these efforts, several efforts in advancing the state of the art in techniques for data acquisition from electronic devices [5] have been reported. Some recent works have addressed challenges in the effective acquisition of volatile memory [14, 15, 17] and specifically in Windows based memory analysis in a computer [13, 18], while Buchholz and Spafford have studied the role of file system metadata in digital forensics [4]. Since digital forensics has predominantly been reactionary, some research contributions have been reported in formal methods for event reconstruction [10] and building theoretical foundations [12] to digital forensics. Turner has applied the DEB model to selective imaging of hard disk drives [20] and Beebe and Clark [3] introduce a text string search engine in for thematic searching in digital evidence.

The models and techniques described above have independently viewed the challenges in evidence analysis but are only stepping stones to integrate collected evidence from different sources. We require a framework that enables the development of new tools for interpretation of diverse data. Our work derives motivation from work reported in [8] and presents the FIA architecture as a means for abstracting technology dependence of evidentiary data and integrating and composing information from different sources.

3 FIA for Composing Digital Evidence

We introduce a new architecture called the forensic integration architecture (FIA) that consists of 4 layers. The architecture is illustrated in Figure 2. The layers that constitute the FIA are:

1. *evidence storage and access layer;*
2. *representation and interpretation layer;*
3. *meta-information layer;* and
4. *evidence composition and visualization layer.*

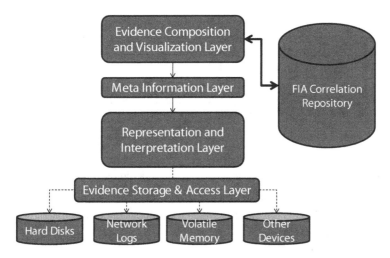

Fig. 2. Illustration of FIA evidence composition architecture

The FIA architecture is consistent with forensic principles. Based on a preliminary version of Turners DEB model, the FIA architecture pads the layers with added functionality that enhances its features and promises a natural transition towards automation. The layers are designed to allow scope for future extensions and selective modifications during analysis.

3.1 Evidence Storage and Access Layer

The *evidence storage and access layer* provides a binary abstraction to all data seized during an investigation. Acquisition of digital evidence is outside the scope of this work and the layer assumes that the evidence sources are forensically imaged copies stored on persistent media. All media must comply with *read only* semantics to maintain integrity of the data at all stages of an investigation. The layer supports registration interfaces for the acquired sources and their interpreters to be registered with FIA.

Once registered, the layer guarantees forensically secure access to the registered media. The layer also appends case specific metadata information prior to commencing analysis.

3.2   Representation and Interpretation Layer

The types of data that the *representation and interpretation layer* will be capable of supporting hard disk images and memory dumps from various operating systems (Windows OS, Linux, UNIX, Mac OS, etc.), network and system logs, and mobile devices with third party file systems (Nokia mobile with Symbian file system, iPod/iPhone with HFS+, etc.). The layer exploits interpreter semantics to extract logical blocks of data from the evidence sources for further analysis. For a file system image, this operation might correspond to extracting directories and files, for a memory dump it might correspond to extracting process control blocks (PCB) from the various processes resident in memory at the time of imaging and for network or system logs, it might correspond to extracting records of entries and their attributes from the log files. The extracted blocks are passed to the layer above. Figure 3 is indicative of some types of evidence semantics that different evidence sources require. The functionalities of this layer can be mapped to the file system support provided by most forensic tool suites which interpret the clusters and sectors of a disk system (e.g., FTK, Encase, PyFlag, etc.). However, this layer has the additional capability of interpreting the contents from other digital media and supporting memory and network forensics.

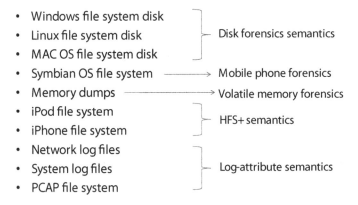

Fig. 3. Some types of evidentiary semantics used by different sources

3.3   Meta-information Layer

The *meta-information layer* supports application interfaces to extract metadata from objects present in the evidence sources. Every logical block of data extracted by the lower layer is represented as a file with properties that define its metadata. The meta-information layer uses a known file signature repository to filter metadata content from these blocks. For example, in hard disk images, files and metadata carry their usual meaning. In memory dumps, PCB metadata might contain its allocated size in kilobytes, assembler type and process schedule information. In log file and packet capture sources, individual entry metadata might contain timestamps, process type, transaction source and destination and protocol information. Information such as the registered application executing a particular file is acquired while extracting metadata from file image. The functionality draws analogy to the file interpretation capabilities provided by existing forensic tool suites while supporting a larger variety of evidence sources.

3.4 Evidence Composition and Visualization Layer

The *evidence composition and visualization layer* is responsible for integrating information from various sources of evidence and composing the components into consistent and comprehensive evidentiary material for presentation to an investigator. This layer is composed of 3 sub-layers, *content indexing sub-layer*, *cross referencing sub-layer* and *knowledge representation and reasoning sub-layer*. The content indexing sub-layer is designed to index all syntactic content, such as keywords, locations, dates and timestamps, etc. in evidence sources and the cross referencing sub-layer cross references indexed data with entries in the FIA repository. This repository can be arbitrarily large and contain any external information that is deemed relevant to the case and be indexed in an identical manner. The knowledge representation and reasoning sub-layer is concerned with the truth value of information and logical inconsistencies in evidence data. The complete layer decomposition is illustrated in Figure 4. While the illustration shows the three sub-layers stacked one above the other, we acknowledge the presence of significant interplay between them and no particular order is pre-conceived in their representation.

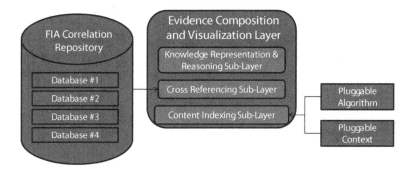

Fig. 4. Illustration of evidence composition and visualization layer

3.4.1 Content Indexing Sub-layer

The *content indexing sub-layer* supports mechanisms to index the logical blocks of data extracted by the lower layers. The indexing mechanism uses pluggable algorithms and pluggable contexts of keywords for indexing all syntactic content in data. The indexing process focuses on individualizing evidence, such as extracting and indexing names, locations, dates and events. We believe that such individualizations are crucial in any investigation and much sought after by investigators. This layer addresses the challenges involved in syntactic indexing and correlation of digital evidence across different sources. Once the data is indexed for each source separately, the indices are integrated to create a comprehensive social calendar of names and events.

3.4.2 Cross Referencing Sub-layer

The *cross referencing sub-layer* is responsible for cross referencing indexed content with external databases to correlate evidence information with real world events. The sub-layer supports indexing a repository containing case relevant content databases using our evidence correlation model and cross referencing with data indexed from the evidence sources. Such a repository is built over a period of time from several investigations. For example, it might represent the collective knowledge of the investigation team learnt over that period. The list of content in the repository can include online dictionaries, automobile registration database, online map index database, calendar of dates and events and a database of social identification for individuals in a given area.

3.4.3 Knowledge Representation and Reasoning Sub-layer

The *knowledge representation and reasoning sub-layer* is concerned with the logical correctness of assertions and theories that are developed based on collected evidence. For example, consider a scenario where investigators discover simultaneous login attempts by a user from Brisbane and Perth into a corporate mail server. The information renders itself to the development of two independent assertions "*The user was in Brisbane at time X*" and "*The user was in Perth at time X*". Clearly, information regarding user login attempts themselves, either from Brisbane or Perth, cannot be held against the user. However, correlating semantic information regarding the simultaneous attempts from two different cities provides a suspicious flavor to the actions and warrants further investigation. This sub-layer enables the development of such assertions and validating their truth value based on correlating information from multiple sources which is an integral part of any investigation. Any evidence to the contrary is flagged and presented to the investigator in an appropriate form which constitutes visualization.

4   Case Study – Car Theft Investigation

To demonstrate the concepts introduced in FIA, we present a case study using a hypothetical case concerning a car theft. The case was developed by Malcolm Corney at Queensland University of Technology as an assignment in a Computer Forensics course. The analysis of the case was carried out using existing forensic tools while following the FIA methodology. The true novelty of this architecture is described in Section 4.3. While the case contains only one disk image, we believe that the case involves sufficient diversity to demonstrate the utility of digital evidence integration. The actual value of this architecture, however, is perceived only when multiple such images are analyzed simultaneously.

4.1 About the Case

The case consists of a disk image containing multiple file system partitions. The case revolves around a chain of email messages recovered from Google Mail using the Thunderbird Client. The image contains several pictures of Australian wildlife with steganographic content containing pictures of car models. These car pictures represent cars recently reported stolen and currently under investigation. Each picture is password protected and the passwords are contained in an encrypted mail attachment. In addition, the disk slack space contains suspect's personal mail account details and a car model sequence that is traced back to the sequence of car thefts reported.

4.2 Extracting the Data

The disk was imaged using dd UNIX imager and the copy was hashed to preserve its integrity. The imaged disk was then registered under a new case with source and semantics information. This action reflects the functionality of the *evidence storage and access layer*. The image was then analyzed using FTK to detect and extract files, mail drafts and inbox messages. These actions reflect the extraction of logical blocks of data from the *representation and interpretation layer*. The same tool was also used to extract file properties or metadata information from the files and wildlife picture files. PRTK was used to crack the password of the encrypted file which contained passwords to the steganographic pictures which in turn provided more metadata. In FIA, this operation is performed at the *meta-information layer*. These operations were repeated with Encase and Sleuthkit to corroborate the results.

4.3 Evidence Composition

Once all the relevant data is extracted, the *evidence composition and visualization layer* takes over and indexes content in the extracted logical blocks. In our case study, the chain of email messages was used as the main source to generate evidence composition as illustrated in Figure 5. The contents were then cross referenced with multiple databases held in FIA repository to determine potential connections. Using directed keyword and metadata searches, an illustration of how FIA might piece the different sources of evidence together is illustrated in Figure 6. The dates of creation of picture files produced a pattern that traced back to the dates in the email chain indexed previously. Metadata analysis of the pictures further revealed the use of a particular camera that was recovered from the suspect's premises. The contact list from Thunderbird client revealed two persons with criminal record history, when their names presented hits in a simulated police database. The car registration numbers were cross referenced with simulated databases containing *automobile registration details* to determine the owners of the cars and *police complaint details* to verify if a stolen complaint has been registered since the theft and whether theft details fitted the description. Further, an address recovered from the email content was searched for a registration log (again, added to the FIA repository) to determine if the owner of the premises had collaborated with the suspect to store the stolen cars until they were shipped offshore.

Fig. 5. Illustrating evidence composition for car theft case

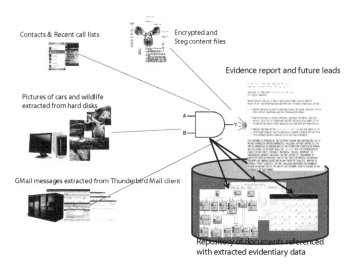

Fig. 6. Correlating data in car theft investigation using FIA

We have thus demonstrated the operation of the FIA architecture on a car theft case to perform evidence integration. FIA views the extracted data as conceptual sources, both at a syntactic and semantic level, and correlates information present in these sources in an attempt to reconstruct the past. In the process, FIA also aids the generation of further investigative leads that enable investigators to build a strong foundation for the case based on scientific evidence and facts.

5 Conclusions and Future Work

In this paper, we presented the FIA architecture for integrating digital evidence from multiple evidence sources in a technology independent manner and composing evidence information. The architecture supports all requirements of forensic security. In addition, FIA also supports indexing content identified as conceptual sources and cross references them with a repository of internal and external databases relevant to a case. To the best of our knowledge, FIA is the only known work that attempts to integrate different sources of evidence and compose comprehensive evidence. The architecture is hierarchical and completely modular and extensible to keep pace with challenges that frequently crop up in this field. The model has been demonstrated with a hypothetical case study involving car theft.

Future work will focus on the design and comprehensive validation of a prototype with real evidence data. Research is currently underway into developing data representation and effective indexing algorithms for content in FIA repository for evidence property identification in different evidence sources.

References

1. Alink, W., Bhoedjang, R.A.F., Boncz, P.A., de Vries, A.P.: XIRAF - XML-based indexing and querying for digital forensics. Digital Investigation. In: The Proceedings of the 6th Annual Digital Forensic Research Workshop (DFRWS 2006), vol. 3(suppl. 1), pp. 50–58 (2006)
2. Beebe, N.L., Clark, J.G.: A hierarchical, objectives-based framework for the digital investigations process. Digital Investigation 2(2), 147–167 (2005)
3. Beebe, N.L., Clark, J.G.: Digital forensic text string searching: Improving information retrieval effectiveness by thematically clustering search results. Digital Investigation 4(suppl. 1), 49–54 (2007)
4. Buchholz, F., Spafford, E.: On the role of file system metadata in digital forensics. Digital Investigation 1(4), 297–308 (2004)
5. Carrier, B.D., Grand, J.: A hardware-based memory acquisition procedure for digital investigations. Digital Investigation 1(1), 50–60 (2004)
6. Case, A., Cristina, A., Marziale, L., Richard, G.G., Roussev, V.: FACE: Automated digital evidence discovery and correlation, Digital Investigation. In: The Proceedings of the Eighth Annual DFRWS Conference, 5th edn., pp. S65–S75 (September 2008)
7. Cohen, M.I.: PyFlag - An advanced network forensic framework, Digital Investigation. In: The Proceedings of the Eighth Annual DFRWS Conference, vol. 5(suppl. 1), pp. S112–S120 (September 2008)
8. Common Digital Evidence Storage Format Working Group. Standardizing digital evidence storage. Communications of the ACM 49(2), 67–68 (Feburary 2006)
9. Garfinkel, S.: AFF: a new format for storing hard drive images. Communications of the ACM 49(2), 85–87 (2006)
10. Gladyshev, P., Patel, A.: Finite state machine approach to digital event reconstruction. Digital Investigation 1(2), 130–149 (2004)
11. Hosmer, C.: Digital evidence bag. Communications of the ACM 49(2), 69–70 (2006)
12. Mocas, S.: Building theoretical underpinnings for digital forensics research. Digital Investigation 1(1), 61–68 (2004)
13. Mee, V., Tryfonas, T., Sutherland, I.: The Windows Registry as a forensic artefact: Illustrating evidence collection for Internet usage. Digital Investigation 3(3), 166–173 (2006)
14. Nikkel, B.J.: Improving evidence acquisition from live network sources. Digital Investigation 3(2), 89–96 (2006)

15. Petroni, J., Nick, L., Walters, A., Fraser, T., Arbaugh, W.A.: FATKit: A framework for the extraction and analysis of digital forensic data from volatile system memory. Digital Investigation 3(4), 197–210 (2006)
16. Schatz, B., Clark, A.: An Open architecture for digital evidence integration. In: Proceedings of the 2006 AUSCERT R&D Stream, pp. 15–29 (2006)
17. Schatz, B.: BodySnatcher: Towards reliable volatile memory acquisition by software. Digital Investigation 4(suppl. 1), 126–134 (2007)
18. Schuster, A.: Searching for processes and threads in Microsoft Windows memory dumps. Digital Investigation. In: The Proceedings of the 6th Annual Digital Forensic Research Workshop (DFRWS 2006), vol. 3(suppl. 1), pp. 10–16 (2006)
19. Turner, P.: Unification of digital evidence from disparate sources (Digital Evidence Bags). Digital Investigation 2(3), 223–228 (2005)
20. Turner, P.: Selective and intelligent imaging using digital evidence bags. Digital Investigation. In: The Proceedings of the 6th Annual Digital Forensic Research Workshop (DFRWS 2006), vol. 3(suppl. 1), pp. 59–64 (2006)

Distinguishing between Camera and Scanned Images by Means of Frequency Analysis

Roberto Caldelli, Irene Amerini, and Francesco Picchioni

Media Integration and Communication Center - MICC,
University of Florence, Florence, Italy
roberto.caldelli@unifi.it
http://lci.det.unifi.it/caldelli.html

Abstract. Distinguishing the kind of sensor which has acquired a digital image could be crucial in many scenarios where digital forensic techniques are called to give answers. In this paper a new methodology which permits to determine if a digital photo has been taken by a camera or has been scanned by a scanner is proposed. Such a technique exploits the specific geometrical features of the sensor pattern noise introduced by the sensor in both cases and by resorting to a frequency analysis can infer if a periodicity is present and consequently which is the origin of the digital content. Experimental results are presented to support the theoretical framework.

Keywords: digital forensic, source identification, scanner, sensor noise.

1   Introduction

Digital images are nowadays used in the majority of the application fields in place of "old" analog images because of their easiness of usage, quality and above all manageability. These favorable issues bring anyway an intrinsic disadvantage: digital content can be simply manipulated by ordinary users for disparate purposes so that origin and authenticity of the digital content we are looking at is often very difficult to be assessed with a sufficient degree of certainty. Scientific instruments which allow to give answers to basic questions regarding image origin and image authenticity are needed [1]. Both these issues are anyway connected and sometimes are investigated together. In particular, by focusing on assessing image origin, two are the main aspects to be studied: the first one is to understand which kind of device has generated that digital image (e.g. a scanner, a digital camera or it is computer-generated) [3,7] and the second one is to succeed in determining which kind of sensor has acquired that content (i.e. the specific camera or scanner, recognizing model and brand) [6,1,4]. The main idea behind this kind of researches is that each sensor leaves a sort of unique fingerprint on the digital content it acquires due to some intrinsic imperfections and/or due to the specific acquisition process. Various solutions have been proposed in literature among these the use of CFA (Color Filter Array) characteristics [5] is quite well-know, nevertheless two

M. Sorell (Ed.): e-Forensics 2009, LNICST 8, pp. 95–101, 2009.

seem to be the main followed approaches. The first one is based on the extraction, from images belonging to different categories (e.g scanned images, photos, etc.), of some robust features which can be used to train a SVM (Support Vector Machine). When training is performed and whether features grant a good characterization, the system is able to classify the digital asset it is asked to check. The second approach is based on the computation of fingerprints of the different sensors (this is particularly used in sensor identification) through the analysis of a certain number of digital contents acquired by a device (e.g. images scanned by a particular scanner, photos taken by a camera and so on). Usually fingerprints are computed by means of the extraction of PRNU noise (Photo Response Non-Uniformity) [1,2] through a digital filtering operation; PRNU presence is induced by intrinsic disconformities in the manufacturing process of silicon CCD/CMOSs. After that the PRNU of the to-be-checked content is compared with the fingerprints and then it is classified. In this paper a new technique to distinguish which kind of device, a digital scanner or a digital camera, has acquired a specific image is proposed. Because of the structure of CCD set, the (PRNU) noise pattern, left over a digital image, will have a completely different distribution: in the scanner case it should show a mono-dimensional structure repeated row after row in the scanning direction, on the other hand, in the camera case, the noise pattern should present a bi-dimensional template. On the basis of this consideration we construct a 1-D signal and by resorting to a DFT analysis, which exploits the possible existence of a periodicity, understanding which has been the acquisition device. The paper lay-out is the following: Section 2 introduces a characterization of the sensor pattern noise and the periodicity is discussed, in Section 3 the proposed methodology is presented and then in Section 4 some experimental results are brought to support theoretical theses; conclusions are drawn in Section 5.

2   Sensor Pattern Noise Characterization

PRNU (Photo Response Non-Uniformity) noise is quite well-known as being an effective instrument for sensor identification because it is deterministically generated over each digital image it acquires. Such a noise is therefore an intrinsic characteristic of that specific sensor. The extraction of this noise is usually accomplished by denoising filters [8] and information it contains are used to assess something on the sensor characteristics. If we focus our attention on the acquisition process, it is easy to comprehend that when a photo is taken by a digital camera, basically a PRNU with a bi-dimensional structure is superimposed to it; on the contrary, when a digital image is created by means of a scanning operation the sensor array which slides over the to-be-acquired asset located on the scanner plate leaves its mono-dimensional fingerprint row by row during scanning. So in the last case, it is expected that a certain periodicity of the 1-D noise signal is evidenced along the scanning direction. This behavior should be absent in the camera case and this difference can be investigated to discern between images coming from the two different kinds of device. Being $R(i,j)$ with $1 \leq i \leq N$ and $1 \leq j \leq M$, the noise extracted by the scanned image of size $N \times M$, and assuming i (row) as scanning direction, it can, at least ideally, be expected that all the rows are equal (see Equation 1).

$$R(i,j) = R(k,j) \quad \forall \ 1 \leq j \leq M, 1 \leq i, k \leq N \tag{1}$$

So if a 1-D signal, $\mathbf{S}$ of $N \times M$ samples, is constructed by concatenating all the rows, it happens that $\mathbf{S}$ is a periodical signal of period M (Equation 2).

$$\mathbf{S} = [R(1,1), \cdots, R(1,M), \cdots, R(N,1), \cdots, R(N,M)] \tag{2}$$

It is also worthy to point out that if the 1-D signal is mounted along columns direction (i.e. this would be right assuming that j is the scanning direction), $\mathbf{S}$ is not periodical anymore, but it is constituted by diverse constant steps each of length M. A periodical signal such as $\mathbf{S}$, represented in Equation 2, contains a number of repetitions equal to N and therefore will have basically a frequency spectrum made by equispaced spikes. Such spikes will be spaced of $(N \times M)/M = N$ and will be weighted by the spectrum of the basic replica of the signal. So most of the energy of such a signal is located in these spikes. Obviously this is what should happen, in practice the 1-D signal will be corrupted and its periodical structure altered. Consequently the spectral spikes will be reduced and their magnitude partially spread over the other frequencies. If it is still possible to individuate such peaks, it will be simple to distinguish between a scanned image and a digital photo.

3   The Proposed Methodology

According to the idea presented in Section 2, let us describe in detail which is the proposed methodology to achieve that aim. The to-be-checked image I (size $N \times M$) is denoise filtered [8] obtaining I_d which is subtracted to the initial image to extract the sensor pattern noise R (see Equation 3).

$$R = I - I_d \tag{3}$$

To improve the possible presence of the deterministic contribution due to the 1-D PRNU pattern noise, R is divided into non-overlapping stripes (both horizontally and vertically, because both possible scanning directions have to be taken into account) and then all the different rows (columns) belonging to a stripe are averaged according to Equation 4 where L is the width of the stripe.

$$R_r(k) = \frac{1}{L} \sum_{i=1}^{L} R[i + (k-1)L] \quad 1 \leq k \leq N/L \tag{4}$$

After that two new noise images, named *bar codes*, respectively R_r (size $N/L \times M$) and R_c (size $N \times M/L$), have been obtained; R_r and R_c have the same number of samples. If an image has been scanned in the row direction, for instance, it is expected that R_r will be composed by equal (ideally) rows, on the

Fig. 1. Bar codes of size $N/L \times M$ (scanning direction = row): camera image (top), scanned image (center) and ideal bar code for a scanned image (bottom)

other side such a characterization can not be expected in the column direction for R_c and, above all, for an image coming from a digital camera (both directions): this circumstance is presented in Figure 1. *Bar codes* are then used to create the mono-dimensional signal by concatenating respectively rows of R_r and columns of R_c and then periodicity is checked. Sometimes to reduce randomness a low pass filtering operation (usually a median filter) is applied to bar codes, along the rows and the columns separately, before constructing 1-D signals.

For the sake of clarity, let us call S_r and S_c the two mono-dimensional signal, obtained as previously described, from R_r and R_c respectively. DFT (Discrete Fourier Transform) is applied to both these signals and the magnitude of the coefficients is considered. After that a selection is carried out on the basis of the following criterion: amplitude values above a threshold T (see Equation 5 where α is a weighting factor usually set to 0.4) and at the same time located in the expected positions within the spectrum (see Section 2) are taken.

$$T = \alpha * max(max(abs(DFT(S_r))), max(abs(DFT(S_c)))) \tag{5}$$

In the end all the values satisfying the previous selection criterion are added, separately for row and column cases, yielding to two energy factors, F_r and F_c respectively and their ratio $RATIO = F_r/F_c$ is computed. If the digital image has been scanned in the row direction, a high value of $RATIO$ is expected (if the scanning direction has been along columns $RATIO$ will be very small), otherwise if the image has been taken by a digital camera the two energy factors should be comparable and a value of $RATIO$ around one is foreseen. Doing so it is possible not only distinguishing between images coming from a scanner or from a camera but, in the scanner case, determining the scanning direction. To improve robustness, this technique is applied to all the three image channels (R, G, B) and three energy contributions are collected in each factor F_r and F_c.

4   Experimental Results

Experimental tests have been carried out to support the theoretical framework. Digital images coming from 4 different scanners (Epson Expression XL 10000 2400x4200 dpi, HP Scanjet 8300 4800x4800 dpi, HP Deskjet F4180 1200x2400 dpi, Brother DCP 7010 600x2.400 dpi) and from 7 commercial cameras (Canon

DIGITAL IXUS i ZOOM, Nikon COOLPIX L12, Fuji Finepix F10, HP Photosmart C935, Nikon D80, Samsung VP-MS11, Sony DSC-P200) have been acquired in TIFF and JPEG format. Because of the diverse size of the contents, the analysis have been done by dividing them into images of fixed dimension $N \times M$ (1024 × 768). Obtained results have confirmed theoretical assumptions as it can be seen in Figure 2 (a) where $RATIO$ values are plotted and a separate clustering is observed (for sake of clarity when $RATIO$ was over 1 the inverse was taken, due to this, information about scanning direction is lost). In Figure 2 (b), only scanned images, correctly detected, are figured: in this case inversion

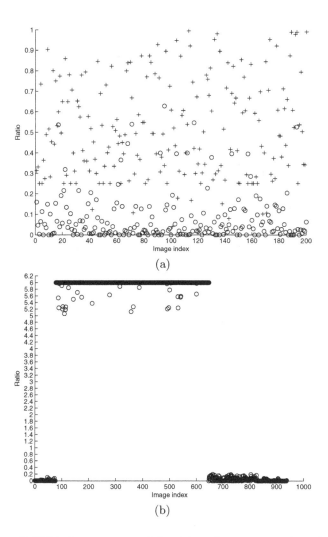

(a)

(b)

Fig. 2. Energy $RATIO$ for 200 scanned (circle) and 200 camera (cross) images (a). Energy $RATIO$ only for 950 scanned images, correctly detected: scanning directions are evidenced (b).

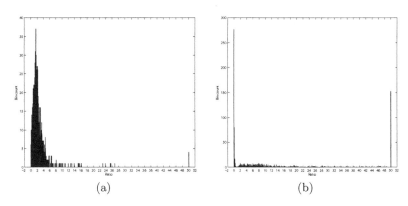

(a)   (b)

Fig. 3. Statistical distribution of $RATIO$: camera (a) and scanned images (b)

Table 1. Confusion matrix for scanned and camera images over a data set of 2000 images (left) and scanning direction recovery for scanner correct answers (right)

	Camera	Scanner
Camera	89.74%	10.26%
Scanner	14.65%	85.35%

	Row	Column
Row	100.00%	0.00%
Column	0.00%	100.00%

of $RATIO$ has not been done and, to make visualization easier, high values are saturated at 6. It is simply to distinguish the two different scanning directions individuated by high and low values of $RATIO$; in particular it is interesting to note the left and the right side of the plot related to column scanning direction and the central part related to row direction. In Figure 3 the statistical distribution of $RATIO$ for 1000 camera images (a) and 1000 scanned ones (b) are pictured where, in this case, higher values have been saturated at 50; a strong concentration is evidenced on the tails of the graph for the scanner case. Finally, a massive test has been carried out on a data set of 2000 images (half scanned images and half photos) by setting a threshold at 0.2 with $RATIO$ normalized between 0 and 1 (as done for Figure 2 (a)): percentages are presented in the rows of Table 1 (left). In Table 1 (right) percentages related to the scanning directions in the scanner successful cases (85.35% of Table 1 left) are reported.

5   Conclusions

In this paper a new technique to distinguish between digital images acquired by a scanner and photos taken by a digital camera has been proposed. Sensor pattern noise periodicity along the scanning direction is checked for classification through a frequency analysis. Experimental results have been presented to support the theoretical framework. Future developments will regard the integration of this feature within a SVM.

References

1. Chen, M., Fridrich, J., Goljan, M., Lukas, J.: Determining Image Origin and Integrity Using Sensor Noise. IEEE Trans. on Information Forensics and Security 3(1), 74–90 (2008)
2. Mondaini, N., Caldelli, R., Piva, A., Barni, M., Cappellini, V.: Detection of malevolent changes in digital video for forensic applications. In: Proc. SPIE, vol. 6505, 65050T (2007)
3. Lyu, S., Farid, H.: How realistic is photorealistic? IEEE Transactions on Signal Processing 53(2), 845–850 (2005)
4. Gou, H., Swaminathan, A., Wu, M.: Robust scanner identification based on noise features. In: Proc. SPIE, vol. 6505, p. 65050S (2007)
5. Swaminathan, A., Wu, M., Liu, K.J.R.: Digital Image Forensics via Intrinsic Fingerprints. IEEE Transactions on Information Forensics and Security 3(1), 101–117 (2008)
6. Khanna, N., Mikkilineni, A.K., Chiu, G.T.-C., Allebach, J.P., Delp, E.J.: Scanner identification using sensor pattern noise. In: Proc. SPIE, vol. 6505, 65051K (2007)
7. Khanna, N., Chiu, G.T.-C., Allebach, J.P., Delp, E.J.: Forensic techniques for classifying scanner, computer generated and digital camera images. In: Proc. IEEE ICASSP, pp. 1653–1656 (2008)
8. Mihcak, M.K., Kozintsev, I., Ramchandran, K.: Spatially Adaptive Statistical Modeling of Wavelet Image Coefficients and its Application to Denoising. In: Proc. IEEE ICASSP, vol. 6, pp. 3253–3256 (1999)

Developing Speaker Recognition System: From Prototype to Practical Application

Pasi Fränti[1], Juhani Saastamoinen[1], Ismo Kärkkäinen[2], Tomi Kinnunen[1], Ville Hautamäki[1], and Ilja Sidoroff[1]

[1] Speech & Image Processing Unit,
Dept. of Computer Science and Statistics, University of Joensuu, Finland
[2] Institute for Infocomm Research (I²R),
Agency for Science,
Technology and Research (A*STAR), Singapore

Abstract. In this paper, we summarize the main achievements made in the 4-year PUMS project during 2003-2007. The emphasis is on the practical implementations, how we have moved from Matlab and Praat scripting to C/C++ implemented applications in Windows, UNIX, Linux and Symbian environments, with the motivation to enhance technology transfer. We summarize how the baseline methods have been implemented in practice, how the results are utilized in forensic applications, and compare recognition results to the state-of-art and existing commercial products such as ASIS, FreeSpeech and VoiceNet.

1 Introduction

Voice-based person identification can be a useful tool in *forensic research* where any additional piece of information can guide the inspections to the correct track. Even if 100% matching cannot be reached by the current technology, it may be enough to get the correct speaker ranked high enough among the tested ones.

A state-of-art *speaker recognition system* consists of components shown in Fig. 1. The methods are based on short-term features such as *mel-frequency cepstral coefficients* (MFCCs), but two longer term features are considered here as well: *long-term average spectrum* (LTAS) and *long-term distribution of the fundamental frequency* (F0). After feature extraction, the similarity of a given test sample is measured to previously trained models stored in a speaker database. In person authentication applications, the similarity is measured relative to a known or estimated *universal background model* (UBM) which represents speech in general, and draw conclusion whether the sample should be accepted or rejected. Sometimes a match confidence measure is also desired. In forensics, it may be enough to find a small set (say 3-5) of the best matching speakers for further investigations by a specialist phonetician.

In this paper, we overview the results of *speaker recognition* (SRE) research done within the Finnish nationwide *PUMS*[1] project funded by TEKES[2]. The focus has been

---

[1] Puheteknologian uudet menetelmät ja sovellukset – New methods and applications of speech technology (http://pums.fi).
[2] National Technology Agency of Finland (http://www.tekes.fi).

M. Sorell (Ed.): e-Forensics 2009, LNICST 8, pp. 102–115, 2009.

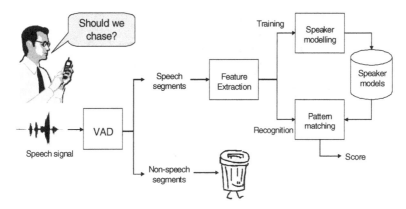

Fig. 1. Overall system diagram for speaker recognition

to transfer research results into practical applications. We studied the existing SRE methodology and proposed several new solutions with practical usability and real-time processing as our main motivations. As results of the project, we developed two pieces of software: *WinSProfiler* and *EpocSProfiler*. The first one is used by forensic researchers in the National Bureau of Investigations (NBI) in Finland, and the second is tailored to work in mobile environment.

The rest of the paper is organized as follows. In Section 2, we review the feature extraction and speaker modeling components used in this study, and study the effect of the voice activity detection by experimenting with several existing techniques and new ones developed during the project. Implementation aspects are covered in Section 3, and results of the implemented software are given in Section 4. The implemented methods are compared against two prototype systems developed for the *NIST*[3] speaker recognition evaluation (SRE) competition[4] in 2006. Conclusions are drawn in Section 5.

2 Speaker Recognition

2.1 Short-Term Spectral Features

Our *baseline method* is based on the *mel-frequency cepstral coefficients* (MFCCs), which is a representation of an approximation of the short-term spectrum (Fig. 2). The audio signal is first divided into 30 ms long frames with 10 ms overlap. Each segment is then converted into spectral domain by the *fast Fourier transform* (FFT), filtered according to a psycho-acoustically motivated *mel-scale* frequency warping, where lower frequency components are emphasized more than the higher ones. The feature vector consists of 12 DCT magnitudes of filter output logarithms. The corresponding 1st and 2nd temporal differences are also included to model the rate and acceleration of changes in the spectrum. The lowest MFCC coefficient (referred to as C0) represents

---

[3] National institute of standards and technology.
[4] http://www.nist.gov/speech/tests/spk/2006

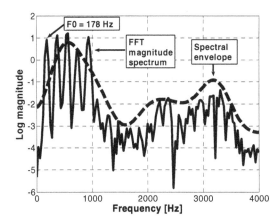

Fig. 2. Illustration of a sample spectrum and its approximation by cepstral coefficients

the log-energy of the frame, and is removed as a form of energy normalization. Mean subtraction and variance normalization is then performed for each coefficient to have zero mean and unit variance over the utterance.

The main benefit of using MFCC is that it is also used in speech recognition, and the same signal processing components can therefore be used for both. This is also its main drawback: the MFCC feature tends to capture information related to the speech content better than the personal speaker characteristics. If the MFCC features are applied as such, there is a danger that the recognition is mostly based on the content instead of the speaker identity. Another similar feature, *linear prediction cepstral co-efficients* (LPCC), was also implemented and tested but the MFCC remained our choice of practice.

2.2 Long Term Features

Besides the short-term features, two longer-term features were studied: *Long-term average spectrum* (LTAS) and *long-term distribution of the fundamental frequency* (F0). The first one is motivated by the facts that it includes more spectral detail than MFCC and as a long time average it should be more robust on changing conditions. On the other hand, it is also criticized by the same reasons: it represents only averaged information over time and all information about variance of the utterance is evidently lost.

Results in [14] showed that LTAS provides only marginal additional improvement when fused with the stronger MFCC features, but at the cost of making the overall system more complex in terms of implementation and parameter tuning, see Fig. 3. Even though LTAS is used in forensic research for visual examination, its use in automatic analysis has no proven motives.

Fundamental frequency, on the other hand, does contain speaker-specific information, which is expected to be independent of the speech content. Since this information is not captured by MFCCs, it can potentially improve recognition accuracy of the baseline system. However, it is not trivial to extract the F0 feature and use it in the matching process. These issues were extensively studied using combination of F0, its

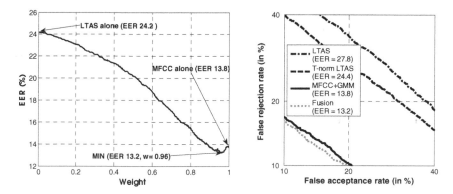

Fig. 3. An attempt to improve the baseline by adding LTAS via classifier fusion. The difficulty of tuning the fusion weights is shown on left. The corresponding results of the best combination are shown on right for NIST 2001 corpus.

derivative (delta), and the *log-energy* of the frame. This combination is referred to as *prosody vector*, and it was implemented in WinSProfiler 2.0.

The results support the claim that the recognition accuracy of F0 is consistent under changing conditions. In clean conditions, no improvement was obtained in comparison to the MFCC baseline. In noisy conditions (additive factory noise with 10 dB SNR), the inclusion of F0 improved the results according to our tests [12]. It is open whether this translates to real-life applications. With the NIST corpora (see Section 4) the effect of F0 is mostly insignificant, or even harmful, probably because the SNR of the NIST files is better than the 10 dB noise level of our simulations.

2.3 Speaker Modeling and Matching

After feature extraction, the similarity or dissimilarity of a given test sample to the trained models in a speaker database must be measured. We implemented the traditional *Gaussian mixture model* (GMM), where the speaker model is represented as a set of cluster means, covariance matrixes, and mixture weights, and a simpler solution based on *vector quantization* (VQ): estimated cluster centroids represent the speaker model. In [7], we found out that the simpler VQ model provides similar results with significantly less complex implementation than GMM. Nevertheless, both methods have been used and implemented in WinSProfiler 2.0. In the mobile implementation, only the VQ model was implemented at first. Later a new compact *feature histogram* model has been implemented as well.

The background normalization (UBM) is crucial for successful verification. Existing solution known as *maximum a posteriori* (MAP) adaptation was originally formulated for the GMM [21]. The essential difference to clustering-based methods is that the model is not constructed from scratch to approximate the distribution of feature vectors. Instead it is an iteration which starts from the background model. Similar solution for the VQ model was then formulated during the project [7].

In addition to modeling a single feature set, a solution is needed to combine the results of independent classifiers. A *linear weighting* scheme optimized using *Fisher's criterion* and *majority voting* have been implemented. On the other hand, fusion is not necessarily wanted in practical solutions because the additional parameter tuning is non-trivial. In this sense, the performance of the method in WinSProfiler 2.0 could be improved but it is uncertain if it is worth it, or whether it would work in practical application at all. The use of data fusion is more or less experimental and is not considered as a part of the baseline.

2.4 Voice Activity Detection

The goal of *voice activity detection* (VAD) is to divide a given input signal into parts that contain speech and the parts that contain background. In speaker recognition, we want to model the speaker only from the parts of a recording that contain speech.

We carried out extensive study of several existing solutions, and developed a few new ones during the course of the project. Real-time operation is necessary in VAD applications such as speaker recognition where latency is an important issue in practice. The methods can also be classified according to whether separate training material is needed (trained) or not (adaptive). Methods that operate without any training are typically based on short-term signal statistics. We consider the following non-trained methods: *Energy*, LTSD, *Periodicity* and the current telecommunication standards: G729B, AMR1 and AMR2, see Table 1.

Trained VAD methods construct separate speech and non-speech models based on annotated training data. The methods differ in both the type of used feature and model. We consider two methods based on MFCC features (SVM, GMM), and one based on *short-term time series* (STS). All of these methods were developed during the PUMS project. We also modified the LTSD method to adapt the noise model from a separate training material instead of using the beginning of the sound signal.

Figure 4 shows an example of the process, where the speech waveform is transformed frame by frame to the speech/non-speech decisions using the Periodicity-based method [8]. First, features of the signal are calculated, and smoothed by taking

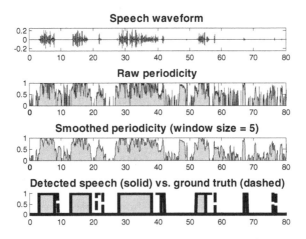

Fig. 4. Demonstration of voice activity detection from frame-wise scores to longer segments using Periodicity method [8]

Table 1. Speech detection rate (%) comparison of the VAD methods with the four data sets

	VAD method	NIST 2005	Bus stop	Lab	NBI
Adaptive	Energy [24]	1.5	14.6	16.8	30.0
	LTSD [20]	40.0	19.2	14.4	31.8
	Periodicity [8]	3.2	21.9	9.9	21.4
	G729B [9]	8.9	6.5	7.9	**13.3**
	AMR1 [5]	5.5	5.7	7.2	21.8
	AMR2 [5]	8.4	7.4	**5.1**	16.1
Trained	SVM [14]	11.6	5.2	19.5	---
	GMM [10]	8.8	7.5	9.7	---
	LTSD [20]	**1.3**	6.2	14.9	---
	STS (unpublished)	7.1	**3.9**	8.6	---

into account the neighboring frames (five frames in our tests). The final decisions (speech or non-speech) are made according to a user select threshold. In real applications, the problem of selecting the threshold should also be issued.

The classification accuracy of the tested VAD methods is summarized in Table 1 for the four datasets as documented in [25]. For G729B, AMR, and STS, we set the threshold when combining individual frame-wise decisions to one second resolution decisions, by counting the speech and non-speech frame proportions in each segment.

For the NIST 2005 data, the simple energy-based and the trained LTSD provide the best results. This is not surprising since the parameters of the method have been optimized for earlier NIST corpuses through extensive testing, and because the energy of the speech and non-speech segments is clearly different in most samples. Moreover, the trained LTSD clearly outperforms its adaptive variant because the noise model initialization failed on some of the NIST files, and caused high error values.

The NBI data is the most challenging, and all adaptive methods have values higher than 10%. The best method is G729B with the error rate of 13%. It is an open question how much better results could be reached if the trained VAD could be used for these data. However, in this case the training protocol and the amount of trained material needed should be studied more closely.

For WinSProfiler 2.13, we have implemented the three VAD methods that performed best in NIST data: *LTSD*, *Energy* and *Periodicity*. Their effect on speaker verification accuracy is reported in Table 2. The advantage of using VAD in this application with NIST 2006 corpus is obvious, but the choice between *Energy* and *Periodicity* is unclear.

Table 2. Effect of VAD in speaker verification performance (error rate %)

	NIST 2001		NIST 2006
	Model size 512	Model size 64	Model size 512
No VAD	13.6	16.0	44.4
LTSD	12.4	13.7	35.8
Energy	9.3	10.4	**16.6**
Periodicity	**8.5**	**9.6**	16.8

3 Methods Implemented and Tested

Experimentation using Praat and Matlab is rather easy and convenient for quick testing of new ideas, but that is not true for technology transfer or larger scale development. Our aim was to have the baseline methods implemented in C/C++ language for software integration with real products, and also for performing large scale tests. Applications were therefore built for three platforms: UNIX/Linux (*SProfiler*), Windows (*WinSProfiler*) and Symbian (*EpocSProfiler*), see Fig. 5.

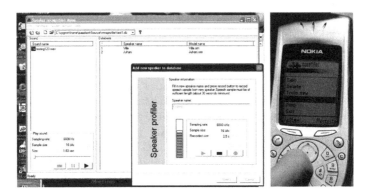

Fig. 5. Constructed applications where the developed SRE system was implemented during the project: *SProfiler* (not shown), *WinSProfiler* (left), and *EpocSProfiler* (right)

3.1 Windows Application: WinSProfiler

First applications (WinSProfiler 1.0 and EpocSProfiler 1.0) were developed based on speaker recognition library called *Srlib2*, which had clear specifications of the functionalities of the training and matching operations. However, the functionality was too much tied with the user interface making porting to other platforms complicated.

In order to avoid multiple updates for all software, the library was then reconstructed step-by-step, ending up to a significant upgrade in 2006 and 2007, which was renamed to PSPS2 (*portable speech processing system 2*). Main motivation of this large but invisible work was that the software should be maintainable, modular, and portable. The following life cycle of the recognition library appeared during the project: Srlib1 (2003) → Srlib2 (2004) → Srlib3 (2005-2006) → PSPS2 (2006-2007).

As a consequence, all the functionality in WinSProfiler was re-written to support the new architecture of the PSPS2 library so that all unnecessary dependencies between the user interface and the library functionality were finally cleared, and above all that the software would be flexible and configurable for testing new experimental methods. This happened as a background project during the last project year (2006-07). Eventually a new version (WinSProfiler 2.0) was released in Spring 2007, and a series of upgrades were released since then: 2.1 (June-07) → 2.11 (July-07) → 2.12 (Aug-07) → 2.13 (Oct-07) → 2.14 (June-08).

The current version (WinSProfiler 2.14) is written completely using C++ language, consisting of the following components:

- Database library to handle storage of the speaker profiles.
- Audio processing library to handle feature extraction and speaker modelling.
- Recognition library to handle matching feature streams against speaker models.
- Configurable audio processing and recognition components.
- Graphical user interface.

The GUI part is based on 3rd party C++ development library *wxWidgets*. Similarly, 3rd party libraries *libsndfile* and *portaudio* were used for the audio processing, and *SQLite3* was used for the database. The rest of the system is implemented by us: signal processing, speaker modeling, matching and graphical user interface. The new version was extensively tested, and the functioning of the recognition components was verified step-by-step with the old version (WinSProfiler 1.0). The new library architecture is show in Fig. 6.

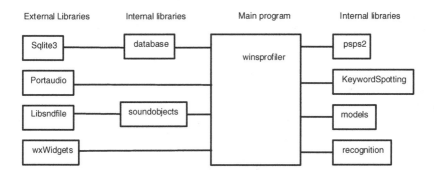

Fig. 6. Technical organization of the WinSProfiler 2.0 software

3.2 Symbian Implementation: EpocSProfiler

During the first project year, the development of a *Symbian* implementation was also started with the motivation to implement a demo application for Nokia *Series 60* phones. Research was carried on for faster matching techniques by speaker pruning, quantization and faster search structures [13]. The existing baseline (Srlib 2) was converted to Symbian environment (Srlib 3) in order to have real-time MFCC signal processing, as well as instant on-device training, identification, and text-independent verification from spoken voice samples.

The development of the *EpocSProfiler* software was made co-operatively with Nokia Research Center during the first project year, and the first version (EpocSProfiler 1.0, based on Srlib 2) was published in April 2004. The Symbian development was then separated from PUMS and further versions of the software (EpocSProfiler 2.0) were developed separately, although within the same research group, using the same core library code, and mostly by the same people.

The main challenge was that the CPU was limited to fixed-point arithmetic. Conversion of floating point algorithms to fixed-point itself was rather straightforward but the accuracy of the fixed-point MFCC was insufficient. Improved version was developed [22] by fine-tuned intermediate signal scaling, and more accurate 22/10 bit allocation scheme of the FFT.

Two voice model types were implemented: centroid model with MSE-based matching as the baseline and a new faster experimental *feature histogram modelling* with entropy-based matching was developed for EpocSProfiler 2.0. In identification, training and recognition response of the new histogram models on a Nokia 6630 device is about 1 second for a database of 45 speakers, whereas the training and identification using the centroid model are both more than 100 times slower.

3.3 Prototype Solutions for NIST Competition

In addition to the developed software, two prototype systems were also considered based on the NIST 2006 evaluation. NIST organizes annually or bi-annually a speaker recognition evaluation (NIST SRE) competition. The organizers have collected speech material and then release part of it for benchmarking. Each sample has an identity label, gender, and other information like, for example, the spoken language. At the time of evaluation, NIST then sends to the participants a set of verification trials (about 50.000 in the main category alone) with claimed identities of listed sound files. The participants must send their recognition results (accept or reject claim, and likelihood score) within 2-3 weeks. The results are released in a workshop and are available for all participants.

For this purpose, we developed a prototype method for the NIST 2006 competition in collaboration with Institute for Infocomm Research (IIR) at Singapore[5]. This method is referred here as *IIRJ*. The main idea was to include three independent classifiers, and calculate overall result by classifier fusion. A variant of the baseline (SVM-LPCC) [4] with T-norm [1] was one component, F0 another one, and GMM tokenization [18] the third one (Fig. 9). In this way, different levels of speaker cues are extracted: spectral (SVM-LPCC), prosodic (F0), and high-level (GMM tokenization). The LPCC feature showed slightly better results at IIR and replaced MFCC.

As a state-of-art, we consider the method reported in [2]. It provided the best recognition performance in the main category (1conv-1conv) and is used here as a benchmark. This system was constructed by a combination of several MFCC-based subsystems similar to ours, combined by SVM-based data fusion [2]. Based on analytical comparison with our MFCC baseline, the main components missing from our software are *heteroscedastic linear discriminant analysis* (HLDA) [17], [3] and *eigenchannel normalization* [11].

The authors at the Brno University of Technology (BUT) later reported simplified variant of the method [3], showing that similar result can be achieved based on the carefully tuned baseline method without fusion and using multiple sub-systems. The authors of the method in [11] have also expressed the same motivation, i.e. to keep the method simple and avoid the use data fusion. The problem of data fusion in practical applications is that the additional parameter tuning is non-trivial, and its role is more or less for demonstrating theoretical limits that given system can reach. The fusion implemented in *WinSProfiler* is therefore mainly for experimental purposes and not considered here as a part of the baseline.

---

[5] Institute for Infocomm Research (I^2R).

4   Summary of the Main Results

Even though usability and compatibility are important issues for a practical application, an important question is the identification accuracy the system can provide. We have therefore collected here the main recognition results of the methods developed during the project, and made an attempt to compare them with the state-of-the-art (according to NIST evaluation), and provide indicative results from comparisons with existing commercial programs. The corpora used are summarized in Table 3.

Table 3. Databases that have been used in the evaluation

Corpus	Trials	Speakers	Length of training data	Length of test data
NIST 2001 (core test)	22,418	174	2 min	2-60 s
NIST 2006 (core test)	53,966	731	5 min	5 min
Sepemco	494	45	12-60 s	9-60 s
TIMIT	184,900	430	15-35 s	5-15 s
NBI data	62	62	42-150 s	10-93 s

4.1   Recognition Results

The following methods have been included in the tests reported here:

- **WinSProfiler 1.0:** An early demo version from 2005 using only the raw MFCC coefficients without deltas, normalization, and VAD. VQ model of size 64 is used.
- **WinSProfiler 2.0:** A new version released in May 2007 based on the PSPS2 recognition library developed already in late 2006. Main differences were use of GMM-UBM, deltas, and normalization. The first version did use neither VAD nor gender information (specific for NIST corpus).
- **WinSProfiler 2.11:** Version released in June 2007, now included gender information (optional) and several VADs, of which the periodicity-based method [8] has been used for testing.
- **EpocSProfiler 2.1:** Symbian version from October 2006. Corresponds to WinSProfiler 1.0 except that the histogram models are used instead of VQ.
- **NIST-IIRJ:** Our joint submission with IIR to NIST competition based on the LPCC-SVM, GMM tokenization and F0 features, and fusion by NN and SVM, using Energy-based VAD. This system does not exist as a program, but the results have been constructed manually using scripting.
- **NIST state-of-the-art:** The results released by the authors providing the winning method in NIST 2006 competition as a reference.

The main results (verification accuracy) are summarized in Table 4 as far as available. The challenging NIST 2001 corpus has been used as the main benchmark since summer 2006. Most remarkable lesson is that, even though the results were reasonable for the easier datasets (TIMIT), they are devastating for the *WinSProfiler* 1.0 when NIST

Table 4. Summary of verification (equal error rate) results (0 % is best) using the NIST 2001, NIST 2006 and the *Sepemco* database

Method and version	Sepemco	TIMIT	NIST 2001	NIST 2006
EpocSProfiler 2.1 (2006)	12 %	8 %	---	46 %
WinSProfiler 1.0 (2005)	24 %	---	33 %	48 %
WinSProfiler 2.0 (no-vad)	7 %	3 %	16 %	45 %
WinSProfiler 2.11 (2007)	13 %	9 %	11 %	17 %
NIST submission (IIRJ)	---	---	---	7 %
State-of-art [2]	---	---	---	4 %

2006 was used. The most remarkable improvements have been achieved in the latter stage of the project since the release of the PSPS2 library used in *WinSProfiler* 2.11.

Another observation is that the role of VAD was shown to be critical for NIST 2006 evaluation (45% vs. 17%), but this did not generalize to *Sepemco* data (7% vs. 13%). This arises the questions whether the database could be too specific, and how much the length of training material would change the design choices and parameters used (model sizes, use of VAD). Although NIST 2006 has a large number of speakers and huge amount of test samples, the length of the samples is typically long (5 minutes). Moreover, the speech samples are usually easy to differentiate from background by a simple energy-based VAD. The background noise level is also rather low.

4.2 Comparisons with Commercial Products

Speaker identification comparisons with three selected commercial software (*ASIS*, *FreeSpeech*, *VoiceNet*) are summarized in Table 5 using NBI material obtained by phone tapping (with permission). Earlier results with WinSProfiler 1.0 for different dataset have been reported in [19]. The current data (TAP) included two samples from 62 male speakers: the longer sample was used for model training and the shorter one for testing. The following software has been tested:

- WinSProfiler, Univ. of Joensuu, Finland, www.cs.joensuu.fi/sipu/
- ASIS, Agnitio, Spain, http://www.agnitio.es
- FreeSpeech, PerSay, Israel, http://www.persay.com
- VoiceNet, Speech Technology Center, Russia, http://www.speechpro.com
- Batvox, Agnitio, Spain, http://www.agnitio.es

The results have been provided by Tuija Niemi-Laitinen at the Crime laboratory in National Bureau of Investigation, Finland. The results are summarized as how many times the correct speaker is found as the first match, and how many times among the top-5 in the ranking. WinSProfiler 2.11 performed well in the comparison, which indicates that it is at par with the commercial software (Table 5).

Besides the recognition accuracy, *WinSProfiler* was highlighted as having good usability in the NBI tests, especially due to its ease of use, fast processing, and the capability to add multiple speakers into the database in one run. Improvements could be made for more user-friendly processing and analysis of the output score list though.

Table 5. Recognition accuracies (100% is best) of WinSProfiler 2.11 and the commercial software for NBI data (TAP)

Software	Used samples	Failed samples	Top-1	Top-5
ASIS	51	11	67 %	92 %
WinSProfiler 2.11 (*)	51	11	53 %	100 %
WinSProfiler 2.11	62	0	53 %	98 %
FreeSpeech	61	1	74 %	98 %
VoiceNet	38	24	29 %	52 %

(*) Selected sub-test with those 51 samples accepted by ASIS.

Overall, the results indicated that there is large gap between the recognition accuracy obtained by the latest methods in research, and the accuracy obtained by available software (commercially or via the project). In NIST 2006 benchmarking, accuracy of about 4 to 7% could be reached by the state-or-the-art methods such as in [2], and by our own submission (IIRJ).

Direct comparisons to our software WinSProfiler 2.11, and indirect comparisons to the commercial software gave us indications of how much is the difference between *"what is"* (commercial software, our prototype) and *"what could be"*. It demonstrates the fast development of the research in this area, but also shows the problem that tuning towards one data can set lead undesired results for another data set.

5   Conclusions

Voice-based recognition is technically not mature, and the influence of background noise and changes in recording conditions affects too much the recognition accuracy to be used for access control as such. The technology, however, can already be used in forensic research where any additional piece of information can guide the inspections to the correct track. Even if 100% matching cannot currently be reached, it can be enough to detect the correct suspect high in ranking.

In this paper, we have summarized our work that resulted in software called *WinSProfiler* that serves as a practical tool supporting the following features:

- Speaker recognition and audio processing.
- Speaker profiles in database.
- Several models per speaker.
- Digital filtering of audio files.
- MFCC, F0 + energy and LTAS features.
- GMM and VQ models (with and w/o UBM).
- Voice activity detection by energy, LTSD and periodicity-based methods.
- Keyword search (support for Finnish and English languages).
- Fully portable (Windows, Linux and potentially Mac OS X).

Extended version of this report appears in [6].

Acknowledgements

The work has been supported by the *National Technology Agency of Finland* (TEKES) as the four year project *New Methods and Applications of Speech Technology* (PUMS) under the contracts 40437/03, 49398/04 40356/05, 40195/06.

References

1. Auckenthaler, R., Carey, M., Lloyd-Thomas, H.: Score normalization for text-independent speaker verification systems. Digital Signal Processing 10(1-3), 42–54 (2000)
2. Brummer, N., Burget, L., Cernocky, J., Glembek, O., Grezl, F., Karafiat, M., van Leeuwen, D.A., Matejka, P., Schwarz, P., Strasheim, A.: Fusion of Heterogeneous Speaker Recognition Systems in the STBU Submission for the NIST Speaker Recognition Evaluation 2006. IEEE Trans. Audio, Speech and Language Processing 15(7), 2072–2084 (2007)
3. Burget, L., Matejka, P., Schwarz, P., Glembek, O., Cernocky, J.H.: Analysis of Feature Extraction and Channel Compensation in a GMM Speaker Recognition System. IEEE Trans. Audio, Speech and Language Processing 15(7), 1979–1986 (2007)
4. Campbell, W.M., Campbell, J.P., Reynolds, D.A., Singer, E., Torres-Carrasquillo, P.A.: Support vector machines for speaker and language recognition. Computer Speech and Language 20(2-3), 210–229 (2006)
5. ETSI, Voice Activity Detector (VAD) for Adaptive Multi-Rate (AMR) Speech Traffic Channels, ETSI EN 301 708 Recommendation (1999)
6. Fränti, P., Saastamoinen, J., Kärkkäinen, I., Kinnunen, T., Hautamäki, V., Sidoroff, I.: Implementing speaker recognition system: from Matlab to practice. Research Report A-2007-4, Dept. of Comp. Science, Univ. of Joensuu, Finland (November 2007), http://cs.joensuu.fi/sipu/pub.htm
7. Hautamäki, V., Kinnunen, T., Kärkkäinen, I., Saastamoinen, J., Tuononen, M., Fränti, P.: Maximum a posteriori adaptation of the centroid model for speaker verification. IEEE Signal Processing Letters 15, 162–165 (2008)
8. Hautamäki, V., Tuononen, M., Niemi-Laitinen, T., Fränti, P.: Improving speaker verification by periodicity based voice activity detection. In: Int. Conf. on Speech and Computer (SPECOM 2007), Moscow, Russia, vol. 2, pp. 645–650 (2007)
9. ITU, A Silence Compression Scheme for G.729 Optimized for Terminals Conforming to Recommendation V.70, ITU-T Recommendation G.729-Annex B (1996)
10. Kay, S.M.: Fundamentals of Statistical Signal Processing, Detection Theory, vol. 2. Prentice Hall, Englewood Cliffs (1998)
11. Kenny, P., Ouellet, P., Dehak, N., Gupta, V., Dumouchel, P.: A study of inter-speaker variability in speaker verification. IEEE Transactions on Audio, Speech and Language Processing 16(5), 980–988 (2008)
12. Kinnunen, T., Gonzalez-Hautamäki, R.: Long-Term F0 Modeling for Text-Independent Speaker Recognition. In: Int. Conf. on Speech and Computer (SPECOM 2005), Patras, Greece, pp. 567–570 (October 2005)
13. Kinnunen, T., Karpov, E., Fränti, P.: Real-time speaker identification and verification. IEEE Trans. on Audio, Speech and Language Processing 14(1), 277–288 (2006)
14. Kinnunen, T., Hautamäki, V., Fränti, P.: On the use of long-term average spectrum in automatic speaker recognition. In: Huo, Q., Ma, B., Chng, E.-S., Li, H. (eds.) ISCSLP 2006. LNCS, vol. 4274, pp. 559–567. Springer, Heidelberg (2006)

15. Kinnunen, T., Chernenko, E., Tuononen, M., Fränti, P., Li, H.: Voice activity detection using MFCC features and support vector machine. In: Int. Conf. on Speech and Computer (SPECOM 2007), Moscow, Russia, vol. 2, pp. 556–561 (2007)
16. Kinnunen, T., Saastamoinen, J., Hautamäki, V., Vinni, M., Fränti, P.: Comparative evaluation of maximum a posteriori vector quantization and Gaussian mixture models in speaker verification. Pattern Recognition Letters (accepted)
17. Kumar, N., Andreou, A.G.: Heteroscedastic discriminant analysis and reduced rank HMMs for improved speech recognition. Speech Communication 26(4), 283–297 (1998)
18. Ma, B., Zhu, D., Tong, R., Li, H.: Speaker Cluster based GMM tokenization for speaker recognition. In: Proc. Interspeech 2006, Pittsburg, USA, pp. 505–508 (September 2006)
19. Niemi-Laitinen, T., Saastamoinen, J., Kinnunen, T., Fränti, P.: Applying MFCC-based automatic speaker recognition to GSM and forensic data. In: 2nd Baltic Conf. on Human Language Technologies (HLT 2005), Tallinn, Estonia, pp. 317–322 (April 2005)
20. Ramirez, J., Segura, J.C., Benitez, C., de la Torre, A., Rubio, A.: Efficient voice activity detection algorithms using long-term speech information. Speech Communications 42(34), 271–287 (2004)
21. Reynolds, D.A., Quatieri, T.F., Dunn, R.B.: Speaker Verification Using Adapted Gaussian Mixture Models. Digital Signal Processing 10(1), 19–41 (2000)
22. Saastamoinen, J., Karpov, E., Hautamäki, V., Fränti, P.: Accuracy of MFCC based speaker recognition in series 60 device. Journal of Applied Signal Processing (17), 2816–2827 (2005)
23. Saastamoinen, J., Fiedler, Z., Kinnunen, T., Fränti, P.: On factors affecting MFCC-based speaker recognition accuracy. In: Int. Conf. on Speech and Computer (SPECOM 2005), Patras, Greece, pp. 503–506 (October 2005)
24. Tong, R., Ma, B., Lee, K.A., You, C.H., Zhou, D.L., Kinnunen, T., Sun, H.W., Dong, M.H., Ching, E.S., Li, H.Z.: Fusion of acoustic and tokenization features for speaker recognition. In: 5th In. Symp. on Chinese Spoken Language Proc., Singapore, pp. 566–577 (2006)
25. Tuononen, M., González Hautamäki, R., Fränti, P.: Automatic voice activity detection in different speech applications. In: Int. Conf. on Forensic Applications and Techniques in Telecommunications, Information and Multimedia (e-Forensics 2008), Adelaide, Australia, Article No.12 (January 2008)

A Preliminary Approach to the Forensic Analysis of an Ultraportable ASUS Eee PC

Trupti Shiralkar[1], Michael Lavine[1], and Benjamin Turnbull[2]

[1] Johns Hopkins University Information Security Institute
4th Floor, Wyman Park Building, 3400 North Charles Street
Baltimore, Maryland, USA 21218
{tshiral1,mlavine}@jhu.edu
[2] Defence and Systems Institute, University of South Australia
University Blvd, Mawson Lakes, South Australia, 5095
Benjamin.Turnbull@unisa.edu.au

Abstract. Subnotebooks, or 'netbooks, are a relatively new consumer market but one that continues to grow significantly worldwide. The aim of this paper is to analyse one of the leading subnotebooks, the 'ASUS Eee PC' from a forensics perspective. Specifically, the work investigates current image creation methods for making image of Eee PCs Solid State Drive and it analyses forensically important artefacts.

1 Introduction and Background

The current generation of subnotebook PCs, epitomised by the Aspire One, Asus Eee PC, One Laptop Per Child OLPC XO-1 and HP 2133 Mini-Note, is eclipsing traditional consumer computers in growth due to their low cost, ease of use and light weight. These ultraportable devices offer fast Internet connectivity with a user-friendly means of performing basic computing tasks. Given this growth, the likelihood that these devices will be misused cannot be ignored. As more criminal investigations include a computer forensic component we can expect that investigators in both the public and private sectors will encounter these and similar devices. Therefore, this work seeks to understand the forensic implications of the subnotebook class of devices through analysis of an Asus Eee PC.

The main purpose of this research is to identify data extraction methods suitable to the Eee PC and seek for forensically interesting features of this device that will benefit to the investigator. Specifically, this work seeks to understand what information can be obtained from the pre-installed applications of the Eee PC that can be used as digital evidence.

2 Technical Overview

The Eee PC 701 is representative of the subnotebook class, with a 7-inch screen and weighing approximately 2 pounds (900g.). Although this device does not offer

M. Sorell (Ed.): e-Forensics 2009, LNICST 8, pp. 116–121, 2009.

support for all applications, it offers a customised set of frequently used applications related to word processing and the Internet. The Eee PC 701 has three USB ports, one SD card slot and a VGA port, but no onboard DVD or floppy drive. The ASUS Eee PC comes in three popular series viz. 700, 900 and 1000 with a range of configurations depending on a user's preference for OS, microprocessor speed, RAM, storage and other specifications. The offerings in this range of products are comparable to competitive products in the marketplace, which have similar specifications in the processor, memory and storage [3][4].

Officially, the ASUS Eee PC officially supports two operating systems: a customized version of Xandros and Microsoft Windows XP. The default Xandros OS comes with two modes: *Easy* and *Advanced*. The Easy Mode uses IceWM window manager and a six tab structured interface. The full desktop mode is the Advanced Mode that uses the KDE Desktop Environment. Both use Debian GNU/Linux 4.0, kernel 2.6.22. The start menu of the Advanced Mode provides an option for switching to the Easy Mode. The Easy mode also provides a special tab to switch to advanced mode. The default file system is ext2. A user can also install various distributions of Linux, such as Ubuntu, Kubuntu, Xubuntu, and EeeBuntu, from a USB connected peripheral. However, the Eee PC driver support for these operating systems is not guaranteed.

With the Eee PC, a traditional hard drive is replaced by solid-state drive (SSD) based on non-volatile NAND flash memory [5]. The Eee PC has options for SSD sizes ranging from 2GB through to 16GB.

3   Forensic Considerations and Research Plan

This work has identified three primary areas for consideration in subnotebook forensic collection and analysis, and these issues will be explored independently. The first issue is related to the on-board SSD. The Eee PC uses solid-state memory instead of a hard drive that soldered directly on to the motherboard. Given this, mechanisms used to forensically copy hard disks from notebooks and other systems are not applicable to subnotebooks, and therefore a process of cloning the SSD without altering data must be developed. The second forensic issue with subnotebooks is the lack of onboard CD or floppy disk drive. The third forensic consideration with these devices is that, by default, the underlying system is abstracted from the user. It is possible that many forensics examiners do not have an in-depth technical knowledge of this unique system. The Eee PC also supports different flavours of Linux operating systems, as previously discussed. Each of these OS' may have a different file system, structure and default storage location. Hence, a forensics investigator should know the suitable forensics tools required for each of these OS and file systems. However, for the purposes of this work, analysis was conducted on an Eee PC with its default Operating System.

3.1   Research Design and Scope

This work was divided into two major phases, *Image Acquisition* and *Analysis*. As the first phase, image acquisition involved an exploration and determination of a reliable method to create a forensically sound image of the SSD. In the second phase, we focused on examining the image with Encase v 6.11 to identify the evidence and the default locations where it may be contained.

As has been noted, it is difficult to physically remove the SSD from an Eee PC. An unsuccessful attempt to remove the SSD could easily damage the SSD, which may irrecoverably destroy forensic evidence as well as the machine itself. Hardware-based data recovery from flash memory is beyond the scope of this paper [6]. Similarly, the process for removing electronics from onboard, soldered systems for forensic purposes has known potential side effects [7]. Therefore, this is not the preferred method for acquisition.

3.2 Image Acquisition

Given the lack of direct access to the SSD that would enable disk imaging through write-blocking hardware, live forensic environments become the only option for access. The lack of CD/DVD drive on these systems initially posed an issue, but the system booted both from USB memory drives and USB-connected DVD drives.

As discussed, not all live environments will boot on an Eee PC. Possibly the best-known live forensic environment is Helix. *Helix version 2*, based on the Knoppix environment, was unable to successfully boot the Eee PC into a live forensic environment. However, *Helix 3* (released September 2008), based on the Ubuntu live environment, did boot the system successfully. Researchers also used *BackTrack 3* to boot the system directly from a USB drive. Although Backtrack contains digital forensics imaging utilities, the environment itself is not considered forensically sound.

Once booted successfully and in a forensically sound manner, it is a relatively simple and well documented process of making a forensic copy of the Eee PC drives. Mounting an external USB disk with read/write permissions, there are several applications that provide forensic copying ability. At a basic level there is *DD*, *DCFLDD* and *DD_Rescue*. However, researchers used *Adepto 2.1*imaging software and Guidance Software's *Linen* to create images of the SSD.

From this point, it was possible to either create a raw image of the entire SSD (**/dev/sda** of 4 GB in size) or create forensic copies of individual partitions. The partitions are as follows:

- /dev/sda1 – system (EXT2, 2.3GB).
- /dev/sda2 – user data (EXT3, 1.4GB).
- /dev/sda3 – BIOS (VFAT, 7.9MB).
- /dev/sda4 – Hidden (boot partition) (FAT, 7.9MB).

The first partition, **/dev/sda1**, contains the variant of *Xandros* operating system. The second partition is mounted as top of first partition. The third and fourth partitions are comparatively small Windows FAT partitions and are less relevant in the analysis of user-created data.

3.3 Forensic Analysis

Acquisition of forensic data provides the framework on which to analyse, and the EeePC (and small scale devices as a class), has considerations associated with it. The use of a custom operating system potentially changes the default storage locations for stored information, and the small size of the SSD potentially limits the possible system files and user-created data saved on the system.

The Easy Mode of an Eee PC environment, which is the default purchased state, provides an application set aimed at a casual user (e.g. word processing, communication and Internet related). The following list summarises the information used by the pre-installed applications and information of potential interest to forensics investigators. Each of these areas is discussed independently.

- **Web browser (Mozilla Firefox) -** Web Browser History, Cookies, iGoogle Settings, Bookmarks and Cache Files.
- **Email (Hotmail, Yahoo, and AOL) -** Email IDs, Chat IDs, Email Archive, History Files, Cache Files, URLs.
- **Instant Messenger: Skype and Pidgin -** Chat IDs, Chat History Logs, Contact Lists, and Phone Numbers. Pidgin Chat program supports: AIM, Google Talk, ICQ, IRC, MSN, QQ, SIMPLE, Sametime, XMPP, and Yahoo.
- **Personal Information Manager (PIM) -** Contacts (Address Book), Journal, To-Do List, Notes and Email.
- **File Manager** (Stores file generated by the following applications) - OpenOffice.org, Notes, Mail, PDF Reader, Digital Camera, Screen Capture application - Word Processing Documents, Spreadsheets, Presentations, Images, and Videos.

Other considerations - Peripheral device connections (e.g. USB, MMC.SD, and Portable Hard Drive), Command Line History, recently accessed documents, installed software, nstalled

- Xandros Anti-Virus Logs, and other application and system Logs

Easy web browsing is one of most attractive features of this computer and could likely be one of the main reasons that a suspect will make use of Eee PC for accessing the Internet. Hence, it is crucial for the forensics investigator to analyse Internet usage. The Eee PC uses *Mozilla Firefox* as the default, pre-installed web browser. The forensic examiner should look at the **/home/user/mozilla/ firefox/** folder to analyse: web browser history, cookies, *iGoogle* Settings, browser cache and bookmarks.

Similarly, Net Books are advertised as internet-capable devices, and the idea that these devices will be used for email and instant messaging is a logical extension. The Web Mail tab provides direct links to the *Hotmail*, *Yahoo Mail* and *AOL* mail programs. For instance, using Encase, Email-IDs can be retrieved from the browser cache even if the IDs are not stored in the web browser. *Skype* and *Pidgin* are the two messengers available for chatting and instant messaging, and between them, can be used for dialling a phone number, voice chatting, and instant messaging. This work was able to identify Chat IDs, Chat history, phone numbers and contact list to be of interest. For example, our work found that an individual's Skype ID is stored at **/home/User/.Skype/ID/chatsync**.

The Eee PC also makes use of a *Personal Information Manager* (PIM). The PIM merges applications like *KOrganizer*, *Kmail* and *KAddressBook* to provide easy access to check e-mails, appointments, and stored contacts. The forensics investigator will be able to obtain To Do List, contact list (Address-book), notes, and journal information which is stored at **/home/user/.kde/share/apps/kabc** which can then be analysed with a number of forensic tools.

By default all documents, spreadsheets, presentations, audio files, video files and images are stored in File Manager. The default location for user-created files is **/home/user/My Documents/**, which stores all Open office, PDF docs and other files. This folder has the sub-folders **/My Pictures/** and **/My Videos/** which store images and videos created using the digital camera and screen capture application respectively.

The files deleted from My Documents are moved to the **/home/user/Trash** folder. If the data stored in these folders is erased, an investigator can still retrieve the names of files recently accessed from **/home/user/.kde/share/apps/Recent Documents**. The information about images including deleted images can be retrieved from the **/home/user/.thumbnail/normal/** folder. It is noted that in its default form, these folders are invisible to the user.

A forensic investigator may also retrieve the list of peripherals (e.g. USB, portable hard drive, external DVD rewriter) attached to the Eee PC at the **/media** and **/disk/removable** folders. From the list provided it will be clear which peripherals where used, all of which can be further examined onsite or in a forensics laboratory.

The **/var/log** folder contains the application logs. For example: *Xandros Antivirus* logs are stored at **/home/user/.XandrosAntivirus/logs/scan.log**. List of all newly installed software can be disclosed at **/var/cache/apt/archives** and at **/usr/bin**. Upon analysing **/dev/shm/resolveconf/interface** folder using EnCase 6.11, the investigator will be able to obtain the IP address(es) of the network(s) to which an Eee PC was connected.

Another forensically interesting item is the command line history. This is stored at **/home/user/.bash_history** and contains a list of all the commands entered and/or executed. The forensics investigator can get information about all the malicious operations performed, such as; installation of anti-forensics tools, downloading root-kits, secure deletion of files and metadata, and disk wiping etc. It is quite possible that an attacker may forget to delete the contents of the bash_history [11]. Hence, the bash_history can play a vital role in understanding the sequence of command line activities and help develop an effective timeline analysis.

4   Conclusion and Future Research

The use and subsequent misuse of new technologies is a known fact, and there is consequently a need for forensics examiners to adapt. Whilst many of the specifics discussed in this paper are unique to the Asus Eee PC, the lessons can be generalised to similar devices. The analysis of small-scale, ultra-portable personal computers will continue to grow as this class of device becomes more popular. Considering the growing market of notebooks and subnotebooks, a comprehensive study of these types of devices should be done and a common investigative framework should be developed to help the forensic investigator's work in this emerging area.

This work has identified a number of areas for future research. One of the areas of research should address how to extract data from an Eee PC that is not operational. Further research is needed to recover data from an intact SSD or one that has been tampered with.

Since this work focussed only on the Eee PC 4G 700 Series model, additional work can verify the outcomes discussed on both the more recent 900 and 1000 series devices within the Eee PC line-up, and also consider the specific analysis issues associated with other, similar devices. Furthermore, since this work was restricted to analyse only one of the default Xandros OS; the second default operating system, Windows XP should be investigated in order to develop an equally important preliminary approach for forensic analysis.

References

1. ASUSTek Pty Ltd, Eee PC, News Release, ASUS Eee PC is America's Most Wanted Christmas Gift, November 21 (2007),
   `http://eeepc.asus.com/global/news11212007.htm`
2. Eee PU USA News Release, ASUS Introduces All-New Eee PC for Complete Mobile Internet Enjoyment (October 16, 2007),
   `http://eeepc.asus.com/us/news101612007.htm`
3. ASUSTek Pty Ltd., Eee PC Specifications (August 19, 2008),
   `http://eeepc.asus.com/us/product.htm`
4. Smith, T.: Subnotebooks and Mini-Laptops (September 18, 2008),
   `http://www.reghardware.co.uk/2008/09/12/rh_bg_subnotebooks/`
5. Eee wiki, eeeuser.com, Asus Eee PC, `http://wiki.eeeuser.com/eee_pc_701`
6. Breeuwsma, M., Jongh, M., Klaver, C., Van der Knijff, R., Roeloffs, M.: Forensic Data Recovery from Flash Memory. Small Scale Digital Device Forensics Journal 1(1) (June 2007)
7. Willassen, S.Y.: Forensic Analysis of Mobile Phone Internal Memory. Presented at the 1st IFIP WG 11.9 Workshop on Digital Evidence, Orlando, Florida (2005)
8. Fogie, S.: PC Forensics Tools, Security Reference Guide (March 18, 2004), `http://www.informit.com/guides/content.aspx?g=security&seqNum=106`
9. Rude, T.: DD and Computer Forensics (August 2000),
   `http://www.crazytrain.com/dd.html`
10. Bezroukov, T.: Unix DD Command and Image Creation (June 05, 2008), `http://www.softpanorama.org/Tools/dd.shtml`
11. Belshaw, G.: Forgetting to lock the back door: A break-in analysis on a Red Hat Linux 6.2 machine (August 04, 2002),
    `http://www.sans.org/reading_room/whitepapers/incident/654.php`

A Provable Security Scheme of ID-Based Threshold Decryption

Wang Xue-Guang and Chai Zhen-Chuan

School of Information Science and Technology, East China University of
Political Science and Law, 555 Long Yuan Road shanghai 201620, China
Samsung electronics R&D center
wangxueguang@ecupl.edu.cn

Abstract. This paper presents an ID-based threshold decryption scheme and proves that it is selective chosen ciphertext secure without random oracles based on solving decisional $(t, q, \varepsilon) - BDHI$ problem assumption.

Keywords: provable security, ID based cryptography, Threshold decryption.

1 Introduction

In general public key certification system, user's public key and ID information are bound by certificates. The fact that authenticity of certificates need be verified before using public key results in increasing the amount of computation. For simplifying certificate management and decreasing additional calculating costs, Shamir [1] proposed identity based(ID-based) public key cryptography in 1984, which let users select their unambiguous information(such as E-mail, telephone number, etc.) as public key, then a trusted Private Key Generator(PKG) generates private key and distributes them to users through secret channel.

But, ID-based encryption (IBE) scheme was proposed using bilinear pairing by Boneh and Franklin [2] until 2001, which could be proved to be secure against adaptive chosen ciphertext attack by random oracle model [3-5]. However, this proof is controversial under assumption of random oracle model, because so-called random oracle does not exist in reality after all, i.e., those schemes will be unsafe after they are put in practice.

The fist IBE scheme without random oracles was proposed by Boneh and Boyen [6] in 2004, which was proved to be secure against selective-ID chosen plaintext attack without random oracle model. We need consider three levels for security of public key system in practice: chosen plaintext security, non-adaptive chosen ciphertext security and adaptive chosen ciphertext security. The last has highest security and is also main research direction at present.

This paper suggests an ID-based threshold decryption scheme based on works of Boneh and Boyen, which can be proved to be secure without random oracles. It was validated that it has ID-based adaptive chosen ciphertext security.

M. Sorell (Ed.): e-Forensics 2009, LNICST 8, pp. 122–129, 2009.

2 Model of ID-Based Threshold Decryption Scheme

There are several roles in the ID-based threshold decryption scheme. A trusted PKG takes charge of generating user private key and threshold private key, also running in the beginning phrase of system, including selecting public parameters, such as bilinear pairing and its corresponding group, etc. A cluster of n decryption servers is denoted by $\Gamma_i (i=1,...,n)$, which has a public ID, generates private keys, executes encryption and decryption, verifies algorithms, and so on.

This scheme includes six algorithms as follow.

① **Start:** this algorithm run by PKG outputs master key - $mkey$, and system's public parameter - cp. cp includes the group selected by PKG, bilinear pairing and so on. cp is public but $mkey$ is secretly saved by PKG.

② **KeyGen($mkey$, ID, t, n):** given PKG's $mkey$, user's ID, number of all decryption - n and threshold t, this algorithm returns n key slices d_{ID_i}, $i = 1,2, ..., n$, which corresponds to public key ID.

③ **KeyVer:** this algorithm returns n public verification message v_i, $i = 1,2, ..., n$, which can be used by decryption server Γ_i for verifying private key slices d_{ID_i}, then PKG secretly sends d_{ID_i} to Γ_i but each message v_i will be public.

④ **Encrypt(cp, ID, M):** given ID and plaintext M, this algorithm returns ciphertext denoted by c.

⑤ **Decrypt(cp, d_{ID_i}, c):** given ciphertext c and key slice d_{ID_i}, this algorithm returns corresponding decryption slice, denoted by δ_i, or returns error information that indicates c is invalid ciphertext. At the same time, it verifies decryption slices.

⑥ **Combin(cp, $\{\delta_i\}_{i \in \phi}$, c):** given t decryption slices $\{\delta_i\}_{i \in \phi}$, this algorithm combines many decryption slices into plaintext M, $\phi \subset \{1, ..., n\}$ and $|\phi| = t$.

3 IND-CCA Security

Given a public key cipher scheme $E = (K, J, D)$, K as secret key generation algorithm, J as encryption algorithm, D as decryption algorithm, consider the procedure as follow. Here, take Q as a assaulter, S as a challenger.

Step 1. Assaulter Q sends ciphertext c to S. S obtains plaintext M by decrypting c and sends M to Q. In this phase, Q can freely select satisfying ciphertext and go to next step.

Step 2. Assaulter Q selects two equal-length messages M_0 and M_1, sends them to challenger S.

Step 3. Challenger S randomly selects a bit-value $\beta \in \{0,1\}$ then calculates c^* and sends it to Q. Here,

$$c^* = \begin{cases} E_{pk}(M_0) & \beta = 0 \\ E_{pk}(M_1) & \beta = 1 \end{cases}, \text{ where } pk \text{ denotes user's public key.}$$

Step 4. After receiving c^*, Q can continue to request decryption services like described in Step 1, but can not question for c^*.

Step 5. Q needs make a guess $\beta' \in \{0,1\}$ about β.

If probability advance that assaulter Q successfully attacks decryption algorithm is $Adv_Q = \left| \Pr[0 \leftarrow Q(c^* = E_{pk}(M_0))] - \Pr[0 \leftarrow Q(c^* = E_{pk}(M_1))] \right|$ and Adv_Q is a negligible value about ε, then E is secure for indistinguishable adaptive chosen ciphertext attack, i.e., IND-CCA security.

4 Building ID-Based Threshold Decryption Scheme

The security of the scheme is built on hard problem of bilinear Diffie-Hellman inversion [6].

Given multiplicative group G and G_1 of the same prime order p, p is a large prime number. And g is the generator of G. The mapping e: $G \times G \rightarrow G_1$ is a computable bilinear pairing. Let plaintexts be all in G_1 and IDs as public keys in Z_p^*.

The process of building six algorithms of the scheme is as follow.

① **Start:** Select x, y, $z \in_R Z_p^*$ and compute $X = g^x$, $Y = g^y$, and $Z = g^z$. Public parameter cp and master key $mkey$ of PKG are respectively:

$$cp = (g, X, Y, Z), \quad mkey = (x, y, z)$$

② **KeyGen(_mkey, ID, t, n_):** To generate n secret key slices for the public key ID, the PKG:

  a) randomly selects a polynomial over Z_p^*: $F(u) = z + \sum_{i=1}^{t-1} u^i a_i$, $a_i \in Z_p^*$

  b) selects random number $r_i \in_R Z_p^*$, computes $K_i = g^{F(i)/(ID+x+r_i y)}$ and outputs secret key slice $d_{ID_i} = (r_i, K_i)$.

③ **KeyVer:** Generate verification message v_i, $v_i = e(g, g)^{F(i)}$, $i = 1, \ldots, n$.

④ **Encrypt(_cp, ID, M_):** To encrypt plaintext $M \in G_1$ using public key $ID \in Z_p^*$, select random number $s \in Z_p^*$ and calculate ciphertext using the expression

$$C = (g^{s \cdot ID} X^s, Y^s, e(g, Z)^s \cdot M)$$

Note that the value of pairing $e(g, Z)$ can be pre-computed and stored for following computation in order to save time.

⑤ **Decrypt(cp, d_{ID_i}, c):** For computing decryption slice δ_i of ciphertext $C = (A, B, C)$, decryption server Γ_i, using its key slice $d_{ID_i} = (r_i, K_i)$, gets that

$\delta_i = e(AB^{r_i}, K_i)$ because of

$\delta_i = e(AB^{r_i}, K_i) = e(g^{s(ID+x+r_iy)}, g^{F(i)/(ID)+x+r_iy}) = e(g,g)^{sF(i)}$.

⑥ **Combin(cp, $\{\delta_i\}_{i\in\phi}$, c):** In order to recovery original plaintext M, a proxy server collects t decryption slices $\delta_i \in G_1$ and calculates M as follow

$$C / \prod_{i\in\phi} \delta_i^{L_i^0} = M .$$

Here, $\phi \subset \{1,...,n\}$, $|\phi| = t$, and $L_i^x = \prod_{j\in\phi, j\neq i} \dfrac{x-j}{i-j}$.

The validity of this computation can be obtained by employing Lagrange interpolation:

$$C / \prod_{i\in\phi} \delta_i^{L_i^0} = C / \prod_{i\in\phi} e(g,g)^{sF(i)L_i^0} = C / e(g,g)^{s\sum_{i\in\phi} L_i^0 F(i)} = C / e(g,g)^{sF(0)} = C / e(g,g)^{s\cdot z} = M$$

After running algorithm KeyGen, PKG secretly distributes key slices d_{ID_i} to decryption server Γ_i, then open all verification message v_i. Γ_i can check the authenticity of $d_{ID_i} = (r_i, K_i)$ by verifying the following equation after receiving d_{ID_i} ,

$$\prod_{i\in\phi} v_i^{L_i^0} = e(g,Z) \text{ and } e(g^{ID}XY^{r_i}, K_i) = v_i .$$

5 Security Proof of ID-Based Threshold Decryption Scheme without Random Oracles

Use reduction to absurdity to prove the security of ID-based threshold decryption scheme. First, assume that threshold decryption scheme is not secure and there is an assaulter who can attack the scheme by probability advance ε under defined attack model. And assume decisional $(t, q, \varepsilon) - BDHI$ problem is hard. Then, construct an algorithm to solve the decisional $(t, q, \varepsilon) - BDHI$ problem. Its result is contrary to the assumption of hard problem. So the threshold decryption scheme is secure.

5.1 Decisional $q - BDHI$ Problem

Decisional $q - BDHI$ problem [6]:

Given $(q+1)$-tuple $(g, g^x, g^{(x^2)}, \cdots, g^{(x^q)}) \in (G^*)^{q+1}$ and $T \in G_1^*$, decide whether equation $T = e(g,g)^{1/x}$ is correct or not.

The advance of algorithm A solves decisional $q - BDHI$ problem is defined as:

$$Adv(A) = \left| \Pr\left[A(g, g^x, \cdots, g^{(x^q)}, e(g,g)^{1/x}) = 0 \right] - \Pr\left[A(g, g^x, \cdots, g^{(x^q)}, T = 0 \right] \right|,$$

where the probability is computed through randomly selecting x on Z_p^*, T on G_1^*, and algorithm A.

If any algorithm can not solve computational/decisional $q - BDHI$ problem in time t with a probability advance which is ε at least, then a computational/decisional $q - BDHI$ problem is said to be hard.

5.2 Construct Algorithm S

The purpose of S is to solve an instance of decisional $BDHI$ problem, i.e., given an input $(g, g^\alpha, g^{\alpha^2}, \cdots, g^{\alpha^q}, T) \in (G^{q+1}) \times G_1^*$ (S doesn't know α), decides whether T is equal to $e(g,g)^{1/\alpha}$, if yes, output 1, otherwise 0.

Considering Q as assaulter, S as challenger, before interacting with Q, S needs prepare for a generator $h \in G^*$, and corresponding $q-1$ pairs of two-tuple $(w_i, h^{1/(\alpha+w_i)})$ (S doesn't know α). These parameters are as follow:

① Randomly select $w_1, \cdots, w_{q-1} \in Z_p^*$,

let $f(\theta) = \prod_{i=1}^{q-1}(\theta + w_i) = \prod_{i=0}^{q-1}(c_i \theta^i)$ such that $c_0 \neq 0$;

② Compute $h = \prod_{i=0}^{q-1}(g^{\alpha^i})^{c_i} = g^{f(\alpha)}$ and $u = \prod_{i=1}^{q}(g^{\alpha^i})^{c_{i-1}} = g^{\alpha f(\alpha)}$. It is easy to know that $u = h^\alpha$ and $h \neq 1$, because $h = 1$ means that there is a $w_j = \alpha$ and S can solve decisional $BDHI$ problem directly;

③ Let $f_i(\theta) = f(\theta)/(\theta + w_i) = \sum_{i=0}^{q-2} d_i \theta^i$

and $h^{1/(\alpha+w_i)} = g^{f_i(\alpha)} = \prod_{i=0}^{q-2}(g^{\alpha^i})^{d_i}$.

S computes:

$$T_h = T^{(c_0^2)} \cdot T_0,$$

where $T_0 = \prod_{k=0}^{q-2} e(g^{(\alpha^k)}, g)^{c_0 c_{k+1}} \prod_{i=1}^{q-1}\prod_{j=0}^{q-2} e(g^{(\alpha^i)}, g^{(\alpha^j)})^{c_i c_{j+1}}$.

Here, if $T = e(g,g)^{1/\alpha}$, then $T_h = e(g^{f(\alpha)}, g^{f(\alpha)})^{1/\alpha} = e(h,h)^{1/\alpha}$.

Otherwise, T_h only is a random value in $G_1 \setminus \{T_0\}$, because T randomly distributes on G_1^*.

5.3 Security Verification

The interaction process between Q and S is as follow:

Select attack ID: Q selects an attack object $ID^* \in Z_p^*$.

Initialization: S executes the following steps.

① Selects random number $a, b \in Z_p^*$ such that $ab = ID^*$;

② Selects random number $z \in Z_p^*$, computes $X = u^{-a}h^{-ab} = h^{-a(\alpha+b)}$, $Y = u = h^\alpha$ and $Z = h^z$;

③ Publishes $cp = (h, X, Y, Z)$.

During above computation, the master key *mkey* is implicitly defined as $mkey = (x, y, z) = (-a(\alpha+b), \alpha, z)$. Though S doesn't know x and y, it knows $x + ay = -ab = -ID^*$.

Phrase 1: Q successfully compromises t-1 out of n decryption servers. Without loss of generality, suppose compromised servers are $\Gamma_1, \cdots, \Gamma_{t-1}$.

Phrase 2: Q starts a series of private key queries and decryption queries.

① Private key query about $ID \neq ID^*$: In order to provide n valid key slices and n verification messages, S operates according to the following for Q's query:

a) Randomly selects a polynomial over Z_p^*:

$$F(u) = z + \sum_{i=1}^{t-1} u^i f_i, \ f_i \in Z_p^*;$$

b) Fetches n unused two-tuples $(w_i, h^{1/(\alpha+w_i)})$, without loss of generality, suppose these tuples' subscripts denote by $i = 1, \cdots, n$. Let $h_i = h^{1/(\alpha+w_i)}$.

c) Computes $r_i = a + \dfrac{ID - ab}{w_i}$, returned secret key slices and verification messages are as follow:

$$d_{ID_i} = (r_i, h_i^{F(i)/(r_i-a)}) \text{ and } v_i = (g, g)^{F(i)}, \ i = 1, \cdots, n.$$

It is easy to know, $h_i^{F(i)/(r_i-a)} = h^{F(i)/(r_i-a)(\alpha-w_i)} = h^{F(i)/ID+x+r_i y}$. d_{ID_i} is valid secret key slice because w_i is randomly selected by S. So also is $r_i = a + \dfrac{ID - ab}{w_i}$ from view of Q.

② Private key query about ID^*: In order to provide t-1 valid key slices and n verification messages, S operates according to the following for Q's query:

a) Randomly selects $r_i \in Z_p^*$ and $K_i \in G$, $i = 1, \cdots, t-1$;

b)   Computes $v_i = \begin{cases} e(g^{ID^*} X \cdot Y^{r_i}, K_i), & i = 1, \cdots, t-1 \\ e(g,g)^{L_0^i z} \prod_{k=1}^{t-1} v_k^{L_k^i} & i = 1, \cdots, n \end{cases}$,   where

$L_k^x = \prod_{j=0, j \neq k}^{t-1} \dfrac{x-j}{k-j}$;

c) Returned t-1 secret key slices and n verification messages are as follow:

$$d_{ID_i} = (r_i, K_i) \quad i = 1, \cdots, t-1 \text{ and } v_i \quad i = 1, \cdots, n.$$

In fact, S implicitly selects a polynomial $F(u)$, such that $e(g^{ID^*} X \cdot Y^{r_i}, K_i) = e(g,g)^{F(i)}$ and $F(0) = z$ for $i = 1, \cdots, t-1$.

Challenge: Once assaulter Q thinks phrase 2 can be over, Q will output two equal bit-length plaintexts (M_1, M_2). After received those plaintexts, S randomly selects a bit $\beta \in \{0,1\}$ and $l \in Z_p^*$, computes challenge ciphertext $c = (h^{-al}, h^l, T_h^{zl} \cdot M_\beta)$ and then sends it to Q.

Here, if $T_h = e(h,h)^{1/\alpha}$, then c is a valid ciphertext on M_β. Because:

let $s = l/\alpha$ (l is randomly selected, so s also is random distribution on Z_p^*), then

$$h^{-al} = h^{-a\alpha(l/\alpha)} = h^{(x+ab)(l/\alpha)} = h^{(x+ID^*)(l/\alpha)} = h^{sID^*} \cdot X^s$$

$$h^l = Y^{l/\alpha} = Y^s$$

$$T_h^{zl} = e(h,h)^{zl/\alpha} = e(h,h)^{zs} = e(h,Z)^s$$

If T_h only is a random number on $G_1 \setminus \{T_0\}$, then c is completely independent of bit β from view of Q.

Phrase 3: According to its requirement, Q continues to send private key queries like phrase 2, whose time qs is limited by $qs < \lfloor q/n \rfloor$. The challenger still replies Q's queries like phrase 2.

Hypothesize: Q output its guess $\beta' \in \{0,1\}$ for β. If $\beta' = \beta$, then S returns 1, which means $T = e(g,g)^{1/\alpha}$. Otherwise S returns 0, which means $T \neq e(g,g)^{1/\alpha}$.

During above interaction process, if input T satisfies $T = e(g,g)^{1/\alpha}$, then the probability advance of Q satisfies $Adv = |\Pr[\beta = \beta'] - 1/2| > \varepsilon$, which results in the advance that S solves hard problems satisfies $\Pr\left[S(g, g^x, \cdots, g^{(x^q)}, e(g,g)^{1/x}) = 1 \right]$ $> 1/2 + \varepsilon$. If $T = P \neq e(g,g)^{1/\alpha}$, then the probability advance of Q satisfies

$\Pr\left[S(g,g^x,\cdots,g^{(x^q)},e(g,g)^{1/x})=1\right]>1/2+\varepsilon$, because ciphertext is also random number. In this situation, the advance that S solves hard problems only is a guess, i.e., $\Pr\left[S(g,g^x,\cdots,g^{(x^q)},P)=1\right]=1/2$.

In summary, the probability advance that algorithm S solves decisional $q-BDHI$ problem is

$$Adv_s=\left|\Pr\left[S(g,g^x,\cdots,g^{(x^q)},e(g,g)^{1/x})=1\right]-\Pr\left[S(g,g^x,\cdots,g^{(x^q)},P)=1\right]\right|\geq\left|(1/2+\varepsilon)-1/2\right|=\varepsilon$$

This is contrary to the assumption.

According to above proof and IND-CCA's definition, the ID-based threshold decryption scheme has IND-CCA security, that is, it is secure for indistinguishable adaptive chosen ciphertext attack.

6 Conclusions

Through reviewing related researches, this paper proposes an ID-based threshold decryption scheme built on Boneh and Boyen's works. After defining IND-CCA and solving decisional $(t,q,\varepsilon)-BDHI$ hard problem, we proved the scheme is secure for selective-ID adaptive chosen ciphertext attack without random oracles.

Acknowledgements. This work is supported by Chinese Society and Science Foundation under Grant No. 06BFX051.

References

1. Shamir, A.: Identity-based cryptosystems and signature schemes. In: Blakely, G.R., Chaum, D. (eds.) CRYPTO 1984. LNCS, vol. 196, pp. 47–53. Springer, Heidelberg (1985)
2. Boneh, D., Franklin, M.: Identity based encryption from the Weil pairing. In: Kilian, J. (ed.) CRYPTO 2001. LNCS, vol. 2139, pp. 213–229. Springer, Heidelberg (2001)
3. Bellare, M., Rogaway, P.: Random oracles are practical: A paradigm for designing efficient protocols. In: Proceedings of the first ACM Conference on Computer and Communication Security, ACM Conference, pp. 62–73 (1993)
4. Bellare, M., Boldyreva, A., Palacio, A.: An uninstantiable random oracle model scheme for a hybrid-encryption problem. In: Cachin, C., Camenisch, J.L. (eds.) EUROCRYPT 2004. LNCS, vol. 3027, pp. 171–188. Springer, Heidelberg (2004)
5. Nielsen, J.B.: Separating random oracle proofs from complexity theoretic proofs: The noncommitting encryption case. In: Yung, M. (ed.) CRYPTO 2002. LNCS, vol. 2442, pp. 111–126. Springer, Heidelberg (2002)
6. Boneh, D., Boyen, X.: Efficient selective-ID secure identity based encryption without random oracles. In: Cachin, C., Camenisch, J.L. (eds.) EUROCRYPT 2004. LNCS, vol. 3027, pp. 223–238. Springer, Heidelberg (2004)

Analysis of Sensor Photo Response Non-Uniformity in RAW Images

Simon Knight, Simon Moschou, and Matthew Sorell

School of Electrical & Electronic Engineering,
The University of Adelaide, Australia

Abstract. The focus of this paper is a review of a digital camera identification technique proposed by Lukas et al [1], and a modification of the denoising filter, allowing it to be used for raw sensor data. The approach of using raw sensor data allows analysis of the noise pattern separate from any artefacts introduced by on-board camera processing. We use this extension for investigating the reliability of the technique when using different lenses between the same camera and between cameras of the same manufacturer.

Keywords: digital forensic, source identification, sensor noise, reference noise pattern.

1 Introduction

The recent growth of digital devices used among society today has led to the expansion of forensics into the digital domain. In particular, digital cameras are a source for forensic applications which include; camera identification, proving a photograph came from a camera or a type of camera, grouping photographs from a large database by their processing history, providing baseline evidence to prove or disprove image tampering and fast-tracking the physical evidence retrieval process.

In this study we review a method for camera identification, [1] using JPEG and extend the technique for raw images. We apply the extension in both a controlled laboratory and outdoor environment using different lenses between cameras of the same manufacturer. The aim is to verify the significance of the image sensor for camera identification by eliminating artefacts introduced by on-board processing.

The EXIF [5] format can be used to embed information such as timestamps and camera details inside an image file. However this can be easily edited using a text editor or software packages such as ExifTool [6], making it unreliable for camera identification in a forensic context. This provides a motivation for studying the technique proposed in [1] in further detail.

M. Sorell (Ed.): e-Forensics 2009, LNICST 8, pp. 130–141, 2009.

2   Background

2.1   Technique Overview

The approach begins with an implementation of the digital camera identification technique proposed by Lukas et al [1] [2] [3]. These papers make the assumption that the high-medium frequency component (HMFC) of the sensor noise pattern is an equivalent bullet scratch for the camera, and thus can be used for camera identification.

Their proposed method involves calculating the reference noise pattern (RNP) for a camera by averaging the noise components of multiple images. This process is implemented using the denoising filter explained in [1, Appendix A]. The RNP is unique to a digital camera and its presence can be found in an image using correlation detection.

In related work, Lukas et al [3] and in [1], found that the HMFC of the noise pattern for both CCD and CMOS sensors are stable over the life of the camera. This supports its suitability for use in camera identification.

2.2   Noise Model

The classification of noise outlined in [1] is based on noise in a digital image a component of both the shot noise or photonic noise (random) and the pattern noise (deterministic). The process of averaging multiple images suppresses the random shot/photonic components and enhances the pattern noise, which remains constant across all images. This allows use of the pattern noise for camera identification and is the focus of the noise breakdown.

As stated in [1], the pattern noise is both a component of the fixed noise pattern (FPN) and the photo-responsive non-uniformity (PRNU). The FPN is due to dark currents, and increases with exposure duration and temperature. The FPN can be removed by subtracting a dark frame from an image and is performed by a number of middle to high-end cameras.

The PRNU is the more dominant component due to pixel non-uniformity (PNU). PNU is the variation of sensitivity between pixels for a uniform level of light intensity, and occurs from differences and imperfections in the silicon wafer used to manufacture the imaging sensor. These physical differences provide the unique sensor fingerprint on which the identification technique is based.

Lower frequency components such as light refraction on dust and camera lenses also contribute to the PRNU, but are independent of the sensor. For this reason, [1] establish that these lower frequency components should not be used for sensor identification and that only the sensor dependent PNU component should be used.

2.3   Camera Identification

Using the techniques described in [1] for JPEG-compressed images as both the reference and test data, we successfully identified one camera from seven different camera reference patterns. Each reference pattern was generated using a data set

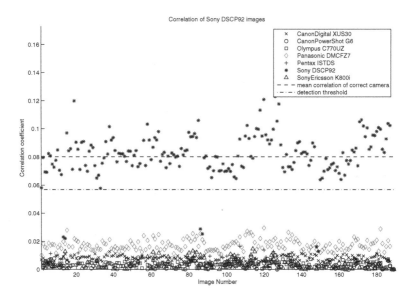

Fig. 1. Camera Identification by RNP correlation

of approximately 50 JPEG images for each camera. A further 190 JPEG images from one test-camera (a Sony DSC-P92) were used to test the identification technique. It was found that the correlation coefficient of just six of those images were too low to conclude a match, and that none of the other noise patterns matched the test images, corresponding to a detection rate of 97% and a false match rate of 0. Hence we conclude from our experimental results that the technique is effective. The results can be seen in Figure 1.

2.4 Identification After Resampling

The performance of the technique for different resolution images was verified. The Sony DSC-P92 reference pattern was generated using images taken at 3 Megapixel (MP) resolution.

A set of images were taken using the same Sony DSC-P92 at 5MP, and correlated against the 3MP reference pattern. The results can be seen as the first set of 50 data points in Figure 2, where the images taken at 5MP are not successfully identified. To address this, the 5MP images were downsampled to 3MP using bicubic interpolation and an anti aliasing filter, and then correlated against the 3MP reference pattern. The results of this can be seen as the second set of 50 data points in Figure 2, where identification is now successful after the images were downsampled to the same resolution as the RNP. This is an important result as digital photos are commonly taken across a range of resolution settings.

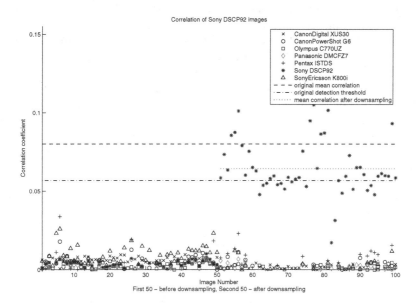

Fig. 2. Before and After Downsampling

3   Extension Using RAW Sensor Data

3.1   Original Image Format (JPEG)

The images used for camera identification were taken in the JPEG format. This is the most common image format, but involves post sensor processing including colour interpolation, white balance and gamma correction. This processing may be unique to a manufacturer's implementation and often will add additional noise components to the image. These noise components may be unique to a manufacturer or camera model, but could not be used reliably to differentiate between two identical model cameras. Additionally the camera firmware can often be upgraded, potentially changing the noise characteristics over time.

The technique proposed in [1], outlines that the identifier for a camera is due to its pixel non uniformity (PNU) unique to the sensor. This is separate from any on-board processing. In order to establish the sensor alone as a fingerprint for the camera, we investigated the denoising filter using the raw sensor output.

3.2   Bayer Matrix and Conversion of Raw Sensor Data

Digital camera image sensors measure only light intensity, and are unable to distinguish between different colours. In order to measure colours, most digital cameras use colour filters before the sensors. The most common arrangement is known as a Bayer matrix, where the colour pattern in a 2 by 2 block alternates between Red (R), Green (G) and Blue (B) filters.

The RAW image format stores the sensor readings directly, before the on-board processing and compression stages in the camera. This is suitable for our investigation of the camera sensor alone. There is no industry standard for RAW formats. The Pentax *ist DS and DL cameras discussed in this paper save their sensor data using the proprietary Pentax .*PEF* format.

The Bayer Matrix was extracted in Matlab by reverse engineering the binary structure of a saved .PEF RAW image. The data was extracted as a 12-bit number and up shifted to 16-bit, allowing the image to be saved in the 16-bit lossless TIFF format. Upon close inspection of the extracted image, the Bayer pattern of the image was visible, confirming the technique.

An alternative method to extract the RAW image is a tool such as the open source software package *dcraw* [7]. This software is designed to process a RAW format file into a final image, but can also be used to extract only the sensor readings using the command:

```
dcraw -D -T -4 -W Image.PEF
```

A 4 bit upshift was performed on the extracted 12 bit image to remain consistent with the Matlab extraction approach. This resulted in the same image as using the Matlab approach. The use of a software package such as *dcraw* would allow our RAW technique to be extended to the majority of digital cameras without requiring the camera's RAW format reverse engineered.

3.3   Modified Denoising Filter for RAW Images

The technique proposed in [1] could not be directly applied to converted RAW Bayer pattern images. The large differences in pixel intensity between red, green and blue pixels meant that each surrounding pixel contained edge effects. These high frequency components were extarcted by the denoising filter, and were present with the PNU in the resulting RNP.

The approach taken was to decimate the Bayer matrix into four planes; red, green1, green2 and blue, each of which should share the same pixel sensitivity. Each plane is then a quarter of the size of the original extracted Bayer matrix, and is denoised using the filter described in [1, Appendix A]. Once each plane has been denoised, the Bayer matrix is reassembled from the four planes and subtracted from the original image. This gives the noise pattern for the RAW image. This decimated approach avoids introducing additional noise, which techniques such as interpolation would do.

When decimating the Bayer matrix into the four different planes the starting sequence for the Bayer matrix does not need to be known. The requirement is that every second pixel in both the horizontal and vertical directions belongs to the same colour level (red, green or blue) and should share the same sensitivity. This allows the implementation to be used for different manufacturers which may vary the arrangement of the Bayer matrix pattern.

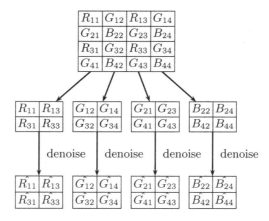

Fig. 3. Bayer matrix decimation method for an 8x8 image

$$\begin{array}{|c|c|c|c|}\hline \hat{R}_{11} & \hat{G}_{12} & \hat{R}_{13} & \hat{G}_{14} \\\hline \hat{G}_{21} & \hat{B}_{22} & \hat{G}_{23} & \hat{B}_{24} \\\hline \hat{R}_{31} & \hat{G}_{32} & \hat{R}_{33} & \hat{G}_{34} \\\hline \hat{G}_{41} & \hat{B}_{42} & \hat{G}_{43} & \hat{B}_{44} \\\hline \end{array}$$

Fig. 4. Reconstructed denoised Bayer Matrix

4   Camera Lenses

4.1   Overview of Optical Effects

This section discusses the motivation for the lens study.

Imperfections in lenses contribute to distortions in the final image, and can be categorised as either high (affecting a small image section) or low frequency components (affecting the whole image).

Modern consumer digital cameras are either compact (point and shoot) cameras which have an inbuilt lens or Digital SLR cameras which have interchangeable lenses. If the lenses had an impact on the RNP, interchangeable lenses would reduce the reliability of the camera identification process. The fixed micro lens which serves to focus incoming light onto each sensor is not studied in this paper, as it is fixed to the camera. [9]

Commonly observed optical aberrations include radial distortion (barrel or pincushion effects), vignetting (darker sections towards edge of image) and chromatic aberration (colour fringing). These distortion effects are typically low frequency [10], and should not be extracted by the denoising filter. Research into the forensics properties of these effects has been conducted in [11], and [12].

Noise sources such as scratches, dust [13] and imperfections in the materials also contribute noise to an image. If they affect a small region of the image, they would be categorised as high frequency noise and be extracted by the denoising filter.

These imperfections are unique to an individual lens and may hold forensic utility in lens identification. Importantly they may be present in methods to extract the sensor pattern noise such as the filter outlined in this paper, which would impact the reliability of the identification technique.

The aim of our lens study was to determine the significance of these lens effects on each RNP found using the technique outlined above.

4.2   Approach

Two similar Pentax camera models, the *ist DS and *ist DL, were used to study the effect of lenses on the noise pattern. These cameras were selected as they allowed the PENTAX-F (small) and Tamron (large) lenses to be used interchangeably between both cameras. All images were taken in the RAW format and processed using the modified RAW denoising filter described earlier. A *baseline* and *merged* RNP set were generated for correlation analysis.

The *baseline* set contained RNPs for each camera and lens combination, consisting of RNPs: DL Large, DL Small, DS Large and DL Small. This set was used to study the correlation result for a camera with the lens used to take the photo versus an alternative lens.

The *merged* set was generated by merging the images unique to each camera and each lens, consisting of RNPs: DL Camera, DS Camera, Small Lens and Large Lens. This allowed the study of the significance of the image sensor versus the significance of the lens, based on the correlation results.

4.3   Data Sets

Both *baseline* and *merged* RNP sets were generated in both controlled laboratory and outdoor environments.

Indoor Controlled Laboratory. An indoor imaging laboratory was used as a controlled environment, in which images were taken of a suspended blank sheet of white paper. A low fan setting was used to vary the image content between images, ensuring any effects of the image content would be averaged out of the resulting RNP. Light and temperature were maintained at a constant level and the cameras were powered using either a constant voltage power supply, or freshly charged batteries. These environmental conditions may affect the noise present in an image, so it is important their effect is minimsed.

The zoom was varied between 18mm, 35mm and 50mm for each camera and lens combination. This reduced the effect of the secondary (zoom) lens. The following table shows the data set taken for the laboratory environment.

PENTAX-F Lens	*18mm*	*35mm*	*50mm*
DL Camera	Subset A	Subset B	Subset C
DS Camera	Subset D	Subset E	Subset F
Tamron Lens	*18mm*	*35mm*	*50mm*
DL Camera	Subset G	Subset H	Subset I
DS Camera	Subset J	Subset K	Subset L

Each *baseline* RNP was generated using 75 images for each zoom setting. The *merged* RNPs used 20 images from each zoom setting for a total of 120 images used. For example, to generate a *merged* RNP unique to just the DL camera, 20 images from subset A, B, C, G, H, I would be used. For a *merged* RNP unique to the Tamron lens, 20 images from subset G, H, I, J, K and L would be used.

Outdoors. The outdoors data set was taken around the university campus, to provide a level of randomness and variability of image content typical of real world images. The zoom setting was also varied arbitrarily. The following table shows the data set captured for outdoors.

	PENTAX-F Lens	**Tamron Lens**
DL Camera	Subset M	Subset N
DS Camera	Subset O	Subset P

Each *baseline* RNP was generated using 75 images for each subset and the *merged* RNPs where generated by combining two subsets common to either the camera or lens for a total of 150 images used. For example, to generate a *merged* RNP unique to just the DS camera subsets O and P would be combined. A *merged* RNP unique to the PENTAX-F lens would combine subsets M and O.

5   Results

5.1   Indoor Controlled Laboratory

The baseline results in Figure 5 show a clear correlation with the correct camera. The mean correlation is stable which is expected for images with uniform image

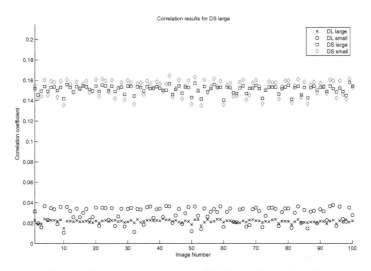

Fig. 5. Scatterplot for Indoor DS Large Lens Baseline

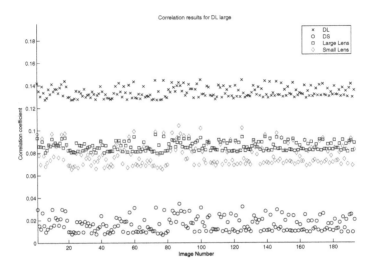

Fig. 6. Scatterplot for Indoor DL Large Lens Merged

content (controlled). Determining the lens however is inconclusive. The small lens has greater variance than the large lens, but both have a similar mean.

The merged set was used to compare the significance of the sensor against the lens, by averaging a common component (camera or lens). The results in Figure 6 show clearly a result for the correct camera. Under controlled lab conditions this shows that the sensor has a greater significance on the noise pattern than the lens. In the common middle tier there is a slight bias for the correct lens.

5.2   Outdoors

Baseline and merged results were also considered for the outdoor data set. Again for the baseline results in Figure 7 there is strong correlation for the correct camera but with greater variance than observed for the indoor set. This is likely due to the image content varying between images. The temperature and battery level of the cameras also varied over the outdoor data, which may have contributed to greater variance in correlation.

The merged results in Figure 8 again confirm that the sensor is more dominant for identification than the lens. This is followed by the correct lens, the incorrect lens and then the incorrect camera giving the lowest correlation. This was also confirmed by the outdoor CDF shown in Figure 9.

In both indoor and outdoor sample sets we have established that camera sensor is more dominant than lens although within the middle tier it may be also be possible to identify the correct lens. Note that some of our results did not have clear speration between lenses for merged sets which could be due to a number of reasons such as random image content for outdoors.

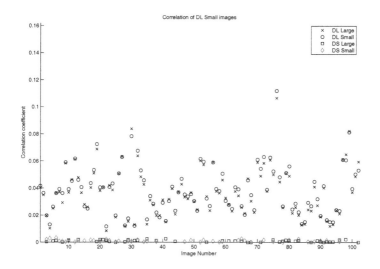

Fig. 7. Scatterplot for Outdoor DL Small Lens Baseline

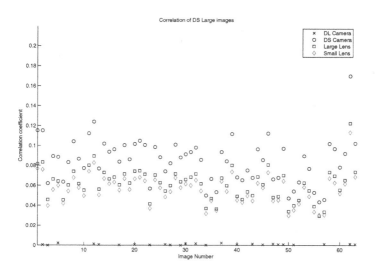

Fig. 8. Scatterplot for Outdoor DS Large Lens Merged

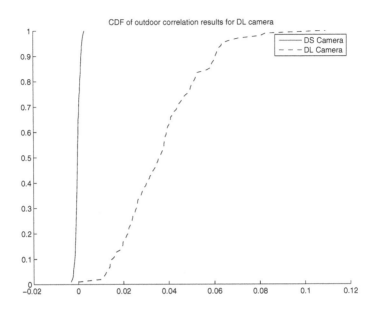

Fig. 9. CDF of outdoor DL Small Lens dataset

6   Conclusion

In this paper we have reviewed a technique for digital camera identification [1] using the JPEG format. We have also tested the robustness of the technique for images at different resolutions. The technique is extended for raw sensor data by modifying the denoising filer. The purpose of this is to eliminate post sensor processing artefacts and focus on the noise pattern unique to the sensor.

For both controlled indoor and outdoor data sets, the correlation results show clear correlation with the correct camera. Further, the merged results show that the camera sensor is more dominant than the lens for identification. This is strong evidence to support the assumption that the reference noise pattern found for a camera is unique to that camera's sensor.

Other applications of the developed extension for RAW images may include measuring the noise pattern of images in different temperature environments or for cameras with different battery levels. This may allow for more information associated with an image to be determined. In the case of temperature, the time of day or typical environment could be determined and in the case of battery, images could be ordered chronologically to determine a sequence of events.

References

1. Lukáš, J., Fridrich, J., Goljan, M.: Digital Camera Identification from Sensor Pattern Noise. IEEE Transactions on Information Security and Forensics 1(2), 205–214 (2006)

2. Lukáš, J., Fridrich, J., Goljan, M.: Digital 'Bullet Scratches' for Images. In: Proc. ICIP 2005, Genova, Italy (September 2005)
3. Lukáš, J., Fridrich, J., Goljan, M.: Determining Digital Image Origin Using Sensor Imperfections. In: Proc. SPIE Electronic Imaging, Image and Video Communication and Processing, San Jose, California, January 16-20, pp. 249–260 (2005)
4. Mihcak, M.K., Kozintsev, I., Ramchandran, K.: Spatially adaptive statistical modeling of wavelet image coefficients and its application to denoising. In: Proc. IEEE Int. Conf. Acoustics, Speech, and Signal Processing, Phoenix, AZ, vol. 6, pp. 3253–3256 (March 1999)
5. Standard of Japan Electronics and Information Technology Industries Association, Exchangeable image file format for digital still cameras: Exif Version 2.2, http://www.exif.org/Exif2-2.PDF (accessed on 7-11-2008)
6. ExifTool by Phil Harvey, http://www.sno.phy.queensu.ca/~phil/exiftool/ (accessed on 1-11-2008)
7. Decoding raw digital photos in Linux, http://www.cybercom.net/~dcoffin/dcraw/ (accessed on 7-11-2008)
8. Stanford University, WAVELAB, http://www-stat.stanford.edu/~wavelab/ (accessed on 7-11-2008)
9. Holst, G.C.: CCD Arrays, Cameras, and Displays, 2nd edn. JCD Publishing & SPIE Pres, USA (1998)
10. Janesick, J.R.: Scientific Charge-Coupled Devices, SPIE PRESS Monograph, vol. PM83. SPIET The International Society for Optical Engineering (January 2001)
11. Choi, K.S.: Automatic source camera identification using the intrinsic lens radial distortion. Optics express (1094-4087) 14(24), 11551 (2006)
12. Johnson, M.K., Farid, H.: Exposing Digital Forgeries Through Chromatic Aberration. In: ACM Multimedia and Security Workshop, Geneva, Switzerland (2006)
13. Zamfir, A., Drimbarean, A., Zamfir, M., Buzuloiu, V., Steinberg, E., Ursu, D.: An optical model of the appearance of blemishes in digital photographs. In: Proc. SPIE, Digital Photography III, vol. 6502, pp. 0I10I12 (Feburary 2007)

Audit Log for Forensic Photography

Timothy Neville and Matthew Sorell

School of Electrical and Electronic Engineering,
University of Adelaide SA 5005, Australia
matthew.sorell@adelaide.edu.au

Abstract. We propose an architecture for an audit log system for forensic photography, which ensures that the chain of evidence of a photograph taken by a photographer at a crime scene is maintained from the point of image capture to its end application at trial. The requirements for such a system are specified and the results of experiments are presented which demonstrate the feasibility of the proposed approach.

Keywords: Digital photography, crime investigation, forensic investigation, digital negative.

1 Introduction

In legal terminology, the chain of evidence (or chain of custody) refers to "the ability to guarantee the identity and integrity of the specimen from collection through to reporting of the test results" in a Court of Law [1]. As technology continues to evolve, the ability to both maintain and break the chain of evidence has become increasingly easy. One example of this is in the area crime scene photography.

Since 1840 traditional analogue photography has involved both a negative and positive image, with the latter developed using the former [2]. While important in developing a viewable picture, the negative image, to law enforcement agencies, has also allowed the chain of evidence of a crime scene photograph to be easily secured. This is because image manipulation of a negative photograph is both relatively difficult to achieve and relatively easy to identify.

The advent of more sophisticated technology has, however, provided law enforcement with the ability to use digital cameras in the course of their investigations, and indeed the lack of technical support for film cameras is accelerating this migration. As digital forensic photographs provide investigators with high quality images with quicker access, at a cheaper cost than traditional analogue photographs, a significant benefit exists for the use of this technology. There is, however, one significant drawback to the use of digital photography: the inherent insecurity of a digital image and the ease at which the chain of evidence can be broken.

While it is unlikely that law enforcement officials would manipulate digital evidence, it is nevertheless important that a secure chain of evidence is maintained that is similar to its physical evidence counterpart. Indeed, digital photographs tendered in a speeding fine case in New South Wales were found to not include the

M. Sorell (Ed.): e-Forensics 2009, LNICST 8, pp. 142–152, 2009.

appropriate watermarks needed to prove authenticity and were thus deemed inaccessible as evidence [3]. Similarly, from an international point of view, the jury in the case of *State of Florida v Victor Reyes* (2003) acquitted Victor Reyes of murder after the validity of a digitally enhanced photograph was challenged by the defence attorney [4].

Current practices for the secure storage of digital data in law enforcement involve software packages such as Foray's Authenticated Digital Asset Management System used by the FBI and DEA in the United States [5]. These packages track and monitor every access to the digital data once it has been uploaded to a secure storage device. For example, a crime scene investigator takes a series of digital photographs at a crime scene then travels back to the crime lab and uploads the photographs to a secure server running data management software. Once these photographs enter the system their access can be tracked.

In the above scenario, while the photographs can be tracked once uploaded, there is no electronic confirmation that the image taken at the scene is the same as the image uploaded at the crime lab. The only assurance in the chain of evidence during this period is the integrity of the camera operator. This gap in the electronic chain of evidence is a direct consequence of digital technology. In the case of an analogue photograph a negative image is produced at the moment of capture; for a digital photograph no negative is needed, and thus no negative is produced.

2   The Need for a Digital Negative

Whilst there appears to be little demand for a digital negative by the everyday user, the aforementioned scenario indicates a need for law enforcement. One novel yet cumbersome approach suggested by Blythe and Fridrich [6] is to create a secure digital camera that takes a biometric image of the user's iris. The iris image information would then be included in the metadata of the captured photograph. While this approach identifies the person who took the photograph it still fails to secure the digital image from the time it is taken to the time it is stored on a secure storage device. This approach also renders a camera specific-approach to authentication, providing limitations on what how secure authentication process.

It is from the idea of creating a secure digital camera, that the aims of this project were developed. There is a definite need to prove, beyond a reasonable doubt, that the photograph taken at a crime scene is the same as the image uploaded at the crime lab. Following from traditional analogue photography, one approach to this would be to create a digital negative of the image at the time of capture. This image should immediately be stored securely and accessed at a later time to prove authenticity.

We propose that a digital negative need not be a secure copy of the complete digital image or digital image file, but rather a secure data structure against which an image or set of images can be audited. In the application outlined in this paper, it should be noted that once a digital file is stored in a conventional auditable logging system such as Foray, it is possible to keep track of subsequent image processing and analysis; we are concerned with ensuring that the chain of custody extends from the point at which the photograph is taken to the point at which it enters such a conventional logging system. It is thus sufficient to consider four components of an audit trail record:

- A record of the nature of the transaction and operating-system specific parameters including the file name and its location on a memory device
- A decipherable metadata record, if possible, which allows independent matching of a file with its record
- A thumbnail or miniature version of the image, if possible, which allows visual confirmation of a file match, and
- A cryptographic hash code, to verify that an image file is a complete and untampered copy of the original file.

In order to construct a record at the front-end of the chain of evidence, it is necessary to capture the above components at the camera. We have identified two broad approaches where the image file is effectively quarantined and so the audit file can be constructed with certainty of security. The first is to embed the Audit Log System in the firmware of a Digital Still Camera; the second is to monitor and capture the required data as it is transferred to and from a memory card, provided that the camera under consideration only supports an external memory.

The first approach is impractical for the simple reason that modern Digital Still Cameras are highly optimized devices with little processing overhead available in which to consider the separate processing of an audit log record. The development of such an implementation would result in a camera with a very specific and relatively small market which would contribute prohibitively to the cost of the product to an end user.

The second approach has the advantage that it can be implemented and customized, at least in theory, for any of the finite combinations of cameras and memory devices under consideration, with the cost of development and production significantly reduced for two reasons – the one generic device (economy of scale) is not necessarily specific to just one make and model of camera (economy of scope). However an external device adds bulk to the camera, might require an independent power source, and might, if not designed properly, prevent or inhibit normal use of the camera. With these limitations in mind, we consider the requirements of our proposed system.

2.1 File Transaction Component

The file transaction component of the record includes the name of the file, the timestamps and other operating-specific parameters available to the data monitoring device. It is also important to consider the nature of the transaction, which might be, for example:

- The transfer of a file onto a memory device (writing)
- The reading of the file from a memory device (reading)
- The deletion of a file from a memory device (deletion)
- The changing of the name or other file records (renaming)

Other memory device transactions which might be of interest include identification of when a device is switched on or off, and when a memory device is swapped in or out of a logging system. While it is desirable to maintain an associated timestamp, for a low-power unit it might not be feasible to maintain an accurate real time clock, in which case it is at least necessary to ensure that the order of transactions is accurately recorded.

2.2 Metadata Record and Thumbnail

Unlike traditional negatives, which only show a colour-inverted, snapshot of the photograph taken, a digital negative has the ability to provide greater information to the user. Images are most often stored in JPEG format [7], but other formats (particularly proprietary so-called *raw* formats) are also used. JPEG, and many of the proprietary formats, also support the Exif metadata standard [8] within the file structure, and the Exif standard is ubiquitously supported by all Digital Still Cameras the authors have examined. Metadata stored in Exif format includes the time and date at which an image was taken, the make and model of camera, and a wide range of standard camera settings. A thumbnail or miniature version of the image is often included. Proprietary extensions include specific camera parameters. The Exif data structure, which is limited in size to 64 Kilobytes, is thus a very good encapsulation of the characteristics of a digital image file, especially if it includes a thumbnail image.

2.3 Cryptographic Hash

A cryptographic hash function generates a number based on a complete file input to it, which is virtually unique to that file. Hash functions are best known for their application as a digital signature. For our proposal, a hash can be used to verify that an image file is in fact identical to the version originally written to the memory device with a very high level of confidence, without having to permanently store the complete original image.

3 Audit Log System

The proposed architecture of the Audit Log System (ALS) is given in Figure 1. The proposed system is an external device which is physically attached to the camera, interfacing to the camera through the memory device socket. A number of form factors were considered in conceiving the proposed system. It would be ideal for such a log system to be implemented in the form of a full-sized memory adaptor which accepts a micro-form memory. For example, adaptors which allow micro-SD memory devices to be used in a full-sized SD-card slot exist, and there are similar adaptors for related devices such as Sony's Memory Stick. Implementation in such a package would be ideal because the photographer would not be inconvenience by having to manage a separate device. However, our investigation of technical requirements suggests that such a package is not currently viable, although this may change in the future. In particular, we recognize the need for an independent power supply and electrical interface for accessing the audit records.

We therefore visualize the proposed system as a small form factor package similar in size to a miniaturized music player, sufficiently large to contain a rechargeable

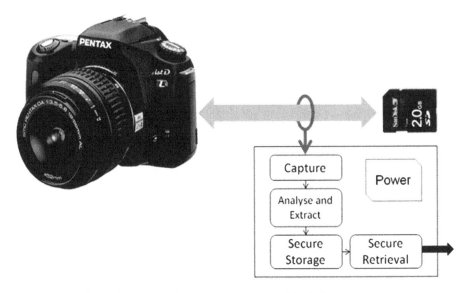

Fig. 1. System Architecture of the proposed Audit Log System

battery, electrical sockets for memory access and power, and a socket for the normal memory device such as SD-card or Memory Stick. A universal memory socket would allow the device to be used on a wider range of cameras, although multi-format support would complicate firmware. A memory plug, similar to a port extender, is relatively easy to implement. The key complication is that most cameras completely encapsulate the memory device and so minor physical modification of the camera might be necessary to allow a thin cable to extend from the memory socket to the ALS, such as drilling a small hole or cutting a slot in a panel.

It is also necessary to support an external memory plug to connect into the camera, and a means of physically securing the device to the camera. In the latter case, it would be a relatively simple matter to design the package to be screwed into the universal tripod thread, and provide a further thread for a tripod to be used.

Taking the concept further, it is necessary to consider the electronic requirements based on the proposed architecture. For the purpose of discussion of specifics, we consider the widely used SD-card memory to illustrate the challenges of implementation.

3.1 Passive Capture

The proposed system is located between the camera and the memory and interprets communications between the two devices. Both an active and a passive architecture can be considered.

An active architecture would mean that the ALS would interface directly to the camera and mimic the functions of the memory. The memory would be connected separately and in this case the ALS would mimic the role of the camera. Such an active architecture has some advantages, particularly in determining which of the two devices (the memory or the camera) is transmitting, and allows translation between memory protocols, enhancing the compatibility of an old camera with a contemporary memory device for example. However the latter function is not critical to our consideration, and the disadvantages are manifold. These include the need to implement sophisticated mimicry and translation of operating system characteristics such as compliant communication when the external memory is full, but most critically if the ALS fails then the photographer cannot continue working.

A passive architecture on the hand means that the memory is connected directly to the camera and receives power and communication signals exactly as intended. All that is required is for the ALS to monitor the communications between the two devices and interpret events of interest for analysis and storage. There are some complications because full interpretation of the handshaking protocol between the memory and the camera is needed to determine the direction of transmission, but on the other hand there is no need to mimic communications, and if the ALS fails the photographer can continue working.

A more important consideration however is that a passive implementation does not interfere with the chain of evidence and is thus more trustworthy.

In the case of SD memory, there are a total of five data lines which need to be monitored, consisting of a four-bit bus and a single bit command line, plus a clock which operates at up to a nominal speed of 25MHz (in addition to circuitry which detects whether power has been applied). The most appropriate architecture for the capture circuitry is a First-In-First-Out (FIFO) buffer which uses the SD-card clock signal to write to the memory. The subsequent analysis processor needs to be able to read data out of the FIFO buffer at a somewhat higher speed to ensure real-time analysis; alternatively a very large buffer is needed to allow more leisurely processing. The latter case is highly undesirable however because unless the command channel is interpreted with low delay, memory is wasted and may overflow during idle periods when the clock continues to cycle. It should be noted that emerging standards operate at higher clock speeds, and so it is likely that higher operating speeds will be needed to support new memory devices.

3.2 Analysis and Extraction

The ALS is not intended to store a complete record of all communications but rather a secured summary of transactions. It is therefore necessary for the ALS to interpret communications, and this function requires a combination of data communications at a reasonable speed, computationally tractable analysis, and low power embedded computing.

It would be possible in theory to implement an automatic configuration algorithm in the analysis process, so that the device would automatically determine the make and model of the camera and the memory type and behave accordingly. However, it is sufficient here to consider only the case in which a known camera communicates through a known protocol to a known memory device. In this case, the analysis processing is required to perform the following functions:

- Determine the status of the communication channel, so that the ALS is only armed when the camera is on, memory is connected and power is applied to the memory.
- Interpret file transaction instructions and parameters in order to extract the file construction parameters for the audit record

- Determine when a memory device is removed or inserted
- Interpret operating system instructions and parameters including the amount of free memory on the memory card, based only on passive capture of data communication between the camera and the memory.
- When an image file is transferred, capture the Exif metadata file component, and generate a cryptographic hash of the full image file.

It should be noted that contemporary low-powered microprocessors designed for battery-driven consumer electronics such as cameras and mobile phones, for example an ARM RISC processor, would be capable of delivering the data transfer bandwidth and processing power to meet the current and emerging technical requirements of the ALS.

3.3 Secure Storage and Secure Retrieval

We note that the security of auditable transaction records is an active area in computer security, particularly in the field of security of financial records, and propose that an off-the-shelf solution for secure storage would be sufficient to meet the requirements of the device. However, it is worth considering some of the requirements of the secured data records.

Simply put, the secure record should be relatively easy to extract, and once extracted, effectively impossible to modify without detection. The secure memory of the ALS may either be an un-erasable WORM (Write Once Read Multiple) memory, in which case the ALS has a finite life, or else a secure protocol is required to allow the secure memory to be erased and over-written.

It is worth considering that it is very much in the interest of the investigator to ensure that the chain of evidence is maintained, and in the latter case this means that such a secure protocol is supported by the investigator's requirement to retain the audit log before erasure. However, just as anyone can dispose of a film negative, it is always possible to dispose of an audit file.

There are significant disadvantages in specifying a WORM solution, notably that the device has a finite life and that such memory is becoming increasingly rare, requiring a proprietary silicon solution. For these reasons, we reject the WORM approach and advocate a secure erasure protocol.

It should also be noted that once the audit log is extracted it can be entered into a conventional digital chain-of-custody system and is then subject to conventional procedures. It is however necessary to note that a secure but conventional cryptographic communication solution is required for tamper detection, so that the chain of evidence is maintained from the ALS to the point of entry.

3.4 Power

There are two options for providing power to the ALS. Either the ALS can operate on the same power supply as the memory card, provided by the camera's battery, or it can have its own independent power supply. The use of the camera's power supply is undesirable for two key reasons. Firstly, the ALS draws additional power which reduces battery life and thus interferes with the photographer's function. Secondly, ALS processing would only be possible when the memory device is powered by the camera, thus reducing the scope for functionality of the device such as the implementation of an internal real-time clock.

It is therefore necessary to specify the use of a separate power supply. However this raises other concerns. Firstly, batteries have a finite size placing a limit on the size and form factor of the ALS. Secondly, a simple mechanism for either charging an internal rechargeable battery, or changing out disposable batteries, becomes a requirement, further complicated by the desirability to have identical batteries to the camera to reduce the amount of equipment required by the photographer. Thirdly, it needs to be recognized that the ALS power can fail independently of the camera, and in this case the camera needs to continue to operate. This latter point is another strong argument in favour of a passive capture implementation, since active intervention would prevent the camera from working.

4 Proof-of-Concept Demonstration

In order to develop the ALS concept the transfer of data between a digital camera and an SD Card needed to be understood. Four basic experiments were conducted to show that this was not the case. As the basic function of the ALS is to monitor the copying of files from one device to another, the experiments conducted were limited to this one mode of operation.

The aims of the experiments were to demonstrate that it is possible to monitor communications between a Digital Still Camera and an SD-Card memory, and in particular to show that a JPEG image file could be detected and reconstructed from the data captured during file transfer.

4.1 Equipment

The experiments required the following equipment:

- SD Extender Card, providing direct access to signals between the SD Card and the SD Card port in a camera or computer.
- Commercial Logic Analyser – Combined with the SD Extender Card, the logic analyser allows the data flow to be captured and examined
- SD Card Reader – in this case integrated within a laptop computer
- Digital Still Camera – A digital camera with an easily accessible SD port.

4.2 Results

Early experiments showed that the command line structure for a SD card copy operation is a series of write block and write multiple block operations. Each write command (a series of file setup instructions) is preceded by a status check which checks the current status of the SD Card, while the write multiple blocks (the file payload transfer) is followed by a stop command. Although the information gained from this experiment was minimal, it did show that the command line of an SD Card is independent of the SD Card's data lines. The communications during the setup of a file transfer onto the memory were interpreted according to the SD card standard, demonstrating that it is possible to interpret file transaction information which can usefully be included in an audit record.

Having confirmed that the communication standard was being interpreted correctly, we implemented a post-capture analysis program in Matlab to automatically detect and extract a JPEG image. This was relatively simple to implement, noting that a JPEG image, according to the standard, starts with the byte sequence FF D8. Similarly, it is relatively easy to identify the Exif metadata sequence, which begins with FF E1. While there were some complications during capture, due primarily to the limitation of operating the available logic analyser at a fixed clock rate and with limited memory, it was possible to capture a significant proportion of the JPEG image by triggering the storage of the logic levels once FF D8 was detected on the data lines.

Figure 2 demonstrates that it is possible to recover the JPEG image file from the data lines captured during the file transfer process. This experiment was done using a file transferred from a laptop rather than a camera for simplicity.

Fig. 2. The original image (left) was transferred from a laptop to an SD memory card. Although incomplete, it can be clearly seen that a significant proportion of the file was captured and reconstructed, resulting in a useable JPEG image fragment.

It is worth making the observation that experimental results using a Digital Still Camera were disappointing, but for interesting reasons. It was possible to trigger the logic analyser when the start of the JPEG image was detected, but after writing some Exif metadata to the file, there was a significant delay before the rest of the file was transferred. This delay meant that the logic analyser's memory was exhausted before any further data was transferred. However this delay does demonstrate that the implementation of the camera's file compression and transfer firmware is such that the camera transfers what it is able to construct directly to the external memory as soon as it is composed, rather than constructing the entire JPEG image file and transferring as a single operation. While the latter approach would be more efficient, due to the external memory being powered for a shorter period, there is also a need for larger internal memory in the camera which increases costs, albeit marginally. The implications for implementation of the ALS are similarly important, because it is clearly necessary for the data capture system to either capture a very large amount of data and then process it, requiring a large FIFO memory, or a sufficiently large FIFO buffer to allow the ALS's microprocessor to transfer and analyse communications without overflow.

5 Future-Proofing and Extensions

An important issue the ALS shall need to consider through its development is the ability to implement future proofing functionality to its design. As storage technology continues to evolve, memories will become larger and different standards will be introduced. One example of this is the new High Capacity Secure Digital Card (HCSD Card) which operates at four times the speed and has a greater storage capacity when compared to current SD Cards. While not all digital cameras have the ability to use HDSD Cards, new digital cameras will be able to utilise this new standard. Thus, the ALS design must take this into consideration.

Furthermore, while the experiments conducted examined the copying of an image from one device to the SD Card, the ALS can be extended to monitor the removal of images from the SD Card and also the copying of images from a SD Card to another device. These uses allow the ALS to be designed not just for a digital camera but also for other devices that require data monitoring.

The main purpose of the ALS is to preserve the chain of evidence of a digital image from the moment it is taken at crime scenes. However, the ALS could also be implemented in other law enforcement activities. One particular operation could be to track the photographs, or even video, taken at surveillance location. By recording the time, date and thumbnail of every photograph taken, the ALS can prove timeline of the photographs for investigators in court.

6 Conclusions

The Audit Log System for digital forensics is one solution to creating a digital negative. With the creation of a digital negative the chain of evidence of digital images can be strengthened, providing an extra layer of authenticity to evidence tendered in court. From a theoretical standpoint, the ALS idea can be achieved; with experimentation showing that the SD Card protocol is workable, with images able to be recreated. From this understanding, the design can be taken further to include hardware design, power and packaging.

References

[1] West Midland Toxicology Laboratory: Chain of Custody (June 21, 2003),
http://www.toxlab.co.uk/coc.htm (accessed, March 2008)

[2] National Geographic: History of Photography,
http://photography.nationalgeographic.com/photography/
photographers/photography-timeline.html (accessed, September 2008)

[3] Pelly, M., Norrie, J.: Speedcam slip puts $100m fines in doubt. Sydney Morning Herald (March 26, 2006),
http://www.smh.com.au/news/national/
speedcam-slip-may-cost-100m/2006/03/23/1142703456320.html
(accessed, March 2008)

[4] Bergstein, B.: Digital Photos Pose Issues in Court. CRN -Channel Web (February 8, 2004),
http://www.crn.com/digital-home/18831429 (accessed, March 2008)

[5] Foray Technology: Foray Technology - Clients (2008), http://www.foray.com/
company/clients.php (accessed, September 2008)

[6] Blythe, P., Fridrich, J.: Secure Digital Camera. Digital Forensic Research Workshop (2004)

[7] ITU: CCITT T.81 information technology – Digital compression and coding of continuous-tone still images – Requirements and guidelines. International Telecommunications Union (1993)

[8] JEITA: JEITA CP-3451 Exchangeable image file format for digital still cameras: Exif Version 2.2. Japan Electronics and Information Technology Industries Association (2002)

Authenticating Medical Images through Repetitive Index Modulation Based Watermarking

Chang-Tsun Li and Yue Li

Department of Computer Science, University of Warwick, Coventry CV4 7AL, UK
{ctli,yxl}@dcs.warwick.ac.uk

Abstract. In this work we propose a Repetitive Index Modulation (RIM) based digital watermarking scheme for authentication and integrity verification of medical images. Exploiting the fact that many types of medical images have significant background areas and medically meaningful Regions Of Interest (ROI), which represent the actual contents of the images, the scheme uses the contents of the ROI to create a content-dependent watermark and embeds the watermark in the background areas. Therefore when any pixel of the ROI is attacked, the watermark embedded in the background areas will be different from the watermark calculated according to the attacked contents, making the authentication unsuccessful. Because the creation of the watermark is content-dependent and the watermark is only embedded in the background areas, the proposed scheme can actually protect the content without distorting it.

Keywords: Medical image authentication, digital watermarking, data hiding, digital forensics, integrity verification.

1 Introduction

Due to the privacy concerns and authentication needs, many digital watermarking schemes [1, 2, 3, 6, 12] have been proposed to embed authentication data into the contents of medical images. Most methods [1, 2, 6, 11] require the least significant bits (LSBs) of the image pixels to be replaced with the authentication codes or watermarks. Although the distortion due to this kind of "lossy" watermark embedding is usually visually insignificant, medical images with watermarks embedded with this type of irreversible watermarking schemes may not be accepted as feasible evidence in the court of law, should medical disputes occur. Many reversible data hiding schemes [7, 10], although not specifically proposed for the purpose of medical image authentication, have been developed to facilitate reversible data hiding, in which the original images can be recovered after the hidden data is extracted from the watermarked images. A reversible watermarking scheme specifically developed for authenticating medical data has been proposed in [3]. The common problem with these reversible data hiding schemes is that, apart from the actual payload (i.e., the watermark, secret data, authentication codes, etc), side information for reconstructing the exact original image has to be embedded as well. The side information wastes limited embedding capacity and is usually the compressed form of the location map of

M. Sorell (Ed.): e-Forensics 2009, LNICST 8, pp. 153–159, 2009.

the original data that is expected to be affected by the embedding process. The waste of embedding capacity reduces the authentication power of the scheme and the resolution of tamper localization, as explained in [8]. Moreover, authentication schemes are also expected to be resistant against attacks, such as the Holliman-Memon counterfeiting attack, the birthday attack and the transplantation attack, by involving the contents in the watermarking process in a non-deterministic manner [5, 8]. Therefore schemes with high payload, high resolution of tamper localization, high security and zero distortion to the ROI are desirable.

2 Proposed Method

It is observed that, apart from the ROI, which represents the actual contents of images, many types of medical images have significant background areas. Exploiting this characteristic, we propose a new scheme, which uses the contents of the ROI to create a content-dependent watermark and embeds the watermark in the background areas without adding any embedding distortion to the ROI. Without loss of generality, we will use mammograms with gray level range [0, 255] in the presentation of this work. Because the background areas contain no information of interest and the gray levels of their pixels fall in the low end of the intensity range, wherein human eyes are not sensitive to variation, a greater degree of embedding can be carry out to strengthen security and/or increase resolution of tamper localization [8].

2.1 Segmentation

The mission of the image segmentation operation is that when given either the original image, I_o, during the *watermarking* process or the watermarked image, I_w, during the *authentication* process as input, the segmentation function should partition the input image into the same bi-level output image, with one level corresponding to the background areas and the other to the ROIs. Figure 1(a) shows a typical mammogram with intensity represented with 8 bits. We can see that it has a dark background with intensity below 30 and a significantly brighter area of a breast (ROI) with the intensity of most pixels above 100. Since we will embed the watermark in the background area and the distortion due to embedding will not raise the intensity significantly, so a threshold between 50 and 100 for partitioning the images is a reasonable value. However, due to the fact that mammograms may be taken at different times with different equipments under various imaging conditions, using a heuristic constant threshold to segment mammograms is not feasible. So we propose to use *moment-preserving thresholding* [11], which is content-dependent, to perform the segmentation task.

Given a gray-scale image, I, with $X \times Y$ pixels, we define the intensity / gray scale at pixel (x, y) as $I(x, y)$. The ith *moment* of an image is defined [11] as

$$m_i = \left(\frac{1}{X \times Y}\right)\sum_{x=1}^{X}\sum_{y=1}^{Y}I^i(x, y) \tag{1}$$

A transform is called *moment-preserving* if the transformed image, I', still has the same moments as I. In the context of binary segmentation, to divided I into two

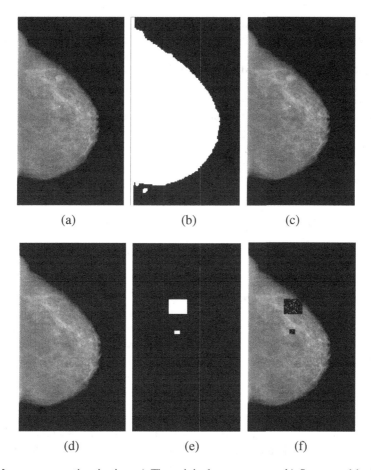

(a)   (b)   (c)

(d)   (e)   (f)

Fig. 1. Mammogram authentication. a) The original mammogram, b) Segmented background and ROIs, c) the watermarked mammogram, d) tampered mammogram, e) the black spots indicate the tampered areas, f) authentication result with the noisy areas indicating tampering.

classes of p_0 and p_1 pixels with gray scale z_0 and z_1, respectively, we can find a threshold t by first solving Eq. (2), as formulated below

$$\begin{cases} p_0 z_0^0 + p_1 z_1^0 = m_0 \\ p_0 z_0^1 + p_1 z_1^1 = m_1 \\ p_0 z_0^2 + p_1 z_1^2 = m_2 \\ p_0 z_0^3 + p_1 z_1^3 = m_3 \end{cases} . \qquad (2)$$

Once z_0, z_1, p_0 and p_1 are obtained, setting the threshold t to a value between the gray scales of p_0th and $(p_0 +1)$th pixels will yield segmentation result I' that preserves the first four moments (i.e., m_0 to m_3) of I [11]. From the above description, we know that to make sure the algorithm uses the same segmentation result in both watermarking and authentication processes, when given the original image I_o and watermarked image I_w, respectively, as the input image I, the algorithm should yield the same values for p_0 and p_1. Because the significant gap between the background and ROI in both I_o and I_w, our experiments have proved the feasibility of the use of the moment-preserving thresholding method. The reader is referred to [11] for more details about moment-preserving thresholding.

After moment-preserving thresholding, some pixels with low intensity in the ROI may be classified as background pixels. Moreover, the smoother intensity transition across the boundary separating the background and the ROI may also cause misclassification. To compensate for these two types of misclassifications, a morphological operation of 'dilation' with a disk of radius equal to 5 pixels is applied to the segmented ROI so as to allow the ROI to grow and the background area to shrink.

2.2 Watermarking

The steps as described in the next three subsections have to be taken in order to watermark mammograms.

2.2.1 Establishing Non-deterministic Dependence

In order to authenticate the ROI pixels without distorting them, we involve the gray levels of the ROI pixels in the creation of the watermark (authentication code). As discussed in [5,8], non-deterministic block-wise dependence is crucial in thwarting various types of attacks, such as the cut-and-paste attack, the Holliman-Memon counterfeiting attack, the birthday attack and the transplantation attack. Once the segmentation is completed, the ROI pixels are group into overlapping blocks of multiple pixels. By allowing overlapping, each pixel of the ROI appears in multiple ROI blocks, which in turn gets involved in the watermarking process of multiple background pixels, and as a result, get authenticated by multiple background pixels. If the ROI area is greater than the background, we make the number of ROI blocks the same as the number of background pixels and uniquely associate each background pixel with a ROI block in a key-controlled manner. If the ROI area is smaller than the background, only the same number of background pixels as the ROI blocks are selected as *embeddable*, each uniquely associated with a ROI block. The selection of embeddable background pixels and the association between those background pixels and ROI blocks are also key-controlled. The size of the ROI blocks, as discussed in [8] partially determines the resolution of tamper localization and security, and is to be determined by the user according to the application needs.

2.2.2 Watermark Creation

Suppose we want to embed b bits of watermark (authentication code) in each background pixel. To create the b-bit content-dependent watermark, we first convert the gray levels of the pixels of the corresponding ROI block into binary form, rearrange the bits of each binary gray level under the control of a secret key and perform a bit-wise Exclusive OR operation on those rearranged binary values. Finally, b bits from the result of the Exclusive OR operation are chosen, under the control of the secret key, as the watermark.

Fig. 2. RIM-based watermarking with b equal to 3

2.2.3 Watermark Embedding

Distortion resulted from data hiding is always a major concern [4]. We employ the RIM embedding method reported in [10] to embed the b-bit watermark into a background pixel. The idea of embedding the b-bit watermark w in a pixel, with its gray level equal to x, is to assign a modulation index $r(x)$, $r(x) \in \{0,1, 2, ... , 2^b-1\}$), to each gray level x of the image, with gray level 0 corresponding to a key-generated random modulation index $r(0)$, as shown in Figure 2 with $r(0) = 3$. Since the range of $r(x)$ is smaller than the range of the gray levels, the modulation indexes can be *repeatedly* used to index the gray levels. To embed the b-bit watermark, the gray level, x, of the background pixel is modulated so that the new value x' lands on an index $r(x')$ equal to the value of the b-bit watermark w. Because the indices repeat, watermarking can be achieved by modulating the pixel in question upward or downward, depending on which way results in lower distortion (see Figure 2). The relationship between the gray level x of each pixel and its corresponding random modulation index $r(x)$ can be formulated as

$$r(x) = \left[r(0) + x\right] \bmod 2^b \tag{3}$$

where "mod" is the modulo operation. For example, suppose $x = 17$ and the 3-bit watermark $w = 7$. We could hide w in x by changing x to either 12 or 20 because $r(12) = r(20) = w = 7$. However, we can see that changing x to 20 incurs less distortion, therefore, the algorithm will choose to change x to $x' = 20$.

Note that, in order not to provide security gaps to attackers, the inherent characteristics of medical images of various modalities have to be taken into account when watermarking. We observed that, on average, 80% of the pixels in the background areas of mammograms have a gray level of 0. So it is quite easy for an attacker to guess the embedded watermark without knowing the secret key. For example, if the gray level of a background pixel of a *watermarked* mammogram equals 4, the probability that the embedded information equals 4 is 0.8. This is an apparent security gap to be closed. To circumvent this problem, for each zero-valued pixel, we modify its gray level by assigning it a random number in the range of $[0, 2^{b-1}-1]$ generated with the secret key. This pre-processing, if necessary, should be carried out before the watermarking process.

2.3 Authentication

To authenticate a watermarked image, the scheme performs the same operations as described in Section 2.1, 2.2.1 and 2.2.2 to calculate the *"original"* b-bit watermark w for each background pixel. To extract the *embedded* watermark w' from each watermarked background pixel x', the scheme simply establishes the correspondence between the elements of the gray level range, with gray level 0 corresponding to a key-generated random modulation index $r(0)$, as described in Section 2.2.3 and shown in Figure 2, and takes the index $r(x')$ corresponding to the gay level of the watermarked pixel x' as the *embedded* watermark w' (i.e., $w' = r(x')$). If $w = w'$, background pixel and the corresponding ROI block are regarded as authentic, Otherwise, they are regarded as manipulated. A bi-level authentication map, with value 255 (0) indicating the authenticity (inauthenticity) of the ROI block could be produced to show the authentication result.

3 Experiments

We have applied the proposed algorithm to various mammograms. Figure 1 demonstrates the process. The size of the images is 460×792 pixels. Figure 1(a) to (c) are the original image, segmented ROIs and background, and the watermarked image (with $b = 3$ and the size of the ROI blocks equal to 4×4 pixels), respectively. The distortion to the background region is so insignificant that we cannot see it (PSNR = 39.65dB). Figure 1(d) shows the attacked watermarked image, with a small bright spot and a larger mass removed. The two white rectangles in Figure 1(e) show the actually locations where the tampering has taken place. By superposing the authentication map on the attacked image, we can locate the manipulations, as shown in Figure 1(f). For comparison purpose, we also use LSB embedding, in which the *b*-bit watermark is embedded by directly replacing the *b* least significant bits of the background pixel with the watermark, in place of the RIM embedding method described in Section 2.2.3. The embedding distortion added to the background area in terms of PSNR is 36.19dB, which is worse then RIM embedding. As discussed in [9], apart from greater distortion, another drawback of LSB embedding is that the very location where the watermark is hidden is known.

4 Conclusions

In this work, we have proposed a novel scheme for authenticating medical images using RIM watermarking technique, which is capable of protecting the region of interest (ROI) without distorting it. The main features of the scheme are:

- By involving the ROI in the creation of a content-dependent watermark and carrying out the embedding in the background area only, the scheme can not only embed higher payload to strengthen security and to increase resolution of tamper localization, but also prevent adding any distortion to the ROI.
- It can resist existing attacks such as the Holliman-Memon counterfeiting attack, the birthday attack and the transplantation attack due to the merit of non-deterministic dependence.
- The balance between security, tamper localization, and embedding distortion can be adjusted by varying the size of the ROI block and the number of watermarkable bits according to the needs of the applications.

References

[1] Bao, F., Deng, R.H., Ooi, B.C., Yang, Y.: Tailored Reversible Watermarking Schemes for Authentication of Electronic Clinical Atlas. IEEE Transactions on Information Technology in Biomedicine 9(4), 554–563 (2005)

[2] Coatrieux, G., Maitre, H., Sankur, B.: Strict Integrity Control of Biomedical Images. In: Proc. Security and Watermarking of Multimedia Contents III, SPIE, vol. 4314, pp. 229–240 (2001)

[3] Guo, X., Zhuang, T.G.: A Region-Based Lossless Watermarking Scheme for Enhancing Security of Medical Data. Journal of Digital Imaging (July 10, 2007), doi:10.1007/s10278-007-9043-6

[4] Ker, A.D.: Locally Square Distortion and Batch Steganographic Capacity. International Journal of Digital Crime and Forensics 1(1), 29–44 (2009)

[5] Kim, H.Y., Pamboukian, S.V.G., Barreto, S.S.L.M.: Authentication Watermarking for Binary Images. In: Li, C.-T. (ed.) Multimedia Forensics and Security, IGI Global (2008)

[6] Kong, X., Feng, R.: Watermarking Medical Signals for Telemedicine. IEEE Transactions on Information Technology in Biomedicine 5(3), 195–201 (2001)

[7] Li, C.-T.: Reversible Watermarking Scheme with Image-independent Embedding Capacity. IEE Proceedings - Vision, Image, and Signal Processing 152(6), 779–786 (2005)

[8] Li, C.-T., Yuan, Y.: Digital Watermarking Scheme Exploiting Non-deterministic Dependence for Image Authentication. Optical Engineering 45(12), 127001-1–127001-6 (2006)

[9] Li, C.-T., Li, Y.: Protection of Digital Mammograms on PACSs Using Data Hiding Techniques. International Journal of Digital Crime and Forensics 1(1), 60–75 (2009)

[10] Thodi, D.M., Rodriguez, J.J.: Expansion Embedding Techniques for Reversible Watermarking. IEEE Transactions on Image Processing 16(3), 721–730 (2007)

[11] Tsai, W.H.: Moment-Preserving Thresholding: a New Approach. Computer Vision, Graphics, and Image Processing 29(3), 377–393 (1985)

[12] Zhou, X.Q., Huang, H.K., Lou, S.L.: Authenticity and integrity of digital mammography images. IEEE Transactions on Medical Imaging 20, 784–791 (2001)

Cyber Forensics Ontology for Cyber Criminal Investigation

Heum Park, SunHo Cho, and Hyuk-Chul Kwon

AI Lab. Dept. of Computer Science, Pusan National University, Busan, Korea
parkheum2@empal.com, sean@pusan.ac.kr, hckwon@pusan.ac.kr

Abstract. We developed Cyber Forensics Ontology for the criminal investigation in cyber space. Cyber crime is classified into cyber terror and general cyber crime, and those two classes are connected with each other. The investigation of cyber terror requires high technology, system environment and experts, and general cyber crime is connected with general crime by evidence from digital data and cyber space. Accordingly, it is difficult to determine relational crime types and collect evidence. Therefore, we considered the classifications of cyber crime, the collection of evidence in cyber space and the application of laws to cyber crime. In order to efficiently investigate cyber crime, it is necessary to integrate those concepts for each cyber crime-case. Thus, we constructed a cyber forensics domain ontology for criminal investigation in cyber space, according to the categories of cyber crime, laws, evidence and information of criminals. This ontology can be used in the process of investigating of cyber crime-cases, and for data mining of cyber crime; classification, clustering, association and detection of crime types, crime cases, evidences and criminals.

Keywords: ontology, cyber crime, digital evidence, criminal investigation, cyber forensics.

1 Introduction

Crime has increased amid the explosion of information technology, Internet services and digital equipments, as criminals have used those tools and environments on the cyber space as well as in the real word. Typical cyber crimes are Internet fraud, such as credit card and advance fee fraud, fraudulent web sites, and illegal online gambling and trading; network intrusion and hacking; virus spreading; cyber piracy and cyber terrorism; child pornography distribution; identity theft. The Internet's pervasiveness likewise makes identity theft, network intrusion, cyber piracy, and other illicit computer-mediated activities a challenge for many law-enforcement agencies. [1],[6] It is difficult to collect evidence in cyber space, to investigate crime in cyber space, and to connect cyber evidence together with general evidence. Thus, professional engineers are required for collection of cyber evidence as well as crime analysis. Recently, cyber crime and digital data forensics have been studied for the purposes of cyber criminal investigation and data mining of cyber crime. In investigating cyber

M. Sorell (Ed.): e-Forensics 2009, LNICST 8, pp. 160–165, 2009.

crime, it is necessary to collect cyber evidence and digital equipment as evidence, to investigate connections with general crime, to classify documents, and to apply relevant relational laws. In addition, data mining technology is requisite. Detecting cyber crime can likewise be difficult because heavy network traffic and frequent online transactions generate huge amounts of data. Thus, data mining of crime (including cyber crime) can be a powerful tool enabling criminal investigators who may lack extensive training as data analysts to explore large databases quickly and efficiently [1]. For the efficient investigation of cyber crime, it is necessary to integrate the various cyber crime concepts.

Recently, knowledge representation systems and information systems using cyber forensics ontology have been studied for criminal investigations and evidences investigation process. However, those studies have concerned only general criminal cases and digital evidence, and have focused exclusively on database-based retrieval systems. In 2007, the cyber crime forensics ontology was presented by A. Brinson, A. Robinson and M. Rogers. The purpose of this ontology was to find specialization, certification, and education within the cyber forensics domain [2]. However, this ontology was designed only for specialization, certification, and education within the cyber forensics domain, thus it is necessary to apply real-world investigation of cyber crime and data mining of crime cases.

Therefore, we focused on building a cyber crime forensics ontology for investigation of real-world cyber crime that can be applied to data mining of cyber crime. We constructed the ontology by including the categories cyber crime, evidence, laws, information on criminals and crime cases, based on the cyber crime in *the cyber division of the Korean National Police Agency (KNPA: http://www.netan.go. kr)*. In the following Section 2, we discuss related studies concerning ontology, the existing cyber forensics ontology, and data mining technology. In Section 3, we introduce the cyber crime forensics ontology for cyber criminal investigation, along with the areas in which the ontology can be applied. In Section 4, we draw conclusions.

2 Related Studies

Ontology for the present context was originally proposed in 1992 by Tom Gruber who defined it as "a specification of a conceptualization." The word "ontology" seems to generate a lot of controversy in discussions about AI. It has a long history in philosophy, in which it refers to the subject of existence. That is, an ontology is a description (like a formal specification of a program) of the concepts and relationships that can exist for an agent or a community of agents. The definition is consistent with the usage of ontology as set of concept definitions, but is more general. The representational primitives are typically classes, attributes, and relationships. The definitions of the representational primitives include information about their meaning and constraints on their logically consistent application. [3] [4].

The most recent development in standard ontology languages is OWL from the World Wide Web Consortium (W3C). OWL is used for formal description of conceptual meanings and relations. Like Protégé OWL makes it possible to describe concepts but it also provides new facilities. Also, many ontology building tools are introduced and used. OWL ontologies may be categorized into three species or sub-languages: OWL-Lite, OWL-DL and OWL-Full. A defining feature of each sub-language is its expressiveness [5]. We created the ontology using OWL-DL as a description language and Protégé as a tool.

D. Dzemydiene presented Knowledge Representation in Advisory Information System of Crime Investigation Domain in 2002 and also developed a helpful criminalistics information system. He used an ontology by concepts and relations of crimes; serious crime, theft, illegal keeping of firearm, and others, all of which suggests a forensic intelligence process for criminal investigation [9]. In addition, D. Dzemydiene and E Kazemikaitiene proposed an Ontology-Based Decision Support System for Crime Investigation Processes in 2005, an ontology helps to create the framework and thus to ensure the collection, accumulation, storage, treatment, and transmission, in proper form, of important investigation information, which establishes the conditions to make optimal decision in criminal investigation [8].

C. M. Donalds and K. Osei-Bryson proposed the Criminal Investigation Knowledge System (CRIKS) in 2006, in order to assist security forces in gathering, storing and easily retrieving of information/intelligence/knowledge and reports on criminal activities obtained from members of the public and other local and overseas security forces. They created a domain ontology OntoCRIKS for the criminal investigation, by defining and identification of related concepts and relationships of the ontology can disambiguate idea of concepts and relationships in an organization. The concepts and relationships of this ontology were derived from document base, case base, operations base, discussion base, cognitive base and scenario base, and they applied the text mining technique [7].

The cyber forensics ontology of Ashley Brinson et al was created for the purpose of finding the correct layers for specialization, certification, and education within the cyber forensics domain in 2007. This ontology consisted of tow subtopic; technology and profession, and has five layers; Hardware, Software, Law, Academia, and Military and Private Sector. The hardware section of this model should be broken into Large Scale Digital Devices, Small Scale Digital Devices, computers, and others. The software section of this model contains three categories: analysis tools, operating systems, and file systems. The law section focuses on law enforcement and the involvement of the court and legal system within a cyber forensic investigation. The academia section focuses on curriculum development track within the ontology. The military category focuses on what cyber forensic duties military personnel perform. The military has many needs including data protection, data acquisition, imaging, extraction, interrogation, normalization, analysis, and reporting. The private sector was broken down into consulting and industry [2]. However, it was designed only for specialization, certification, and education within the cyber forensics domain.

H. Chen et al. introduced data mining for general crime applicable to entity extraction, clustering, association, deviation detection, classification, string comparison and social network analysis. In addition, they introduced a general framework for crime data mining that draws on experience and various proven techniques to analyze different types of crimes. Significantly, understanding the relationship between analysis capability and crime type characteristics can help investigators to more effectively use those techniques to identify trends and patterns, address problem areas, and even predict crimes [1]. We can apply the ontology to the data mining of cyber crime, classification, association, detection, clustering and retrieval systems.

3   Cyber Forensics Ontology for Cyber Criminal Investigation

In criminal investigations, first, the process by which the investigation of the crime will be conducted is planned, the crime scene and environment are secured, and evidence is collected by processes. Next, the evidence is examined and analyzed, and the outlines of the crime-case and the exact crime type are discerned. Then, write documents and the pertinent relational laws are determined, and the criminal is arrested [8][9]. Based on the criminal investigation process guidelines of the KNPA (Korea), in the process of investigating cyber crime, first, the scene is secured and evidences (volatile evidence and nonvolatile evidence in both cyber space and the real word) are collected according to the evidence-collection processes (or rules). Second, that evidence is examined and analyzed, after which it is securely stored. Third, the relational laws are applied to the crime for prosecution, and reports of the crime case are written. In cyber forensics, the crime type, the relational laws and the cyber crime type are closely related to each other, so relational crime types and laws can be found easily in the process of collecting evidences.

Accordingly, we defined the concepts and relations among crime types, evidence collection, criminals, and crime case and law, based on the processes of the cyber criminal investigations. We constructed a cyber crime forensics ontology for the cyber criminal investigation, which ontology consists of five concepts; Law, Crime_Case, Criminal, Crime_Type and Evidence. Figure 1 shows a concept diagram of these subclasses. The class 'Cyber_Crime' has the subclass 'Crime_Case' with the property 'hasCrimeCase', along with the subclass 'Law' with the property 'hasBaseLaw'. 'Law' is a collection of relational laws, and the class 'Crime_Case' has the subclasses 'Crime_Type', 'Evidence' and 'Criminal'. In addition, the domain 'Crime_Case' is linked to the range 'Criminal' with the property 'hasCriminal' and conversely with the property 'hasCrimeCase'. Also it linked to the range 'Evidence' with the property 'hasEvidence' and to 'Crime_Type' with the property 'hasCrimeType'. 'Crime_Type' has the subclasses 'CyberTerror' and 'GeneralCrime'.

Law. The Class 'Law' has subclasses 'Criminal Act', 'Act on Promotion of Information and Communications Utilization and Information Protection, etc', 'Information Communication Infrastructure Protection Act', Protection of Communications Secrets Act', 'Framework Act on Telecommunications', 'Telecommunications Business Act', 'Location Information Protection Act', 'Copyright Act', 'Radio Waves Act',

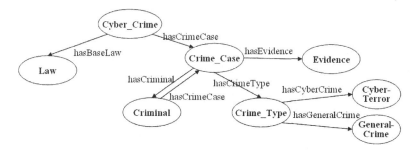

Fig. 1. Concept diagram of cyber forensics ontology for investigation of cyber crime

'Digital Signature Act' and 'Computer Programs Protection Act'. And each subclass has individuals of provisions and items.

Crime_Case. The 'Crime_Case' class includes subclasses 'Crime_Type', 'Evidence', 'Criminal' and 'Law' from above concepts diagram. This class is connected with all concepts; Cyber_Type, Law, Evidence and Criminal.

Criminal. The 'Criminal' class includes Evidence, Crime type and relational Laws as crime information through the Crime_case class. This class is connected all concepts through another concept, and has individuals of criminal.

Crime_Type. The Crime_Type class is a compendium of crime types, it consist of subclasses; Cyber Terror and General Cyber Crime. The Cyber Terror is broken down into three sub classes; Hacking, Distribution Virus and Distribution Spam. Hacking includes the subclasses; Intrusion, Dos, Information Theft, Logical bomb, and others. Distribution Virus has the subclasses; Worm, Virus, Spyware and Adware. Distribution Spam has the subclasses; Mail, Message and Call. As for General Cyber Crime, it is broken down into nine classes; Fraud, Illegal Site, Illegal Reproduction, Defamation, Infringement of Private, Stalking, Sexual Violence, Threatment and CopyRights. Each subclass has individuals.

Evidence. The 'Evidence' class is a collection of processes and evidence types, and has subclasses 'Collection' and 'EvidenceType'. Evidence type has subclasses 'Nonvolatile Evidence' and 'Volatile Evidence'. Nonvolatile evidence includes H/W; computer, scanner, Disk, CD, memory stick, and others, and S/W; illegal S/W, application program, hacking tool et al. Volatile evidence includes memory dump, CPU log, routing history, Disk imaging and blog board et al. Cyber evidence is a compendium of data and history in the cyber space and digital equipments (parts).

Figure 2 shows the subclasses and relations of evidence class. The 'Collection' class has subclass 'OrderedProcessSet' and 'CollectionInfo', and 'CollectionInfo' has subclasses 'Specialist', 'Investigator', 'Time' and 'Location', and 'OrderedProcessSet' has subclass 'Process'; process of collection evidence. 'Process' has subclasses 'takePicture', 'recordVideo', 'drawSketch', 'getCache', 'getRouting', 'getmemoryDump', and others. Each subclass has order of activities and has individuals. 'EvidenceType' has subclasses

Fig. 2. Subclasses and Relations among Evidence and Collection of process

'VolatileEvidence' and 'NonvolatileEvidence'. We applied to store and retrieve documents and evidences of cyber crime using this ontology for experimental test. In addition, we can apply this ontology to data mining of cyber crime, specifically, to entity extraction, clustering, association, deviation detection, classification, string comparison and social network analysis. Significantly, when we begin a criminal investigation, we can obtain the relational crime type, suspects, similar crime cases and many documents as well as collection evidence and legal-admissibility verification of evidences using the ontology. After completing a crime-case, we can also classify documents, evidence and crime types using this ontology. And also, we can classify (cluster) existing crime documents, and retrieve relational documents of related crime cases and crime types from those existing documents using the data mining techniques.

4 Conclusions

We introduce a cyber forensics ontology for representing concepts of cyber crime and the relations among those concepts in the criminal investigations. Also, we suggest an ontological method for investigation of cyber crimes and a means of applying the ontology to the data mining of cyber crimes. This ontology approach, thereby, can provide comprehensive objective information in the process of conducting forensics. In order to semantically integrate such information, we connected with the concepts and relations of crime case, crime type, criminals, relational law and evidence. This ontology, additionally, can be applied to data mining of cyber crime, extraction of similar crime cases and criminals, clustering (classification, association) of crime types and crime cases, and detection of similar methods of criminal investigation. In the future, we will extend the cyber forensics ontology to make it fully applicable to general purposes. Also we will study automatic concept mapping among ontology and refine the ontology for generalizing.

References

1. Chen, H., Chung, W., Xu, J.J., Qin, G., Chau, M.: Crime Data Mining: A General Framework and Some Examples. Computer 37(4), 50–56 (2004)
2. Brinson, A., Robinson, A., Rogers, M.: A cyber forensics ontology: Creating a new approach to studying cyber forensics. Digital Investigation 3S, S37–S43 (2006)
3. Gruber, T.R.: A Translation Approach to Portable Ontology Specifications. Knowledge Acquisition 5(2), 199–220 (1993)
4. Gruber, T.: http://tomgruber.org/writing/ontology-definition-2007.htm
5. Horridge, M., Knublauch, H., Rector, A., Wroe, C.: A Practical Guide To Building OWL Ontologies Using The Prot'eg'e-OWL Plugin and CO-ODE Tools. Univ. Manchester (2007)
6. The Cyber Terror Response Center (CTRC) of the Korean National Police Agency (KNPA), http://www.netan.go.kr/eng/index.jsp
7. Donalds, C.M., Osei-Bryson, K.: Criminal Investigation Knowledge System: CRIKS. In: The 39th Annual Hawaii International Conference on System Sciences, vol. 7, pp. 152–160 (2006)
8. Dzemydiene, D., Kazemikaitiene, E.: Ontology-Based Decision Support System for Crime Investigation Processes. In: Information Systems Development, pp. 427–438. Springer, Heidelberg (2005)
9. Dzemydiene, D.: Knowledge Representation in Advisory Information System of Crime Investigation Domain. In: Databases and Information Systems II, pp. 135–146. Springer, Heidelberg (2002)

Decomposed Photo Response Non-Uniformity for Digital Forensic Analysis

Yue Li and Chang-Tsun Li

Department of Computer Science
University of Warwick
Coventry CV4 7AL, UK
{yxl,ctli}@dcs.warwick.ac.uk

Abstract. The last few years have seen the applications of Photo Response Non-Uniformity noise (PRNU) - a unique stochastic fingerprint of image sensors, to various types of digital forensic investigations such as source device identification and integrity verification. In this work we proposed a new way of extracting PRNU noise pattern, called Decomposed PRNU (DPRNU), by exploiting the difference between the *physical* and *artificial* color components of the photos taken by digital cameras that use a Color Filter Array for interpolating *artificial* components from *physical* ones. Experimental results presented in this work have shown the superiority of the proposed DPRNU to the commonly used version. We also proposed a new performance metrics, Corrected Positive Rate (CPR) to evaluate the performance of the common PRNU and the proposed DPRNU.

Keywords: Digital forensics, PRNU noise pattern, integrity verification, source device identification.

1 Introduction

Among many areas of non-intrusive forensic analysis, extracting and examining the Photo Response Non-Uniformity noise pattern (PRNU), which is a unique fingerprint of image sensors, is one of the most effective methods for digital forensic analysis. As a signature of digital cameras, a PRNU noise pattern is applicable to digital forensic areas such as source device identification [1, 2] and integrity verification [3]. The basic idea of using the PRNU noise pattern for identifying source devices is as follows. Firstly, the PRNU noise patterns of imaging devices, e.g., digital cameras, are extracted from a number of low-contrast images and then the average of them are calculated to serve as the reference fingerprints of the devices. Secondly, the PRNU of the image under investigation is extracted and compared against the reference fingerprint of each device available to the investigator in hope that it would match one of the reference fingerprints, thus identifying the source device that has taken the target image [1, 2]. For integrity verification, a window is slid across the image, and the PRNU noise from the area covered by the window is compared to the corresponding PRNU block of a reference fingerprint. An authentic block covered by the window is expected to have higher correlation with the reference PRNU block while a forged block should have lower correlation [3].

M. Sorell (Ed.): e-Forensics 2009, LNICST 8, pp. 166–172, 2009.
© ICST Institute for Computer Sciences, Social Informatics and Telecommunications Engineering 2009

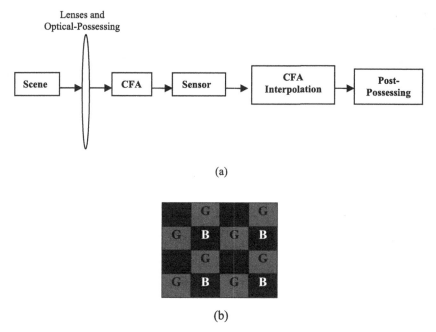

Fig. 1. The processing inside the digital camera, and the typical Bayer CFA. a) The process of capturing a digital. b) Bayer CFA, a typical Color Filer Array.

According to these descriptions, we know that the effectiveness of the aforementioned methods is based on the quality of the PRNU noise. The method for extraction the PRNU noise extraction proposed in [1 – 3]

$$PRNU(i, j) = I(i, j) - I'(i, j) \qquad (1)$$

where $I(i, j)$ is the intensity of pixel (i, j) and $I'(i, j)$ is the intensity of pixel (i, j) in the denoised (low-pass filtered) version of $I(i, j)$. In [1 - 3], the entire filtered noise pattern is treated as the PRNU noise pattern. The PRNU maybe caused either by optical lenses non-uniformity, optical filtering, or by the digital post-processing algorithms. Moreover, details from the scene as well as the noise introduced at the acquisition and storage phases may contribute to the left hand side of Eq. (1).

Another factor worth investigating is the use Color Filter Array (CFA) in most digital cameras. During the image acquisition process of a typical digital camera as illustrated in Fig. 1(a), not every color component of each pixel is physically captured. Instead, for each pixel, only one color component is acquired, depending on a 2 × 2 coordinate pattern – the CFA, as illustrated in Fig. 1(b), pre-defined by the manufacturer. Later an Interpolation Matrix (IM) is utilized to interpolate the missing color components by involving the neighboring pixels according to the CFA [4, 6, 7]. Throughout the rest of this work, we will use the term *physical component* for the color channel/component of each pixel with the same color as that of the corresponding element of the CFA and *artificial component* for the other two color channels/components. Because the *artificial* colors obtained through the interpolation operation is not directly acquired from the scene by *physical* hardware, we expect that the

PRNU noise pattern extracted from the physical components, which are free from interpolation noise, should be more reliable than that from the artificial channels, which carry interpolation noise. Based on this assumption we propose an improved Decomposed PRNU extraction method, which first decomposes each color channel into 4 sub-images and then extracts the PRNU noise from each sub-image. The PRNU noise patterns of the sub-images are then assembled to get the complete Decomposed PRNU (DPRNU).

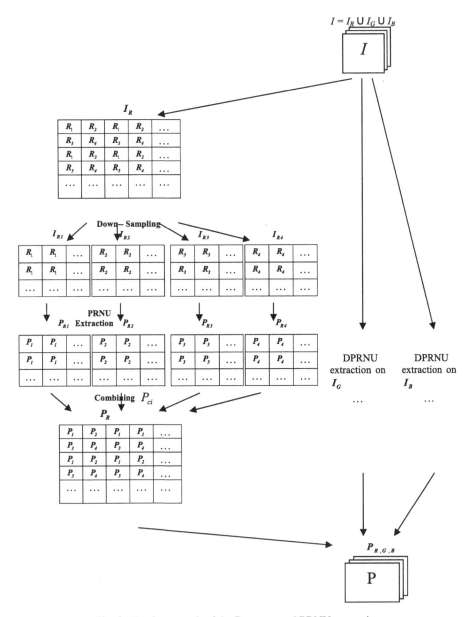

Fig. 2. The framework of the Decomposed PRNU extraction

2   Proposed Decomposed PRNU (DPRNU)

As illustrated in Fig. 2, to extract the DPRNU, we first separate the three color channels I_c, $c \in \{R, G, B\}$ of a color image I. Since a CFA consists of repeating patterns of 2 × 2 pixels as shown in Fig. 1(b) and we know that, for each pixel at the same coordinates of I, only one of the three color components is *physical* and the other two are *artificial*, so the second step is, for each channel I_c, we perform 2:1 down-sampling across both horizontal and vertical dimensions to get four sub-images, I_{ci}, $i \in \{1, 2, 3, 4\}$. A PRNU noise pattern, P_{ci}, is then extracted from each sub-images I_{ci}. Finally the PRNU noise pattern P_c of each channel is formed by combining the four sub-PRNU noise patterns P_{ci}, $i \in \{1, 2, 3, 4\}$. The advantage of the proposed method is that when the PRNU noise patterns of images taken by different cameras with different CFA, the dissimilarity would be enhanced when physical components are compared against artificial components, thus improving performance.

3   Experiments

Fig 3(a) shows a photo of 640 × 480 pixels captured by Olympus C730 and Fig 3(b) is a forged image with the can removed. Fig 3(c) is another forged image with an added can. We use the Haar wavelet and the Wiener filter [5] to perform low-pass filtering in the wavelet domain when extracting PRNU. Both the traditional PRNU [1 – 3] and the proposed DPRNU of the images are extracted and compared block by block as a window of 128 × 128 pixels is slid across the images in a 10-pixel-wide step. We use the commonly adopted True Positive (TP), True Negative (TN), False.

Positive (FP) and False Negative (FN) defined in Eq. (2) – (5) as metrics to evaluate the performance of the two types of PRNU noise patterns.

$$True\ Positive\ Rate\ (\textbf{TP}) = \frac{Number\ of\ True\ Positive}{Total\ Number\ of\ Positive\ Instances} \tag{2}$$

$$True\ Negative\ Rate(\textbf{TN}) = \frac{Number\ of\ True\ Negative}{Total\ Number\ of\ Negative\ Instances} \tag{3}$$

$$False\ Positive\ Rate\ (\textbf{FP}) = \frac{Number\ of\ False\ Positive}{Total\ Number\ of\ Positive\ Instances} \tag{4}$$

$$False\ Negative\ Rate\ (\textbf{FN}) = \frac{Number\ of\ False\ Negative}{Total\ Number\ of\ Negative\ Instances} \tag{5}$$

We use correlation between PRNU noise patterns as the similarity metrics. After the correlations between all pairs of PRNU blocks have been calculated, we deem a block with a PRNU correlation lower than α times of the standard deviation (STD) as forged. We can see from Eq. (2) – (5) that because the denominators are always fixed because they are "ground truth", when the value of α is changed, the numerators may change significantly, making these four metrics less reliable. Therefore, we propose another metrics called *Corrected Positive Rate* (CPR), to measure the fraction of True Positives of the total number of the *detected* Positive instances.

$$Corrected\ Positive\ Rate\ (\text{CPR}) = \frac{True\ Positive}{Number\ of\ Detected\ Positive\ Instances} \qquad (6)$$

When α is greater, less forged blocks will be detected because the threshold for a block to be deemed as forged is lower. That is to say that the detected positives are more likely to be true positives and the number of false reports would become lower. So from Eq. (6) we can see that the value of CPR at greater value of α would be more reliable. We use three different values of α, 1, 1.5 and 2, in our experiments. Table 1 shows the results associated with different values of α. The reader is reminded that according to Eq. (2) – (6), high values of TP, TN and CPR and low values of FP and FN suggest greater performance. We tabulate the performance metrics when the forged images of Fig. 3(b) and 3(c) are tested in Table 1 and 2, respectively. We can see from these two tables that, although for most cases, the proposed DPRNU outperforms the common PRNU in terms of the first 4 metrics (TP, TN, FP and FN), these four metrics do not always reveal the performance difference at different values of α because many differences are marginal. This situation conforms to our concern about the reliability of these four metrics. On the other hand, when α equals 2, the

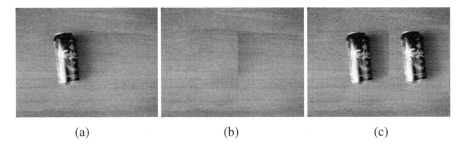

| (a) | (b) | (c) |

Fig. 3. Experimental images of forge detection (image size is 640 × 480). a) The original image, b) The image forged by the removing attacking, c) The image forged by the copy-pasted attacking.

Table 1. Experimental results when the forged image of Fig. 3(b) is tested

α	Noise pattern	TP	TN	FP	FN	**CPR**
2	PRNU	0.0077	0.9467	0.0533	0.9923	**0.0459**
	DPRNU	0.0908	0.9476	0.0524	0.9092	**0.3717**
1.5	PRNU	0.1701	0.8541	0.1459	0.8299	0.2848
	DPRNU	0.1944	0.8939	0.1061	0.8056	0.3848
1	PRNU	0.3529	0.7699	0.2301	0.6471	0.3437
	DPRNU	0.3657	0.7590	0.2410	0.6343	0.3413

Table 2. Experimental results when the forged image of Fig. 3(c) is tested

α	Noise Pattern	TP	TN	FP	FN	**CPR**
2	PRNU	0.0907	0.9433	0.0567	0.9093	**0.2211**
	DPRNU	0.1274	0.9716	0.0284	0.8726	**0.4436**
1.5	PRNU	0.2592	0.8750	0.1250	0.7408	0.2691
	DPRNU	0.2743	0.8574	0.1426	0.7257	0.2545
1	PRNU	0.5313	0.7831	0.2169	0.4687	0.3030
	DPRNU	0.4730	0.7007	0.2993	0.5270	0.2190

proposed metrics CPR (Eq. (6)) clearly indicates the superiority of our proposed DPRNU. However, when α is at lower levels (1 and 1.5), even CPR cannot always provide clear evidence about which types of PRNU is a better candidates. This conforms to our earlier statement that the value of CPR at greater value of α is more capable of providing reliable evaluation.

4 Conclusion

In this work we have briefly reviewed the use of PRNU noise pattern in source camera identification and integrity verification and the role of CFA in the image acquisition process of digital cameras. We then proposed a new way of extracting PRNU noise pattern, called Decomposed PRNU (DPRNU) by exploiting the difference between *physical* and *artificial* components. We also proposed a new performance metrics, Corrected Positive Rate (CPR) to evaluate the performance of the common PRNU and the proposed DPRNU. The experimental results presented in this work have shown the superiority of the proposed DPRNU.

References

1. Chen, M., Fridrich, J., Goljan, M., Lukas, J.: Determining Image Origin and Integrity Using Sensor Noise. IEEE Transactions on Information Security and Forensics 3(1), 74–90 (2008)
2. Chen, M., Fridrich, J., Goljan, M., Lukas, J.: Source Digital Camcorder Identification Using Sensor Photo Response Non-Uniformity. In: Proceedings of SPIE Electronic Imaging (2007)
3. Chen, M., Fridrich, J., Lukas, J., Goljan, M.: Imaging Sensor Noise as Digital X-Ray for Revealing Forgeries. In: Furon, T., Cayre, F., Doërr, G., Bas, P. (eds.) IH 2007. LNCS, vol. 4567, pp. 342–358. Springer, Heidelberg (2008)
4. Gunturk, B.K., Glotzbach, J., Altunbasak, Y., Schafer, R.W., Mersereau, R.M.: Demosaicking: Color Filter Array Interpolation. Signal Processing Magazine 22(1), 44–54 (2005)

5. Mihcak, M.K., Kozintsev, I., Ramchandran, K.: Spatially Adaptive Statistical Modeling of Wavelet Image Coefficients and its Application to Denoising. In: Proceedings of IEEE International Conference on Acoustics, Speech, and Signal Processing, vol. 6, pp. 3253–3256 (1999)
6. Popescu, A.C., Farid, H.: Exposing Digital Forgeries in Color Filter Array Interpolated Images. IEEE Transactions on Signal Processing 53(10), 3948–3959 (2005)
7. Swaminathan, A., Wu, M., Liu, K.J.R.: Non-Intrusive Component Forensics of Visual Sensors Using Output Images. IEEE Trans. on Information Forensics and Security (2007)

Detection of Block Artifacts for Digital Forensic Analysis

Chang-Tsun Li

Department of Computer Science
University of Warwick
Coventry CV4 7AL, UK
ctli@dcs.warwick.ac.uk

Abstract. Although the metadata, such as the header, of a piece of media carries useful information, the metadata may be tampered with for various purposes. It is therefore desirable in the context of forensic analysis that investigators are able to infer properties and information about a piece of media directly from its content without any reference to the metadata. The block size of the block operations that a piece of media has undergone can provide useful clue about the trustworthiness of the metadata and in turn reveals the integrity of the media. In this work, we proposed a novel block artifact detection method for inferring the block size of block-wise operations, such as JPEG compression, that has been applied to the media under investigation. Based on the assumption that block operation create disparities across block boundaries and those boundaries form straight lines, our method exploits the fact that intra-block variance tend to be less than inter-block variance and if most of the pixels along the same vertical line or horizontal line exhibit this relationship then the straight line is believed to be the block boundary.

Keywords: Digital forensics, block detection, computational forensics, block artifacts detection.

1 Introduction

Digital watermarking [2], as a means for authenticating multimedia contents and copyright protection, has attracted enormous efforts in the past decade. Albeit digital watermarking's promising potential, to make it work, a digital watermark has to be embedded into the host media in advance. However, the majority of digital media already produced and to be produced in the near future are not watermarked. This situation poses pressing forensic and security issues as the wide availability and the ease of use of multimedia processing software provide potential offenders convenient avenues for manipulating digital contents for malicious purposes. In response to the needs for analyzing multimedia contents in the context of digital forensics, methods of *non-intrusive forensic analysis* (sometimes called *passive forensic analysis*) of multimedia contents have been proposed in the past few years [3–7] and are expected to draw more attention in the future. As opposite to digital watermarking, which requires a digital watermark to be embedded for later authentication, non-intrusive forensic analysis infers forensic information and implications from the contents

M. Sorell (Ed.): e-Forensics 2009, LNICST 8, pp. 173–178, 2009.

without requiring extra information, such as digital watermark, to be embedded in advance.

Among many areas of non-intrusive forensic analysis, inferring the processing pathways a piece of media, such as image or video, has undergone is one where digital forensic investigators seek traces left by various of multimedia processing tools so as to piece together evidence to support their arguments. For example, without manipulating the content, an offender could modify the metadata / header of a JPEG compressed image to make it appear to be one that has never been compressed with JPEG standards in order to mislead the investigators [6]. In this scenario, because JPEG standards requires that an image be divided into blocks of 8 × 8 pixels before applying DCT to each block, a tool that can detect the trace of 8 × 8 block operation would be helpful in defeating the offender's claim that the image had never been JPEG compressed.

A number of block artifact detection and block operation detection techniques [1, 3, 4, 7, 8] have been proposed in the recent past. The methods reported in [1] and [4] assume that the media is compressed by known standards, such as JPEG and MPEG and attempt to detect block artifacts left by the block operations with fixed block size, e.g., 8 × 8 pixels in JPEG and 16 × 16 in MPEG. This assumption imposes an application limitation of the two methods. On the other hand, without assuming fixed block size, the methods presented in [7] and [8] rely on gradient detectors to pin-point the boundaries between blocks. However, gradient detectors are known to be highly sensitive to texture and linear features such as edges and, as a result, tend to yield false positives. In [3], a pair of cross-differential filters of 2 × 2 pixels is proposed in the hope of reducing the false responses by the linear features. However, in essence the filters are variants of gradient detectors; therefore the responses to them are still prone to the influence of linear features.

In Section 2 we will proposed a new scheme that exploits the fact that *intra-block* variances is expected to be less than *inter-block* variances without assuming the size of blocks and making use of gradient detectors. Experimental results are presented in Section 3.

2   Proposed Method

In the light of the limitations inherent in the methods that rely on gradient detectors to detect boundaries, we proposed in this section a *variance-oriented block artifact detector* (VOBAD). The idea underpinning our proposed VOBAD is that the variance within the blocks boundaries (i.e., *intra-block variance*) is expected to be less significant than the variance of the pixels along the opposite sides of boundaries, (i.e, *inter-block variance*). Therefore, we want the media to respond to the VOBAD positively when the VOBAD is placed right at a block boundary, indicating that the intra-block variance is less than the inter-block variance and negatively when the VOBAD is placed elsewhere, including the places where the linear features of the media appear. Fig. 1 illustrates a 4-pixel-wide VOBAD (oriented horizontally) for detecting vertical block boundaries, as well as another (oriented vertically) for detecting horizontal block boundaries. Each double-headed arrow represents the difference/variance between its two associated pixels. The bold solid lines in the figure represent block boundaries. The response, $r_h(i, j)$, of the horizontal VOBAD is defined as

$$r_h(i, j) = \begin{cases} 1, & \text{if } 2 \cdot |p(i,j) - p(i, j+1)| > \alpha \cdot (|p(i, j-1) - p(i,j)| + |p(i, j+1) - p(i, j+2)|) \\ 0, & \text{otherwise} \end{cases} \quad (1)$$

and the response, $r_v(i, j)$, of the vertical VOBAD is defined as

$$r_v(i, j) = \begin{cases} 1, & \text{if } 2 \cdot |p(i,j) - p(i+1, j)| > \alpha \cdot (|p(i-1, j) - p(i,j)| + |p(i+1, j) - p(i+2, j)|) \\ 0, & \text{otherwise} \end{cases}, \quad (2)$$

where $p(i, j)$ is the intensity at pixel (i, j) and α is greater than 1. $|p(i, j) - p(i, j+1)|$ of Eq. (1) is intended be the *inter block variance*, which correspond to the **thick** arrow in Fig. 1, while $|p(i, j-1) - p(i, j)|$ and $|p(i, j+1) - p(i, j+2)|$ are intended as *intra-block* variances, corresponding to the **thin** arrows. Eq. (2) is to be interpreted the same way. The reason the inter-block variance is multiplied by 2 is because there are two intra-block variances. According to Fig. 1, Eq. (1) and (2), we can see that we only want the horizontal VOBAD and the vertical VOBAD to return 1 when they are placed at

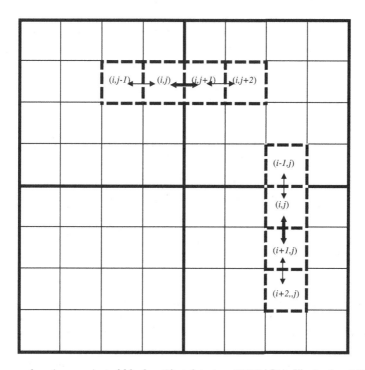

Fig. 1. Proposed *variance-oriented block artifact detectors* (VOBADs). The horizontally oriented 4-pixel-wide VOBAD is for detecting vertical block boundaries while the vertically oriented one is for detecting horizontal block boundaries. Each double-headed arrow represents the difference/variance between the two associated pixels. The bold solid lines represent block boundaries.

the *left*-hand side of and *above* a block boundary, respectively. For example, the horizontal VOBAD in Fig. 1is likely to return 1 because pixel (i, j) is at the left-hand side of the block boundary (i.e., the **thick** arrow straddles the *inter-block* boundary while each of the two **thin** arrows points to the pixels within the same block). But the vertical VOBAD is positioned below the block boundary, as a result, the **thick** arrow, corresponding to the inter-block variance in Eq. (2) points to two intra-block pixels while one of the two thin arrows point to two inter-block pixels. Therefore the response is expected to be 0, instead of 1. If the VOBAD is placed at other positions, the **thick** arrow would point to two intra-block pixels while one of the two thin arrows *may* straddle an inter-block boundary, thus likely to return 0 as well.

When the VOBADs are placed in textured areas or near/at linear features, if the thin arrows straddle inter-block boundaries and/or the thick arrows point to pixels with the same block, they would return 0. Fig. 2(b) and 2(c) show the maps of the responses of the image in Fig. 2(a) to the proposed horizontal and vertical VOBADs. The greater α of Eq. (1) and (2) is, the less noisy the response maps are. However, an α too greater than 1 is not feasible because for any processed media to be deemed acceptable in term of visual quality, the block operations should not result in noticeable difference between intra- and inter-block variances.

However, no matter what value is assigned to α of Eq. (1) and (2), it is inevitable that false responses will be picked up if the conditions match the ones in Eq. (1) and (2). Therefore after convolving the two VOBADs with the media, the next step is to pool the responses horizontally and vertically. Let us take an image of $I \times J$ pixels as an example, we pool the responses according to Eq. (3) and (4).

$$t_h(j) = \sum_{i=1}^{I} r_h(i, j) \qquad , j \in [1, J] \tag{3}$$

$$t_v(i) = \sum_{j=1}^{J} r_v(i, j) \qquad , i \in [1, I] \tag{4}$$

After pooling the responses, we identify n $(1 \geq n \geq J)$ vertical lines and m $(1 \geq m \geq I)$ horizontal lines with the highest t_h and t_v values, respectively, to get a *detection grid* like Fig. 2(d).

3   Experiments

Fig. 2 (a) shows a photo of 512×512 pixels compressed by Adobe Photoshop with JPEG standards at quality level 10 (highest quality level defined by Adobe Photoshop). Fig. 2(b) and (c) show the responses to the horizontal and vertical VOBADs, respectively. Note that to avoid extending the VOBADs beyond image borders we do not apply the VOBADs to the first and last two columns and rows of the images. We set parameter α of Eq. (1) and (2) to 1.5 in the experiment that yields Fig 2(b) and 2(c). Our other experiments suggest that the range [1.0, 2.0] is a reasonable choice. Fig. 2(d) shows the block detection grid after pooling responses vertically and horizontally. The n (=16) vertical lines and m (=16) horizontal lines in

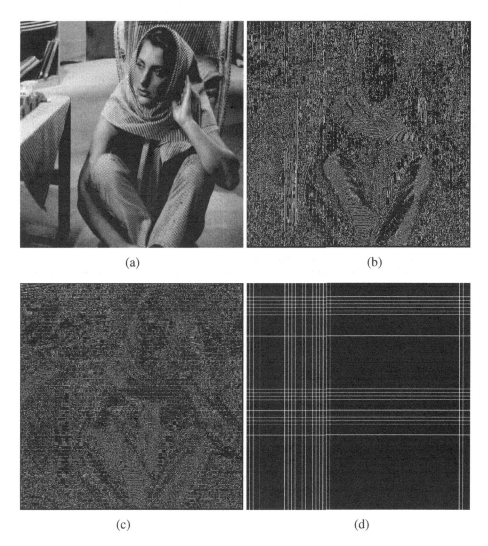

(a)   (b)

(c)   (d)

Fig. 2. Experimental results of block artifact detection (image size is 512 × 512). a) image compressed by Adobe Photoshop at quality level 10 , b) responses to horizontal VOBAD, c) responses to vertical VOBAD, d) block detection grid.

Fig. 2(d) with the highest *pooled* responses t_h and t_v values, respectively, clearly indicate that they correctly appear at the positions of multiples of 8. Although multiples of 8 are also multiples of 2 and 4, but if the correct block size were 2 (or 4), then some of the detected lines should have appeared at positions of multiples of 2, 6 10, 12, etc (or 4, 12, etc), which are not multiples of 8. Being unable to find lines appearing at those positions suggests that the image has undergone an 8 × 8 block operation, which conforms to JPEG standards.

4 Conclusions

In this work we have briefly reviewed a number of non-intrusive forensic methods for detecting block artifacts and pointed out their features as well as limitations. We observed that assuming fixed block size limits the applicability of the schemes while the use of gradient detectors is too sensitive to texture and linear features such as edges. In the light of the limitations inherent in the reviewed methods, we proposed a pair of *variance-oriented block artifact detectors* (VOBADs), which exploit the fact that intra-block variances are less than inter-block variances. The experimental results presented in this work have shown the efficacy of the proposed scheme.

References

1. Fan, Z., de Queiroz, R.: Identification of bitmap compression history: JPEG detection and quantizer estimation. IEEE Trans. on Image Processing 12(2), 230–235 (2003)
2. Li, C.-T., Li, Y., Wei, C.-H.: Protection of digital mammograms on PACSs using data hiding techniques. International Journal of Digital Crime and Forensics 1(1), 75–88 (2009)
3. Luo, W.Q., Huang, J., Qiu, G.: A novel method for block size forensics based on morphological operations. In: International Workshop on Digital Watermarking (2008)
4. Luo, W.Q., Wu, M., Huang, J.W.: MPEG recompression detection based on block artifacts. In: SPIE Electronic Imaging, Security, Steganography, and Watermarking of Multimedia Contents, vol. 6819 (2008)
5. Sorell, M.: Unexpected Artifacts in a Digital Photograph. International Journal of Digital Crime and Forensics 1(1), 45–58 (2009)
6. Sorell, M.: Digital camera source identification through JPEG quantization. In: Li, C.-T. (ed.) Multimedia Forensics and Security, IGI Global, pp. 291–313 (2008)
7. Tjoa, S., Lin, W., Zhao, H., Liu, K.: Block size forensic analysis in digital images. In: IEEE International Conference on Acoustics, Speech and Signal Processing, vol. 1, pp. I-633–I-636 (2007)
8. Wang, Z., Bovik, A., Evan, B.: Blind measurement of blocking artifacts in images. In: IEEE International Conference on Image Processing, vol. 3, pp. 981–984 (2000)

Vocal Forgery in Forensic Sciences

Patrick Perrot[1,2], Mathieu Morel[2], Joseph Razik[2], and Gérard Chollet[2]

[1] Institut de Recherche Criminelle de la Gendarmerie Nationale,
Rosny sous Bois 93110 France
patrick.perrot@gendarmerie.defense.gouv.fr
[2] CNRS-LTCI-Telecom-ParisTech, 37-39 rue Darreau, 75014 Paris France
{chollet,razik,morel}@telecom-paristech.fr

Abstract. This article describes techniques of vocal forgery able to affect automatic speaker recognition system in a forensic context. Vocal forgery covers two main aspects: voice transformation and voice conversion. Concerning voice transformation, this article proposes an automatic analysis of four specific disguised voices in order to detect the forgery and, for voice conversion, different ways to automatically imitate a target voice. Vocal forgery appears as a real and relevant question for forensic expertise. In most cases, criminals who make a terrorist claim or a miscellaneous call, disguise their voices to hide their identity or to take the identity of another person. Disguise is considered in this paper as a deliberate action of the speaker who wants to conceal or falsify his identity. Different techniques exist to transform one's own voice. Some are sophisticated as software manipulation, some others are simpler as using an handkerchief over the mouth. In voice transformation, the presented work is dedicated to the study of disguise used in the most common cases. In voice conversion, different techniques will be presented, compared, and applied on an original example of the French President voice.

Keywords: disguised voices, voice conversion, SVM classifier, identification.

One of the most important issue in the area of forensic speaker recognition is the vocal forgery. How is it possible to detect or to compensate it? What is the influence of disguise on automatic speaker recognition systems? This article tries to give an answer to these questions and raises the question of automatic imitation.

1 Vocal Forgery and Automatic Speaker Recognition in Forensic Sciences

To falsify one's identity or hide it, different possibilities are offered to criminals. They can choose between a transformation of their voice by using simple means like an handkerchief in front of the mouth or speaking with a higher voice, or by using a sophisticated method to imitate the voice of another person in order to compromise him/her.

M. Sorell (Ed.): e-Forensics 2009, LNICST 8, pp. 179–185, 2009.

1.1   Voice Transformation as Forgery

The possibilities for criminals to transform their voice are very numerous. The literature describes different experiments conducted to detect a specific disguise according to a phonetic approach [9][12]. Software manipulation is a very relevant mean to disturb significantly a forensic recognition. The speech is generally dramatically altered. Many parameters can be affected: fundamental frequency, formants, rhythm.

Another disguise which is especially efficient is the whispered voice. This kind of method eliminates the voiced part, the information about fundamental frequency but also alters the intensity. The main drawback for criminals, who use such a disguise, is the difficulty to deliver an audible and intelligible message. Some other techniques are presented in [15][13].

What is interesting to notice is that most general criminals have just used one form of disguise. Masthoff [12]demonstrates that listeners have many difficulties when more than one disguise is used. Impact of disguise in automatic speaker recognition system is presented in [10].

Our work deals with the most common disguises used according to answer of nearly 100 persons to a questionnaire and to the experience of the forensic research institute of the French Gendarmerie. The chosen disguises are, a hand over the mouth,pinched nostrils, high pitch voice, low pitch voice. The impact of these different disguises on speaker recognition performance is presented in [14]. Disguise is a real problem for forensic expert. A preliminary step which consists in detecting if the voice is disguised or not, could be a very useful tool, in order to avoid confusion. The performance of SVM classification is presented in section 2.1 under neutral and degraded conditions.

1.2   Voice Conversion as Forgery

Voice conversion, which consists in producing a sound pronounced by a source speaker to sound like a target speaker, appears as a good way to achieve forgery [11]. A simple way is an imitation of the target by a professional impersonator. This technique of conversion presents the main drawbacks to be difficult to reproduce and thus, is not a universal method. A good mean to compensate this question is to perform an automatic conversion. Different techniques are proposed in the literature. This section describes the main algorithms developed and presents a comparison of two methods. Let us consider a sequence of a spectral vectors pronounced by the source speaker:

$$X = [x1, x2, \ldots, xn] . \tag{1}$$

and a sequence corresponding to the pronunciation of the same utterance by the target speaker:

$$Y = [y1, y2, \ldots, yn] . \tag{2}$$

Voice conversion is based on the calculation of a conversion function F that minimizes the mean squared error:

$$\varepsilon_{mse} = E\left|\|Y - F(X)\|^2\right| . \tag{3}$$

where E is the expectation.

To calculate the conversion function, most representative and relevant techniques, developed in the past decades, are based on Gaussian Mixture Models and related techniques [3][4][2]. Automatic voice conversion is divided into two main steps: training and conversion. First, two speech recordings of the same utterance (one for the source and one for the target) are time aligned by DTW (Dynamic Time Warping), then both signals are analyzed asynchronously by HNM (Harmonic plus Noise Model) as proposed in [3]. MFCC (Mel Frequency Cepstral Coefficient) are extracted from the HNM parameters. The mapping between these two aligned sets of MFCC features (source and target) is based on Gaussian Mixture Models (GMM). The joint density function $P(X,Y)$ as proposed in [4] is estimated with a GMM, i.e. with a probability distribution given by:

$$P(z) = \sum_{q=1}^{Q} \alpha_q \mathcal{N}_q(z, \mu_q, \Sigma_q) . \tag{4}$$

where $z = [x, y]$ is the joint spectral vector, Q the number of gaussians and α_q, μ_q, and $\sum_q$ respectively the weight, the mean, and the covariance matrix of the qth gaussian component. The iterative algorithm EM (Expectation Maximization) is used to estimate the parameters of the GMM on all the joint spectral vectors from the training set. Following the training step the transformation step consists in applying this function to a speech (different from the training data set) of the source. HNM analysis is performed on the speech source and MFCC are extracted from the voiced frames. Then, for each spectral vector x of the source, the corresponding vector of the target y is predicted by finding the expected value of y given x in the joint probability.

Another voice conversion technique based on a client dictionary is possible and presented in [14]. This method consists in using a dictionary of a target voice and replacing speech segments of the source voice by their counterpart of the target voice. It is based on the ALISP (Automatic Language Independent Speech Processing) technique. The principle of ALISP is to encode speech by recognition and synthesis in terms of basic acoustic units that can be derived by an automatic analysis of the signal.

Firstly, a collection of speech segments is constituted by segmenting a set of training sentences, all pronounced by the target client voice. This step is performed using the temporal decomposition algorithm [1] on MFCC speech features. Segments resulting from temporal decomposition are then organized by vector quantization into 64 different classes. The training data is thus automatically labelled, using symbols that correspond to the above classes. The result of the ALISP training is an inventory of client speech segments, divided into 64 classes according to a codebook of 64 symbols. All the speech segments contained in our inventory are represented by their Harmonic plus Noise Model (HNM) parameters. This will allow a smooth concatenative synthesis of new sentences using the stored segments.

The second part of our processing consists in encoding the impostor's voice using the ALISP codebook, and then in performing decoding using synthetic units taken from the segment inventory obtained from client's voice. The different results and the impact of such a conversion on an automatic speaker recognition system is presented in [14]. What is observed is a significant decrease of the performance, that is to say that the target is recognized instead of the source speaker.

2 Experiments and Results

2.1 Identification of Disguised Voices Based on a SVM Classifier

The technique used in this part is a classifier based on VQ (vector quantization) and SVM (support vector machine) dedicated to the identification of disguised voices. SVM is a very efficient discriminant tool in pattern recognition. This method proposes a decision function that only uses a subset of a training database called support vectors. Let us consider a training set

$$A = (x_1, y_1), ...(x_m, y_m) . \tag{5}$$

composed by m couples (attribute vectors and labels) with $x_i \in \Re^n$ and $y_i \in \{-1, +1\}$. SVM algorithm consists in projecting x_i vectors in a new space T from a non linear function:

$$\phi : \Re^n \to T . \tag{6}$$

The second point is to find out the optimal boundary or hyperplane (w, b) of the two class in T. The y class of a new sample x is defined by:

$$y = sign(w.\phi(x) + b) . \tag{7}$$

The optimal hyperplane is the one which maximizes the distance between itself and the closest label vectors. The principle to use a vector quantization prior to the application of a SVM classification is to increase the robustness of noise by building some centroids representative of the sample distribution. The experiment is realized on a training set of 40 people in each disguise and the test is performed on 20 speakers. The training set consists in a reading of the phonetic balanced text: the north wind and the sun, and the test corpus is composed of 10 sentences. Results are presented on DET curves (plotting false acceptance rate against false rejection rate). Fig 1 represents the identification of the four chosen disguises and the normal voice in neutral conditions that is to say without specific noise.

In order to be more realistic, the experiment is carried out by adding different noises on the test set: white and pink noise (Fig 2 and 3) and babble noise (Fig 4). The idea is to measure the impact of degraded conditions on the performance of the classifier.

Noisy conditions affect significantly the results of classification. That is unfortunately not very surprising because data from normal voice and smooth disguised voices are very linked. We notice that voices with a low pitch seem to be the most difficult to discriminate (low pitch voice and hand over the mouth).

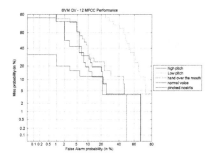

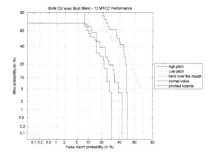

Fig. 1. Neutral conditions   **Fig. 2.** Degraded conditions: white noise

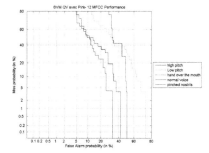

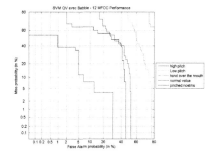

Fig. 3. Degraded conditions: pink noise **Fig. 4.** Degraded conditions: babble noise

2.2   Comparison of Voice Conversion Technique as Forgery

Two different methods of voice conversion have been proposed in section 1.2. A comparison of both methods is performed to measure the level of the conversion quality. The experiment has been based on the voice of the current French President as target speaker in order to be close to a realistic scenario. A 40 minutes speech of the French president was collected and 70 sentences extracted from this discourse are pronounced by a male (the source speaker), for conversion based on GMM in the training task.

A preliminary step consists in aligning both speech segments by DTW and then calculating the conversion function as described in section 1.2. In the case of the conversion based on ALISP, 35 minutes of the discourse have been used to build the dictionary of the target voice. The test has been performed on 10 sentences, different from those of the training set.

Two different comparison methods have been done. The first one is a calculation of the spectral distortion measure between the converted and the target speech (Table 1). After the temporal alignment step of the both signals the distance between MFCC's features is:

$$d = \sum_{t=0}^{n} \sum_{k=1}^{20} (c_k^1(t) - c_k^2(t))^2 \ . \tag{8}$$

where $c_k^1(t)$ and $c_k^2(t)$ are the kth MFCC's coefficient at time t of the converted and the target signal. This measure is normalized by the initial distortion between the source and the target speaker to lie between 0 and 1. 0 means that the converted speech is similar to the target speech and 1 means that the conversion has no effect.

Table 1. Comparison of conversion system

conversion system	GMM	ALISP
spectral distortion	0.77	0.78

The second technique to evaluate the level of the conversion is based on the listening of the result. This kind of technique is subjective and a significant issue is the quality of the speech after conversion. This one is not enough satisfying to allow to recognize significantly the target or the client. A listening of the conversion result will be proposed.

3   Conclusion

Different perspectives of vocal forgery have been presented in this paper. This question appears as a real issue for forensic examination where the risk of confusion between two speakers could have great consequences. Disguised voices considered as a transformation of the voice by simple means alter significantly the performance of automatic speaker recognition. A preliminary detection of disguise before an examination of speaker recognition could be very useful in order to avoid confusion. The presented classification provides interesting results, even if under degraded conditions, the discrimination between disguises is more difficult, especially in the case of low pitch voices. Voice conversion also appears to be an interesting way for impostors to take the voice of a specific person. A comparison of two conversion methods is presented and the results are efficient. This kind of forgery does alter the performance of speaker recognition. An example using the voice of the French president is presented and reveals the threat of such a technique in forensic or terrorism cases.

References

1. Bimbot, F., Chollet, G., Deleglise, P., Montacie, C.: Temporal decomposition and acoustic-phonetic decoding of speech. In: ICASSP, pp. 445–448 (1998)
2. Duxans, H., Bonafonte, A.: Estimation of GMM in voice conversion including unaligned data. In: EUROSPEECH, pp. 861–864 (2003)
3. Stylianou, Y., Cappe, O.: Statistical methods for voice quality transformation. In: EUROSPEECH, pp. 447–450 (1995)
4. Kain, A., Maccon, M.W.: Spectral voice conversion for text to speech synthesis. In: ICASSP, pp. 285–288 (1998)

5. Perrot, P., Aversano, G., Blouet, R., Charbit, M., Chollet, G.: Voice forgery using ALISP: indexation in a client memory. In: ICASSP, pp. 17–20 (2005)
6. Tsuge, S., Shishibori, M., Kita, K., Ren, F., Kuroiwa, S.: Study of Intra-Speakers Speech Variability Over Long and Short Time Periods for Speech Recognition. In: ICASSP (2006)
7. Ortega-Garcia, J., Cruz-Llanas, S., Gonzalez-Rodriguez, J.: Speech variability in automatic speaker recognition systems for forensic purposes In: IEEE 33rd Annual International Carnahan Conference (1999)
8. Benzeghiba, M., De Mori, R., Deroo, O., Dupont, S., Erbes, T., Jouvet, D., Fissore, L., Laface, P., Mertins, A., Ris, C., Rose, R., Tyagi, V., Wellekens, C.: Automatic speech recognition and speech variability: A review. Speech Communication 49(10-11), 763–786 (2007)
9. Kunzel, H.J.: Effect of voice disguise on fundamental frequency. Forensic Linguistics, vol. 7 (2000)
10. Kunzel, H., Gonzalez-Rodriguez, J., Ortega-Garcia, J.: Effect of voice disguise on the performance of a forensic automatic speaker recognition system. In: Odyssey (ed.), pp. 153–156 (2004)
11. Genoud, D., Chollet, G.: Voice transformations: Some tools for the imposture of speaker verification systems. Advances in Phonetics. Franz Steiner Verlag (1999)
12. Masthoff, H.: A report on voice disguise experiment. Forensic Linguistics, vol. 3 (1996)
13. Orchard, T., Yarmey, A.: The effect of whispers, voice sample duration, and voice distinctiveness on criminal Speaker Identification. Applied Cognitive Psychology vo 9(3), 249–260 (1995)
14. Perrot, P., Chollet, G.: The question of disguised voices. In: Acoustics 2008, Paris (2008)
15. Reich, A.R., Duke, J.E.: Effect of selective vocal disguise upon speaker identification by listening. Journal of Acoustical Society of America 66, 1023–1028 (1979)

Complying across Continents: At the Intersection of Litigation Rights and Privacy Rights

Milton H. Luoma[1] and Vicki M. Luoma[2]

[1] Information and Computer Sciences
Metropolitan State University
700 East 7th Street
St. Paul, Minnesota USA 55106-0500
Tel.: 651 793-1481; Fax: 651 793-1246
Milt.Luoma@metrostate.edu
[2] Accounting and Business Law
Minnesota State University
145 Morris Hall
Minnesota State University
Mankato, Minnesota USA 56001
Tel.: 507 389-1916; Fax: 507 389-5497
Vicki.Luoma@mnsu.edu

Abstract. This paper addresses the issues and challenges facing multinational corporations when they become involved in litigation that crosses international borders. The conflict of litigation discovery rights and individual privacy rights in different international jurisdictions can present a very challenging situation for litigants. This paper addresses the conflict inherent between litigation discovery rights versus individual privacy rights and how different nations deal with this conflict. The authors offer several pre-litigation recommendations for those corporations that anticipate the possibility of litigation involving parties in more than one international jurisdiction.

Keywords: multinational litigation, electronic discovery, privacy rights, litigation rights.

Complying with legal restrictions on litigation rights and privacy rights in different international jurisdictions has proven to be one of the most difficult challenges facing multinational corporations. At the heart of this challenge are the different priorities that different nations place upon an individual's right to litigate disputes and an individual's right to privacy. Those countries that place a higher priority on the rights of individuals to seek full satisfaction of their claims against other parties than they do upon the right of privacy tend to have much more liberal discovery rights in the litigation process than do countries that place a higher priority on the rights of individuals to retain their privacy. Those countries that value privacy rights over litigation discovery rights tend to restrict and severely limit the ability of parties to litigation to seek information that may be essential to prosecuting their claims in court.

M. Sorell (Ed.): e-Forensics 2009, LNICST 8, pp. 186–194, 2009.
© ICST Institute for Computer Sciences, Social Informatics and Telecommunications Engineering 2009

It is not difficult to imagine that if one were to ask any citizen of any country whether he or she would want full satisfaction of his or her claims against another party and whether he or she would want complete privacy in his or her dealings, both questions would receive a resounding affirmative response. Unfortunately, the nature of the issues precludes anyone from having a full measure of both of these rights simultaneously. This dichotomy of choices presents extremely difficult choices for multinational corporations that try to operate in diverse cultures when they become involved in litigation. This paper addresses the issues and challenges facing multinational corporations when they become involved in litigation that crosses international borders. A review of privacy rights and litigation rights both within and outside the United States will provide some important background and insights into the nature of the problem as it affects U.S. multinationals. One proposed solution to this problem, namely The Hague Convention, will be reviewed in light of Societe Nationale v. District Court, 482 U.S. 522 (1987). The authors conclude by offering some suggestions for multinationals for surviving the challenges presented by litigation that extends beyond the borders of one country.

1 Litigation Discovery Rights in the United States

In the United States electronic discovery cases and rules are changing, but one thing is consistent in U.S. discovery rules: If something exists, it is discoverable if the information to be obtained might lead to something relevant. This approach to litigation discovery places the highest priority on having disputes fully litigated in the light of all possible facts that might have a bearing on the issues in controversy.

The U.S. Federal Rules of Civil Procedure Rule 26 allow "any matter not privileged that is relevant to the claim or defense of any party"[1] to be discoverable. The rule goes on to explain that "relevant information need not be admissible at trial if the discovery appears reasonably calculated to lead to the discovery of appears reasonably calculated to lead to the discovery of admissible evidence."[2] Such a rule is not only abhorrent to privacy minded countries but illegal in these countries as well. In the countries that guard personal privacy, litigants can obtain information only if they know exactly what they want, where it is located, how it is relevant. Only then might it be ordered produced.

United States discovery allows almost any information requested to be produced. When these early rules and traditions were established, no one anticipated a paperless society in which not only could the document be requested, but the electronic metadata associated with that document, digital artifacts, fragments and multi-versions of data could be requested as well. In addition, these digital electronic footprints are left not only on computer hard drives, but on digital telephones, cell phones, PDAs, copy machines and Internet history files. In the United States information stored on personal computers, phones or PDAs are not considered private if anything relevant to the lawsuit could be stored there. Further, employees who use home electronic equipment for work purposes can have those devices subject to discovery procedures.

---

[1] Federal Rules of Civil Procedure, Rule 26.
[2] Id.

2 Litigation Discovery Rights Outside the United States

Litigation discovery rights outside the United States are generally limited by the laws and customs of countries that value privacy rights over litigation discovery rights. Some countries more severely limit discovery rights than others. In all cases, a country's emphasis on personal privacy rights is the determining factor in the level of restriction of litigation discovery rights. In light of this assertion, it is useful to briefly review the differences in various countries' privacy legislation.

In Europe, countries belonging to the European Union developed the European Union Privacy Directive, which is valid in 25 countries. As part of these directives personal data (data which identifies or concerns a specific named person) cannot be transmitted outside the European economic area (EU nations, plus Iceland, Norway and Lichtenstein) to a country which does not provide by national law protection commensurate with the EU. Presently, only two countries meet these standards outside the EU, namely, Canada and Argentina. These protective directives are not perfect since many of the EU countries interpret them differently.

The EU data directive[3] provides that all computer processed personal data must allow the individual the absolute right to access data concerning themselves, must prove that individuals have freely given consent, the use of the data must be lawful and fair, adequate, relevant and accurate and may be used only as long as necessary and have adequate security. Further discovery of any personal data will be allowed only if the party seeking the information can prove that the document exists and is essential to the litigation.[4] Each member country is then required to adopt laws that comply with the directive and all EU countries have passed these laws.[5] As a result each countries interpretation is somewhat different.

The directives state that personal data is not only information related to a particular person but all information that is identifiable. There are some exceptions including processing all data that is necessary for litigation.[6] However the EU countries have consistently decided that the interests of company subsidiaries are not sufficient legal nexus to be considered an exception under this provision.[7]

Most civil code countries have no custom or laws concerning formal discovery and rarely allow disclosure of evidence that is known to be relevant.[8] In addition, some countries such as France have criminal statutes known as the French Blocking Statute if information is provided that has not met these requirements. Even the common law countries of Australia and United Kingdom have blocking statutes. The Australian Commonwealth Attorney General may prohibit compliance with foreign discovery orders and judgments in foreign antitrust proceedings when Australian

---

[3] Directive 95/46/EC.
[4] Id.
[5] Id.
[6] Council Directive 95/46/EC, art. 2(b), O.J. (L281).
[7] See European Commission, Justice and Home Affairs -- Data Protection, Adequacy of Protection of Personal Data in Third Countries, at http://ec.europa.eu/justice_home/fsj/privacy/thridcountries/ index_en.htm
[8] UK Data Protection Act of 1998, 1998 Chapter 29, Schedule 4(5)(a).

sovereignty is infringed or where the foreign court determines Australia is the correct jurisdiction.[9]

In the defining U.S. case a French bank, Société Générale, was unwilling to examine email of their trader Jérôme Kerviel. Even though Kerviel's actions were about to destroy the company, they were still afraid of the French privacy laws.[10] The defendant sought relief through the Hague convention but the plaintiff refused and the court agreed. The court found that even though the United States had signed The Hague convention participation was voluntary and not mandatory on litigants.

In another case the U.S. courts held that the U.S. Federal Rules should apply even though the Italian litigants argued that to provide the information would be violating Italian laws.[11] In Enron v. J.P. Morgan Securities Inc.,[12] the U.S. Bankruptcy Court held that even though providing the information would be in conflict with the French Blocking Statute the party still had to provide the information requested under U.S. discovery requests. One problem has been that the French government consistently did not actually find anyone guilty under the French Blocking Statute until recently, and accordingly, U.S. courts were not taking the threat seriously. However, in a recent case a French lawyer was held criminally responsible under the statute.[13]

3   Litigation Discovery Rights Versus Privacy Rights

The main reason for this difference in litigation discovery practices is the difference in various countries' views of personal privacy. Privacy has never been a guarantee in the United States Constitution, so privacy rights have developed in a sporadic and unsystematic manner. There is no one comprehensive privacy law in the United States, but rather, privacy law in the United States can be characterized as a myriad of cases, statutes, administrative rules that rule on component of privacy. U.S. privacy laws are general and decentralized. To determine the privacy law in the United States one must examine the Federal Trade Commission rules, a variety of federal regulations, various individual state consumer and fraud acts and some sector specific acts such as the FERPA[14], Gramm Leach Bliley Act[15], HIPAA[16] and others.

---

[9] Foreign Proceedings (Excess of Jurisdiction) Act 1984 No. 3, 1984 (Mar. 21, 2004), *available at* http://www.comlaw.gov.au/comlaw/management.nsf/lookupindexpagesbyid/IP200403254? OpenDocumet Foreign Proceedings (excess of Jurisdiction) Act 1984, s. 6.

[10] London Guardian September 2007 Page 1.

[11] Hagenbuch v. 3B6 Sistemi Elettronici Industriali S.R.L., 2005 U.S. Dist. LEXIS 20049, at *14 (N.D. Ill. Sept. 12, 2005).

[12] Enron v. J.P. Morgan Secur. Inc., No. 01-16034 (Bankr. S.D.N.Y. July 18, 2007).

[13] Commission Nationale de L'informatique et des Libertés, Délibération n°2006-281 du 14 décembre 2006 sanctionnant la société Tyco Healthcare France.

[14] The Family Educational Rights and Privacy Act (FERPA) (20 U.S.C. § 1232g; 34 CFR Part 99) is a Federal law that protects the privacy of student education records.

[15] Financial Modernization Act of 1999, also known as the "Gramm-Leach-Bliley Act" or GLB Act, provides protection of consumers' personal financial information held by financial institutions.

[16] Health Insurance Portability and Accountability Act (HIPAA) enacted in 1996 to address the security and privacy of health data.

In the U.S. electronic data was everywhere before anyone thought of the implications of this free flowing information. No one foresaw hackers, identity thieves, phishers or pharmers. Once the problems surfaced there were too many well established institutions with vested interests and strong lobbyists who prevented any possibility of stopping the information from continuing to flow. Lobbyists[17] are individuals who are paid by special interest groups to make direct contact with members of Congress to influence their views.

A further reason for different rules is countries' views on the collection of information. In the United States discovery is handled entirely by the litigants and outside of the courts involvement unless a conflict occurs. In fact, a litigant "must, without awaiting a discovery request, provide to the other parties... a description by category and location — of all documents, electronically stored information, and tangible things that the disclosing party has in its possession, custody, or control and may use to support its claims or defenses..."[18] In addition, under U.S. Federal Rules even non-parties can be compelled to produce documents to a litigation.[19] In most civil law nations gathering information is a judicial function. The civil law system of courts is based on inquisition rather than the common law adversarial system.[20] The judge normally questions the witnesses and makes a summary of the information. The United States system of discovery is unlike most other common law countries.

The problem arises for multinational corporations when they are involved in litigation that involves the United States and a country with strict privacy and limited discovery laws. If a litigant fails to provide information requested in a USA lawsuit, sanctions can be ordered. These sanctions can be anything from adverse inference instructions, fines, and default judgments. On the other hand providing the information could result in criminal and civil consequences if it involves countries that have laws against providing the information. As a result international cases are often commenced in the United States because of the more liberal discovery laws and larger judgments.

4 The Hague Convention

Some felt The Hague convention on "The taking of evidence abroad in Civil and Commercial Matters" was going to resolve this international legal conflict. The United States, France and 15 other countries agreed to The Hague Evidence Convention. This convention has procedures in which one country can request evidence located in another country. Despite the demand in international litigation, United States courts rarely grant a request to invoke The Hague Convention in litigation. In the leading case of Societe Nationale v. District Court the plaintiffs, the pilot and passenger in a Rallye plane manufactured by the defendants, sued for personal injuries resulting from the crash of an aircraft built by two French

---

[17] Lobbying Disclosure Act (2 U.S.C. § 1601–1612).

[18] Federal Rules of Civil Procedure Rule 26.

[19] Federal Rules of Civil Procedure Rule 45.

[20] Council Directive 95/46/EC, art. 2(b), O.J. (L281) See European Commission, Justice and Home Affairs -- Data Protection, Status of Implementation of Directive 95/46/EC.

corporations. The French corporations submitted answers to the complaint without challenging the jurisdiction of Iowa. Initial discovery was conducted under the Federal Rules of Civil Procedure without objection. Then, when the plaintiffs served additional discovery requests that the defendants claimed would violate French penal laws, the defendants filed for a protective order. The defendants argued that The Hague convention should be followed since the defendants were French. They further argued that the information requested was held in France and so the discovery requested was inappropriate under French law. The Republic of France weighed in on the litigation and stated, "The Hague Convention is the exclusive means of discovery in transnational litigation among the Convention's signatories unless the sovereign on whose territory discovery is to occur chooses otherwise."[21] According to Article 2 of the French Blocking Statute the defendants could attempt to secure a waiver from the French government.[22] In this case there was no indication that the defendants attempted to see the waiver nor is it likely the French government would have consented. The trial magistrate found that he was performing a balancing act between protecting citizens of the United States from harmful foreign products against France's interest in protecting its citizens from "intrusive foreign discovery procedures." When the district court denied the motion on the grounds that when the district court has jurisdiction over a foreign litigant, the Convention does not apply even though the information is physically located in a foreign country.[23] The defendants appealed and argued that the United States had agreed to The Hague Convention. The appellate court held that The Hague Convention does not provide exclusive or mandatory procedures for obtaining documents and information located in a foreign country. The court went on to find that The Hague Convention's plain language and the history of the United States ratification that it was only intended to be an optional procedure.[24] The case was then appealed to the United States Supreme Court.

The Supreme Court concluded that to take the interpretation of the defendants would mean the U.S. was giving up regulation of its courts to the Convention, which would be a serious interference with the jurisdiction of the United States courts. Further, if Congress had meant to give up control of multinational litigation, it would have been clearly stated in the agreement. The Supreme Court found that the American courts should "...take care to demonstrate due respect for any special problem confronted by the foreign litigant on account of its nationality or location of its operations, and for any sovereign interest expressed by a foreign state."[25] However, the Supreme Court confirmed the lower court's findings that the denied the defendants' request for protective orders. The Supreme Court disagrees with the appellate court's finding that The Hague Convention was not appropriate for this litigation. Instead, the Supreme Court found that litigants could use The Hague Convention if they chose to but were not required to do so. As a result of this decision, U.S. courts simply do not refer cases to The Hague Convention.

---

[21] Id.

[22] French Blocking Statue, Section 2.

[23] Id.

[24] 482U.S.529-540.

[25] Id.

5 Recommendations

The authors recommend the following pre-litigation practices:

- Multinational corporations should obtain consent for both the processing and the transfer of personal data. However, this has limited effect since the EU directives require that an individual must have the right to withdraw their consent at anytime.
- Multinational corporations should include clauses in their contracts that require agreement to an alternate dispute resolution process or agree to submit a dispute to The Hague Convention.
- Corporations attempting to acquire interests in foreign corporations or that are involved in cross border outsourcing should review possible legal conflicts before making decisions to acquire or use a particular outsourcing vendor corporation. The acquiring company must determine the organizational litigation risk factor.
- All employees must be educated on both local and international compliance regulations regarding electronic discovery.
- U.S. litigants requesting information must provide state-of-the-art security in the collection of personal data and its transmission.
- Litigants involved in multinational litigation must limit the requested personal data to information that is absolutely essential to the litigation. A litigant might look at the Third Restatement of Foreign Relations Law, which states that before deciding if information is needed a litigant should do a balancing test – how important are the documents, how specific is the request, where did the document originate, what are alternate means to secure information, and what is the importance of the competing governmental interests? [26] Countries with blocking statutes must also release information that is essential to litigation so long as transmission is secure. Along with accepting the benefits from the multi-national corporations some of the burdens must be accepted. These countries must also establish safe harbors for individuals or companies that have no choice but to be in conflict with some countries law.
- U.S. litigants must comply with cross-border data transfer laws to protect personal data. On the other hand, multi-national corporations outside the U.S. need to be as vigilant in retention and deletion of data as U.S. law requires.
- Litigants should seek discovery through the host venue country's court. The problem is that the process can be extremely time intensive. Balancing the requirements of two countries' litigation timetables can be difficult. Courts in either jurisdiction must be willing to cooperate with one another. This discovery request should be a priority since it affects the courts in other countries.

---

[26] Restatement Third, Restatement of the Foreign Relations Law of the United States by The American Institute The American Journal of Comparative Law, Vol. 39, No. 1 (Winter, 1991), pp. 207-213.

- U.S. courts need to review foreign statutes and make every effort accommodate litigants that are under threat of criminal statutes. Corporations need to demonstrate efforts in complying with law and show that actions are taken in good faith.
- Legal representatives and corporate leaders from around the world need to convene at conferences in attempt to solve the problems of conflicting electronic discovery rules and regulations. The Sedona conferences have started this process of meeting and recognizing areas of disagreement.
- Corporations must appoint a technology counsel and establish litigation teams long before litigation occurs. In a recent survey, 67% of large companies (defined as with more than 200 employees) have been involved in litigation in which electronic discovery was requested. Establishing this team would determine the legal requirements of each jurisdiction and the legal penalties for complying or not complying.
- Multinational companies must develop a record-retention policy and schedule based one the top five business drivers of compliance, privacy, litigation readiness, end-user needs and cost. Multinational companies must address country specific requirements on an exceptions basis. Establish a plan that limits access to personally identifiable information and secure the privacy data. Multinational companies must conduct periodic audits to verify compliance and automate as much as possible.
- Companies must review regulations in all possible jurisdictions and prepare for potential litigation. Preparation is important and compliance with as many jurisdictions as possible is essential for preparation. Companies must set up a strategic plan in case of litigation. Multinational corporations may want to keep duplicate sets of data in various locations.

6 Conclusions

There are no easy answers to the problem posed by conflicting electronic discovery and personal privacy laws crossing international borders. At the present time, U.S. courts will continue to put litigants in the precarious positions of violating EU directives and worldwide blocking statutes. Countries with blocking statutes have begun prosecuting violators of their blocking statutes. Multinational companies are left in the middle of these conflicting rules and laws. The American system plays havoc with individual privacy rights, but it provides the best opportunity for a party to prove its case. The problems with international data collection are just beginning to surface and action should be taken to deal with these issues preemptively. Countries vary on retention regulations that affect the ability of litigants to collect and preserve relevant material. It is unlikely either side of the issue will change its mind on what is more important – litigation discovery rights or individual privacy rights – but a spirit of compromise or consideration must prevail with disputes not decided on a parochial basis.

There are ethical issues involved in enforcing one nation's laws over another's with important implications and the other consequences. The present system simply is not working well. Nations and their litigation and privacy policies do not exist in isolation. The nations of the world are too interdependent for any single one to assert supremacy of its particular litigation point of view, customs or traditions. This can happen only if all countries – regardless of whether they are common law or civil law countries, or whether their bias is in favor of privacy protection, or whether their bias is in favor of information disclosure – can find common ground and be willing to compromise.

Ultimately, there are no simple and universal answers to the challenges and issues posed in cases of international litigation where the jurisdictions involved have diametrically opposed laws and customs. All organizations that operate in multiple international jurisdictions must be fully aware of the rights and duties of all potentially interested parties and prepare for the challenges.

References

1. Federal Rules of Civil Procedure, Rule 26
2. Council Directive 95/46/EC, art. 2(b), O.J (L281)
3. European Commission, Justice and Home Affairs – Data Protection, Adequacy of Protection of Personal Data in Third Countries, http://ec.europa.eu/justice_home/fsj/privacy/thridcountries/index_en.htm
4. UK Data Protection Act of, 1998 Chapter 29, Schedule 4(5)(a) (1998)
5. Foreign Proceedings (Excess of Jurisdiction) Act 1984 No. 3, 1984 (March 21, 2004), http://www.comlaw.gov.au/comlaw/management.nsf/lookupindexpagesbyid/IP200403254? Open Document Foreign Proceedings (excess of Jurisdiction) Act 1984, s. 6
6. London Guardian, p. 1 (September 2007)
7. Hagenbuch v. 3B6 Sistemi Elettronici Industriali S.R.L., 2005 U.S. Dist. LEXIS 20049, at *14 (N.D. Ill. September 12, 2005).
8. Enron, v.J.P.: Morgan Secur. Inc., No. 01-16034 (Bankr. S.D.N.Y. July 18, 2007)
9. Commission Nationale de L'informatique et des Libertés, Délibération n°2006-281 du 14 décembre 2006 sanctionnant la société Tyco Healthcare France (2006)
10. The Family Educational Rights and Privacy Act (FERPA) (20 U.S.C. § 1232g; 34 CFR Part 99)
11. Financial Modernization Act of 1999, also known as the "Gramm-Leach-Bliley Act" or GLB Act, provides protection of consumers' personal financial information held by financial institutions (1999)
12. Health Insurance Portability and Accountability Act (HIPAA) enacted in 1996 to address the security and privacy of health data (1996)
13. Lobbying Disclosure Act (2 U.S.C. § 1601–1612)
14. Federal Rules of Civil Procedure Rule 26
15. Federal Rules of Civil Procedure Rule 45
16. Council Directive 95/46/EC, art. 2(b), O.J (L281) See European Commission, Justice and Home Affairs – Data Protection, Status of Implementation of Directive 95/46/EC
17. French Blocking Statue, Section 2
18. Societe Nationale v. District Court, 482 U.S. 522 (1987)
19. Restatement Third, Restatement of the Foreign Relations Law of the United States by The American Institute The American Journal of Comparative Law 39(1), 207–213 (Winter, 1991)

Digital Identity – The Legal Person?

Clare Sullivan[*]

International Graduate School of Business, University of South Australia,
Law School, Ligertwood Building, NorthTerrace, Adelaide SA 5005, Australia
Clare.Sullivan@adelaide.edu.au

Abstract. This paper examines the concept of digital identity which the author asserts is now evident in the United Kingdom as a consequence of the Identity Cards Act (UK) 2006 and the National Identity Scheme it establishes. The nature and functions of the concept, particularly the set of information which constitutes an individual's transactional identity, are examined. The paper then considers the central question of who, or what, is the legal person in a transaction i.e. who or what enters into legal relations. The analysis presents some intriguing results which were almost certainly not envisaged by the legislature. The implications extend beyond the United Kingdom to similar schemes in other jurisdictions, and to countries, like Australia, which may implement such a scheme.

Keywords: Digital identity, legal person, national identity scheme.

1 Introduction

Individuals, businesses and governments are increasingly dependant on technology. Technology is now no longer used just as a means of collecting, storing and processing data and information. It is embedded in processes fundamental to economic and social order and it has created a whole new environment for interaction.[1] As dealings previously conducted in person are replaced by dealings conducted without a history of personal acquaintance, and frequently without face to face interaction, the requirement to establish identity for transactional purposes has increased.[2]

Compared to just a few years ago, it is now a relatively common occurrence to be asked to for proof of identity for transactions. Although rarely defined, the term

---

[*] The author acknowledges with gratitude, the assistance of Professor Ngaire Naffine and guidance provided by Mr Ian Leader-Elliott, both of the Law School University of Adelaide, South Australia, in the preparation of this paper.

[1] As Andrew Feenberg observes, this is the 'substantive impact' of technology. See Andrew Feenberg, *Critical Theory of Technology*, (1991), 5. For a recent example of theory of technology see Arthur Cockfield and Jason Pridmore, 'A Synthetic Theory of Law and Technology' (2007) 8 *Minnesota Journal of Law, Science and Technology*, 491.

[2] The internet, for example, was originally designed for sending data between trusted, known organisations so neither security, nor identity, was considered critical. Now the internet is a critical part of national and international infrastructure. Its distributive nature makes it a crucial communication tool but it founded on, to use Daniel Solove's word's, 'an architecture of vulnerability.' See Daniel Solove, 'Identity Theft, Privacy and the Architecture of Vulnerability (Enforcing Privacy Rights Symposium)' 2003 54 *Hastings Law Journal*, 1227.

M. Sorell (Ed.): e-Forensics 2009, LNICST 8, pp. 195–211, 2009.
© ICST Institute for Computer Sciences, Social Informatics and Telecommunications Engineering 2009

'identity'[3] now appears in hundreds of statutes and regulations in Australia alone, mainly because of the extensive use of identity cards for government employees and contractors working in areas ranging from airports to zoos.[4] As technology becomes more sophisticated and ubiquitous, it is inevitable that identity will assume a crucial role in most, if not all transactions.[5] However, whilst considerable attention has been given to security, particularly by system designers and users, little attention has been given to identity [6] and no attention has been given to identity in a transactional context from a legal perspective. All these factors make analysis of the legal role and nature of identity in a transactional context, particularly important.

Historically, identity has been in the background, resulting in uncertainty about its legal role and nature in a transactional context. Contract law, for example, focuses on whether the transaction is at arms length and generally the parties are assumed to be indifferent to each others' identity.[7] Consequently, what constitutes a person's identity and its precise role in a transactional context at common have been unclear.

In this paper, I analyse the role and nature of an individual's[8] digital identity[9] in a transactional context, [10] from a legal perspective. I argue that a new legal concept of

---

[3] See, however, the Enforcement and National Security (Assumed Identities) Act 1998 (NSW) which is one of the few statutes in Australia to define identity in a context which is broadly relevant to identity for transactional purposes.

[4] See for example, s 234 of the Airports Act 1996 (Cth), s 80 of the ACIS Administration Act 1999 (Cth), s 2B of the Court Security Act 1980 (Vic), s 8 of the Fisheries Act (NT), 9A of the Brands Act (NT), s 151 of The Gene Technology Act 2003 (ACT), s 399A of the Health Act 1958 (Vic), s 145 of the Heritage Act 1995 (Vic),), s 221I of the Transport Act 1983 (Vic) and s 28 of the Zoological Parks Authority Act 2001 (WA).

[5] Especially considering the increase which has occurred just this century, in the requirement to establish identity for transactions.

[6] Identity management has recently become a focus for the IT industry, largely because of system needs which have necessitated the checking and updating of user records but also as a result of concerns about identity fraud especially the use of false identities for terrorist activities and money laundering.

[7] A similar line of reasoning can be found in other branches of the law such as agency, particularly in relation to the doctrine of undisclosed principal. As one commentator observes in relation to identity, 'much legal doctrine obscures the salience of identity qua identity, though when confronted directly with the issue, the law does give substance to the importance of identity.' See Richard R.W. Brookes 'Incorporating Race' (2006) 106 *Columbia Law Review*, 2023, 2097.

[8] 'Individual' is a natural person who has been born, irrespective of whether or not the person is currently alive or is deceased The relevant legislation, particularly the *Identity Cards Act 2006* (UK) also uses the term 'individual.'

[9] In his paper 'digital identity' is an individual's identity which is composed of information stored and transmitted in digital form. 'Information' includes 'data,' unless otherwise indicated.

[10] 'Transaction' is used in this paper to cover a dealing, whether in person (i.e. face to face) or using remote communication (such as a telephone, the internet or a computer network), for which an individual, i.e. a natural person, is required to identify himself/ herself. A transaction may be between an individual and a government department or agency or with a private sector entity, and can range from an enquiry to a contract but does not include transactions and dealings of a non- business nature such as domestic and social interaction. However, when discussed in the context of legal relations such as in relation to the legal person, transaction should be construed to mean a legal transaction such as a contract, for example.

transactional identity is now clearly evident in the United Kingdom as a result of the Identity Cards Act 2006 (UK) c 15 ('Identity Cards Act'} and the United Kingdom National Identity Scheme established by that Act. [11] Although my analysis is based on the Identity Cards Act, the implications of my research extend beyond the United Kingdom to jurisdictions which have enacted, or are likely to enact similar legislation, including Australia. Indeed, the same concept of individual identity is evident in the *Human Services (Enhanced Service Delivery) Bill (Cth) 2007* ('Access Card Bill'), [12] the enabling legislation for the Access Card Scheme proposed for Australia in 2007.[13] Although the Access Card Bill has now been shelved following a change of federal government in Australia,[14] any such scheme must use a concept of transactional identity which consists of a defined set of information which is stored and transmitted in digital form. An individual's transactional identity must be a set of information which is sufficiently detailed in order to single out the individual from a large population, but which is not so detailed as to prevent its efficient use in transactions. The United Kingdom Scheme is the most current model of a national identity registration scheme, particularly in a jurisdiction with a common law heritage.

---

[11] Arguably, a concept of transactional identity which consists of a defined set of information has been evident in commercial practice for several years. However, its presence in legislation which establishes a national identity scheme is a significant development which confirms its emergence as a new legal concept.

[12] The Access Card Bill is remarkably similar to the *Identity Cards Act* especially in the change it proposed to the common law in relation to identity. While both the Act and Bill appear to merely set the criteria for identification of individuals for the purposes of the scheme, they both rely on the same concept of identity. The Access Card Bill contains provisions which are very similar to those in the *Identity Cards Act.*

[13] A similar concept of identity is also evident in other Australian legislation. See for example, the customer identification procedures under the Federal *Anti-Money Laundering/ Counter-Terrorism Financing Act 2006* (Cth) enacted by federal Parliament in Australia on 12 December 2006.

[14] On 15 March 2007 the Bill was delayed following a Senate Inquiry. Like the *Identity Cards Act,* the Bill establishes the framework for the new scheme and operational details including security and privacy aspects were to be covered in subsequent legislation. The Senate Inquiry recommended that the entire legislative package be presented in one Bill, rather than separately as originally planned. The government agreed and the new Bill was to be introduced into Parliament in 2007, with a view to beginning the scheme in April 2008. See Australian Broadcasting Corporation, *'Govt Stands by Smart Card Despite Senate Concerns'*<http//:www.abc.net.au/newsitems/200703s18 7309 3.html>16 March 2007. However, the federal election intervened and the change of government in 2007/8 lead to the Access Card Bill bring shelved as the new government pursued different policy and funding objectives.

2 Registered Digital Identity

Considering the current stated purposes and the longer term objectives of the United Kingdom Scheme[15] and that the Scheme is founded on the basis of 'one person: one identity,'[16] the digital identity registered under the National Identity Scheme, becomes *the* identity of the individual to whom it is attributed in the Register.[17] Registration under the Scheme brings into being an officially recognised identity.[18]

This concept of identity is a collection of digitally stored and transmitted information which is given legal effect by the Identity Cards Act and the Scheme. I call this collection of information, 'database identity.' Database identity is all the data and information digitally recorded about an individual in the database/s accessible under the Scheme.[19] Within database identity is a smaller subset of information which I call 'token identity.' Token identity is a defined and limited set of information which determines an individual's identity for transactional purposes. It is an individual's transactional identity. Under the United Kingdom Scheme, token identity comprises name, gender, date and place of birth, date of death, handwritten signature, appearance through a head and shoulders photograph and biometrics. The biometrics are 10 fingerprints, two iris scans and a face scan, although it seems that only fingerprints will be used, at least initially.[20]

---

[15] As set out in s1 (3), the purpose of the National Identity Register is to set up a 'secure and reliable record of registrable facts about individuals in the United Kingdom.' The information in the register is to be used for a wide range of purposes including provision of public services, crime prevention and detection and national security. See s1 (4). The government wants to make the national identity scheme 'gold standard of identity verification'. See report by the United Kingdom Information Commissioner, *The Identity Cards Bill–The Information Commissioner's Concerns* (June2005),1 <http://www.ico.gov.uk/eventual.html> 10 May 2006. The *Identity Cards Act* is enabling legislation, as was the Access Card Bill. Consequently, the Act does not contain all the detail of the operation of the National Identity Scheme. That detail is contained in the Business Plan and Framework Agreement. See Identity and Passport Service,'*Corporate and Business Plans 2006–2016*'<http//:www.ips.gov.uk/identity/publications-corporate.asp>1 September 2008; and Identity and Passport Service, '*FrameworkAgreement*',14<http//:www.gov./idenity/publications-general.asp.l>1September 2008.

[16] See John Wadham, Coailfhionn Gallagher, Nicole Chrolavicius, *The Identity Cards Act 2006* (2006), 127.

[17] At least on a prima facie basis.

[18] 'Registered identity' is defined in this paper as the identity as registered under the Scheme. Registered identity is an individual's database identity including token identity as recorded for the Scheme.

[19] Information, not the ID card, constitutes identity. See sch 1 *Identity Cards Act* which sets out the information which comprises database identity under the National Identity Scheme.

[20] Home Secretary, '*The National Identity Scheme – Delivery Plan 2008*' Speech by the Right Honourable Jacqui Smith, MP on 6 March 2008, 3.

3 The Role and Nature of Token Identity

Token identity plays a significant role. It is the identity which is used for transactions but it is also the gateway to the information which comprises the remainder of database identity. Most importantly, token identity provides the link between an individual and the information which constitutes his/her database identity, through the 'identifying information' i.e. the registered signature, photograph and biometrics. [21]

The information which comprises token identity is limited. It is summary in nature and is irreducible, although not all the token identity information is used for all transactions.[22] In comparison with the other information which comprises database identity, token identity is also relatively stable. Other than in exceptional cases such as gender re-assignment and changes required under a witness protection program for example, the only birth information which is more commonly subject to change is name, mainly for women in the event of marriage, though also as a consequence of change of name by deed poll. By contrast, the other data and information which makes up database identity is much more extensive, and it is augmented on an on-going basis.

Under the scheme there is a difference between identification and identity. Identification is just one part of the two processes used to establish identity which are firstly, the initial authentication of identity at the time of registration; and secondly, verification of identity which occurs at the time of a transaction. Information collected at the time of registration is used to authenticate identity in the sense that it is used to 'establish the truth of; establish the authorship of; make valid'[23] the identity. Of the information recorded at the time of registration, the signature, photograph[24] and biometrics provide the link to a physical individual, at least notionally. The signature, photograph and biometrics identify an individual under the Scheme in that they are regarded as being 'identical with, or as associated inseparably with,' the individual[25] to whom they are attributed in entry in the National Identity Register.

---

[21] See sch1.

[22] There are basically three levels of identity verification for transactional purposes. The lowest level will be a check using the photograph on the ID card. The highest level check will include biometrics but usually not all the biometrics, i.e. face scan, iris scans and fingerprints, will be used. Depending on the nature of the transaction, the token identity information may be also supplemented by additional information such as a Personal Identification Number ('PIN') or answers to designated questions, although there are conflicting statements as to the use of a PIN and additional questions. This additional information is not part of token identity. It is used to check that the token identity is in the correct hands. Token identity establishes and verifies identity for transactional purposes. See Identity and Passport Service, *'What are the Benefits of the National Identity Scheme?'*, *'Using the Scheme in Daily Life'* and *'What Kind of Organizations will use the Scheme?'* <http://www .identity.cards.gov.uk/scheme.html> 10 May 2006. For a recent statement see also Identity and Passport Service, *'Using the Scheme in Daily Life'*<http://www.ips.gov.uk/ identity/how-idcard-daily-providing.asp >1 September 2008.

[23] Definition of 'authenticate' in the *Concise Oxford Dictionary*.

[24] I refer to a photograph as well as a face scan which I include in biometrics because a face scan will not be used to verify identity for all transactions. Many transactions will only involve matching the appearance of the person present with the photograph.

[25] Identify' is defined in the *Concise Oxford Dictionary* s as '[T]reat (thing) as identical *with*; associate oneself inseparably *with* (party, policy, etc) ; establish identity of.'

Token identity links database identity to an individual, through the 'identifying information'[26] i.e. signature, photograph and biometrics; and is used to access the more extensive data and information which, with token identity, comprises database identity. The relationship between an individual and database identity including token identity, can be depicted diagrammatically:

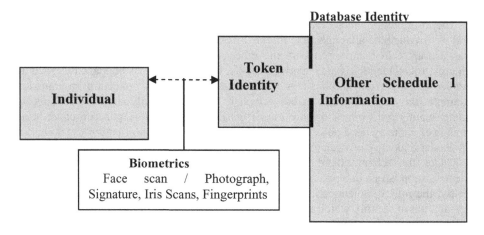

Fig. 1.

At the time of a transaction, identity is verified when all the required token information presented, matches the information on record in the National Identity Register [27] If the token identity information, as presented, matches that on record in the Register,[28] identity is verified under the Scheme.[29]

Matching as a feature of identity is evident in its general definition. The Concise Oxford Dictionary defines 'identity' as 'absolute sameness.'[30] Under the National Identity Scheme, the matching is not with a human being. Identity is verified by matching information about a human being. When presented at the time of a transaction,

---

[26] The signature, photograph and the biometrics are the 'identifying information.' See, sch 1 *Identity Cards Act.*

[27] Verify' as used in the United Kingdom scheme and for the Australian Access Card Scheme accords with *Concise Oxford Dictionary* which definition of '[T]ruth (*of* statement etc); true statement; really existent thing..' though under the schemes this truth is really a *presumption* of truth.

[28] And where applicable, on the identity card, though it is the matching of the token identity information presented, with that on record that is necessary.

[29] This is true for registration too because the individual must establish his/her identity for registration purposes by producing documents such as birth certificate, driver's license and other government issued cards. The information in these documents is cross checked to see if it matches and where possible, it will also be checked against the database of the relevant department/agency.

[30] The definition also adds 'individuality, personality.'

token identity is a token i.e. as a 'sign, symbol, evidence ...serving as proof of authenticity'[31] of identity under the Scheme.

Through this matching process, token identity performs a number of vital, sequential functions at the time of a transaction. First, token identity identifies, by singling out one identity from all the identities registered under the Scheme. The photograph, signature and biometrics are used to identify the individual, though depending on the nature of the transaction and the requirements of the transacting entity, not all the 'identifying information' need be used, nor is it all likely to be used.[32] Secondly, token identity verifies identity by determining whether there is a match between all the token identity information presented, with that on record.[33] These two steps enable the system to recognise and then transact with, the registered identity.

No doubt the role and legal significance of token identity particularly in transactions, exceeds the original intentions and objectives of the government in establishing the scheme. The intention was that dealings be with the individual who is presumed to be correctly represented by the token identity information and who is presumed to present that token identity at the time of the transaction. On this view, a transacting entity deals with that individual. The transaction is via the registered identity, but is with the individual:

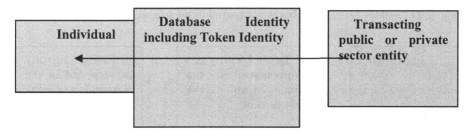

Fig. 2.

The information which constitutes token identity was intended to be just a credential, to be presented by an individual as part of the identification process, in much the same way traditional identity papers are used. However, there are crucial differences between traditional identity papers and token identity. Traditionally,

---

[31] Definition of 'token' in the *Concise Oxford Dictionary*. Although this definition refers to authenticity, under the National Identity Scheme, authentication refers to the registration whereas verification occurs at the time of a transaction. Nevertheless, the plain meaning of 'authenticity' in the definition of 'token' in the *Concise Oxford Dictionary* is clear.

[32] Especially for transactions conducted remotely, using telephone or the internet, for example. Recall that there are basically three levels of verification contemplated by the National Identity scheme.

[33] Such as name, date and place of birth as well as with signature, photograph and biometrics but bear in mind that not all transactions will use all the identifying information. Routine transactions may only require that appearance match the photo or signature may be compared, for example.

identity papers have been used to support claimed identity. Although the identification function of token identity may seek to replicate this traditional function, there are two important distinctions. Firstly, identity papers are presented in person. A human being is not only present, but is central to the identification process. Secondly, although apparently-valid identity papers are needed to support an officer's decision, that decision requires judgment, based on a number of factors including firsthand observation of the individual. Any authorization given by an officer, is based on his/her judgment and to an extent, his/her discretion.[34]

Unlike traditional identity papers, the information which comprises token identity plays the critical role in the transaction, not the individual who presents the information which constitutes token identity, or who is presumed to present it, in the case of transactions which are not in person.[35] The system looks for a match between the information presented and the information on record. Token identity does not just identify. It also enables the system to transact. Regardless of whether the token identity information is presented in person or remotely, if all the token identity information presented, matches the information recorded in the National Identity Register, then the system automatically authorises dealings with that identity.

Within these parameters the system 'can act and will for itself'[36] to recognise the defined set of information which comprises token identity and then transact with the registered identity. The individual who is assumed to be represented by that registered identity is connected to token identity by the signature, appearance (through the photograph) and the biometrics, but is not central to the transaction:

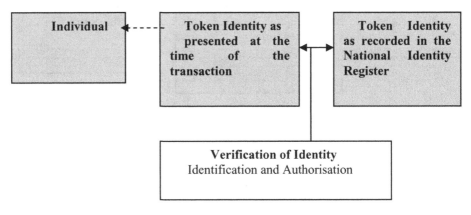

Fig. 3.

---

[34] There is also a further point of difference. Token identity is used for a wide range of transactions including commercial transactions, whereas identity papers were usually used for more limited purposes such as access to defined geographical areas and government entitlements.

[35] The information may be presented remotely and even automatically using computer programming, without any active involvement by an individual *at the time of a transaction,* though of course some human involvement is required at same stage.

[36] David Derham, 'Theories of Legal Personality' in Leicester C. Webb (ed) *Legal Personality and Political Pluralism* (1958) 1, 14.

The system and the transacting entity deals with the registered identity via token identity, not with the individual represented by the token identity:

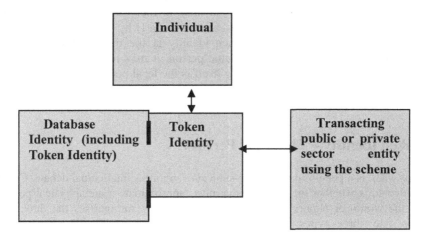

Fig. 4.

Although the intention was to 'reach behind' token identity to deal with the individual presenting it, the system does not actually operate in that way. If the token identity data/information presented at the time of a transaction, does not exactly match the record in the National Identity Register, the system will not recognize the identity and the system will not recognise, nor deal with, the individual presenting that token identity,[37] even if the token identity is otherwise legitimate and authentic.

No doubt procedures will be established for dealing with situations in which the system, through an apparent malfunction, does not recognise what seems to be a legitimate registered identity, and to deal with people who for a variety of reasons are not registered.[38] However, this aspect does not change the role of token identity. It strengthens its significance. If an individual's token identity is not recognized by the system, any protocol designed to deal with that contingency must authorise dealings with the individual, not with his/her token identity.

The automatic authorisation to transact which occurs when the presented token identity information matches that on record in the National Identity Register, raises

---

[37] The authenticity of a registered identity is clearly presumed, primarily on the basis that biometrics are reliable identifiers, and on the overall integrity of the scheme. There is obviously a presumption that the initial registration process is sufficiently robust to ensure authenticity and that subsequent use of the token identity is by the individual to whom it is attributed in the national identity register. However, the 'identifying information' including the biometrics, is not infallible. For a discussion of this aspect see Clare Sullivan, 'The United Kingdom Identity Cards Act 2006 – Proving Identity?' (2006) Vol 3 *Macquarie Journal of Business Law* 259.

[38] Especially since the scheme will be used for government social security benefits. These procedures will require a delicate balance between equity and security concerns, with the balance likely to tip in favour of security, particularly given heightened terrorism concerns.

the question as to the legal nature of database identity, and particularly the legal nature of token identity. These questions raise the central question of who, or what, is the legal person[39] in the transaction i.e. who or what enters into legal relations. Is it the individual who is connected to the identity in the National Identity Register, primarily by the 'identifying information' and particularly by his/her biometrics; or is it the individual who presents the token identity at the time of the transaction? Although it is intended that it be the same person, it may not be. There is also an intriguing third option that token identity itself is the legal person. While this view is controversial because it invests token identity with legal personality, it is a view which sits easily with the functional role of token identity under the Scheme.

4 Token Identity – The Legal Person?

Who, or what, is a person in law, is the subject of vigorous intellectual debate. Central to this debate is whether the legal person must 'approximate a metaphysical person,' to use the words of Ngaire Naffine.[40] Naffine usefully summarises the three main theories into three types of legal persons which she calls P1, P2 and P3, respectively.[41]

As Naffine explains, P1 is the orthodox positive view. Personality arises from rights and duties, rather than from intrinsic humanity.[42] In the words of Alexander Nekam: '[E]verything…. can be the subject- a potential carrier – of rights.'[43] '[T]here is nothing in the notion of the subject of rights which in itself, would necessarily, connect it with human personality, or even with anything experimentally existing.'[44] Once a legal right is in evidence, so is a (legal) person.[45] According to Derham, '[I]t follows of course, that any 'thing' which is treated by the appropriate legal system as capable of entering legal relationships 'is' a legal person, whether it can act and will

---

[39] The 'legal person' is the entity or unit which bears legal rights and duties and so possesses what is called legal personality.

[40] Ngaire Naffine, 'Who are Law's Persons? From Cheshire Cats to Responsible Subjects' (2003) May *The Modern Law Review* , 346.

[41] Ibid, 350.

[42] In Nekam's words, '[T]he rights themselves are given not for human personality or will but for the interests which the law-maker wants to protect. It is the socially protected interests which in legal abstraction we call rights. Since any conceivable interest attributed to any conceivable entity may be regarded as socially important by some community, anything may become a subject of rights – anything existing or anything to which the lawmaking community attaches any existence at all; and human personality or will is by no means a preliminary condition to its formation.' Alexander Nekam, *The Personality Conception of the Legal Entity* (1938), 27.

[43] Ibid, 26. See also Derham, above n 36,13-15.

[44] Ibid, 26 and 28. Nekam asserts that the proposition that every individual is a natural subject of rights by virtue of his/her inherent humanity is flawed. However, as Nekam asserts, a connection between a right and a human being is inevitable. Nekam distinguishes the subject of the right from its administrator. While it is inevitable that the administrator of the right be human, the subject of the right need not be human.

[45] Margaret Davies and Ngaire Naffine, '*Are Persons Property? Legal Debates Debates About Property and Personality*' (2001), 54.

for itself or must be represented by some designated human being.'[46] In other words, a 'thing' can be transformed into a legal person through the legal endowment of rights and duties.

By contrast, P2 theorists maintain that that inherent humanity is absolutely necessary for true peronhood. The abstract, artificial nature of P1 troubles P2 legal theorists who regard '[T]he human being as the paradigmatic subject of rights'[47] which begin at birth and cease on death. The rationale for the P2 view is that 'a human does not have to be sentient to be a (legal) person; his moral and hence legal status comes from being human.'[48] (my addition). This view of the legal person is the basis for fundamental human rights which include the right to privacy and the right to identity which are important rights in the context of the Scheme[49] but it does not fit as well as P1 with the transactional role of token identity.

Token identity is even further removed from P3. P3 theorists insist that the legal person must be human and further assert that the human being must be legally competent.[50] P3 theorists 'maintain that those who lack the will personally to enforce their own rights cannot be truly said to possess those rights and so, it follows that they cannot properly be regarded as legal persons.'[51] Richard Mohr takes this argument one step further to include judgment and responsibility. Mohr asserts that '[T]he legal subject must be capable of acting and of judging actions, must be prudent for the future and responsible for the past. He or she must have experience and must learn from it.'[52]

The theoretical underpinnings of P2 and P3 are not features of, nor prerequisites for, the effective functioning of token identity. Token identity is indeed abstract and artificial. While a human being is linked to the registered identity and specifically to token identity, through signature, appearance (photograph) and biometrics, the

---

[46] Derham, above n 36,13-15. Derham asserts that 'the wrong questions have been asked in the process of resolving many problems concerning legal personality.' He suggests that the appropriate questions are:

'[I]s there personateness? (a) Do the rules of the legal system establish that this entity.....is to be recognized as an entity for the purposes of legal reasoning (is to have the capacity to enter legal relations)?

What is the personality? (b) If so, do the rules of the legal system establish just what kinds of legal relations this entity may enter, or more commonly, do those rules establish whether or not this entity may enter the legal relation claimed or denied on its behalf?

Should there be personateness? (c) If the rules of law in (a) above are silent or ambiguous, should this entity be recognized as an entity for the purposes of legal reasoning?

What kind of personality should there be? (d) If either the rules of law in (a) or (b) above are silent or ambiguous and if (c), being relevant , is answered in the affirmative, then should the entity be recognized as having a personality which includes the capacity claimed or denied on its behalf to enter the legal relation concerned ?'

[47] P. Ducor, 'The Legal Status of Human Materials' (1996) 44 Drake Law Review 195 at 200 cited by Naffine, above n 41,358.

[48] Naffine, above n 40, 361.

[49] For a further discussion see, Clare Sullivan, 'Identity or Privacy?'(2008) Vol 2 No 3 International Journal of Intellectual Property Management 289.

[50] As Naffine points out that this concept of the legal person as both an intelligent and moral subject is particularly evident in criminal jurisprudence. Naffine, above n 40, 362.

[51] Naffine, above n 40,363.

[52] Richard Mohr, 'Identity Crisis: Judgment and the Hollow legal Subject,' (2007) 11 Passages – Law, Aesthetics, Politics, 106,118.

transactional functions of token identity under the Scheme are not necessarily dependant on inherent humanity, nor on a legally competent, rational human actor (though a human administrator is required). While many transactions will be in person, and will include comparison of appearance with a photograph, a signature and/or matching a biometric,[53] the Scheme clearly envisages remote transactions where these links with a physical person are either not required, or are provided on-line, not in person. Rationality and legal competency are also not part of the information which collectively comprises token identity. Rationality and legal competency also do not impact on the functions of token identity under the Scheme, except perhaps in the case of individuals who are minors (which is obvious from the date of birth) and those who are flagged by system as not being competent.

As Naffine observes:

> P1 has neither biological nor psychological predicates; nor does it refer back to any social or moral idea of a person and it is to be completely distinguished from those philosophical conceptions of the person which emphasise the importance of reason. ... The endowment of even one right or duty would entail recognition of their ability to enter into legal relations and so be a person, even though a human would necessarily be required to enforce any right. [54]

To strict legalists who adhere to this P1 view of the person, the legal person should not be confused with flesh and blood people. As F. H. Lawson explains '[A]ll that is necessary for the existence of the person is that the lawmaker..... should decide to treat it as the subject of rights or other legal relations.'[55]

Unlike other notions of the legal person, i.e. P2 and P3, the potentially expansive and inclusive nature of P1 also accords with the enduring nature of identity. Identity, unlike privacy for example, does not necessarily cease on death,[56] though of course death affects the way in which rights and duties are enforced.

5   Token Identity Is the Legal Person

In many ways, P1 fits the concept of token identity now established under the legislation and the actual functions of token identity under the scheme. Indeed, token

---

[53] Depending on the nature of the transaction.

[54] Naffine, above n 40, 351. Alexander Nekam also maintains that 'everything.... can be the subject- a potential carrier – of rights. 'everything.... can be the subject- a potential carrier – of rights.' 'There is nothing in the notion of the subject of rights which in itself, would necessarily, connect it with human personality, or even with anything experimentally existing. In other words, legal personality arises from rights and duties, rather than from inherent humanity. Nekam, above n 42, 26-28.

[55] F.H.Lawson, 'The Creative Use of Legal Concepts' (1957) 32 *New York University Law Review* 909, 915.

[56] Neither database identity nor token identity cease on death and this is reflected in the fact that token identity under the National Identity scheme includes date of death as well as date of birth. S 1(7) (d) *Identity Cards Act*. This feature distinguishes identity from closely related concepts, particularly privacy.

identity is a relatively pure example of P1. Although date of birth and death and gender, appearance, signature and biometrics are part of token identity information, token identity need not be coloured by what Naffine refers to as 'metaphysical notions of what it means to be a person.'[57] Although there is a notional connection with a human being, it is the information which plays the crucial role in the transaction, not the individual to whom it is presumed to relate.

Token identity 'exists only as an abstract capacity to function in law, a capacity which is endowed by law because it is convenient for law to have such a creation.'[58] Although the lawmaker may not have made a conscious decision to create token identity, let alone endow it with legal personality, the legislation has crystallized the concept and through the operation of the scheme, it has been endowed with legal personality.

Richard Tur's description of P1 as 'an empty slot'[59] that can be endowed with legal capacity resonates with the role of token identity under the National Identity Scheme. Verification of identity involves two steps; and an analogy can be drawn with a key being used to open a door. First, the token identity information is presented to establish identity; [60] like inserting the key into a lock - or a slot, to use Tur's metaphor. In the second step, the presented information is compared with that on record in the chip on the ID card[61] and/or in the National Identity Register, to see if it matches. The slot remains empty and non- functional until the key is inserted. If the information matches, it is like the indentions on the key aligning with the indentations in the slot which enable the key to open the door. When the token identity information presented matches that on record in the Register, rights and duties such as those arising under contract for example, then endow the 'empty slot', i.e. token identity, with legal personhood. [62]

On this view, legal relations are between the registered identity through token identity, and the transacting public or private sector entity. Transactional rights and duties initially attach to token identity and then to the registered identity, not to the notional individual (who is associated with that registered identity because his/her signature, photograph and/or biometrics are so recorded in the National Identity Register):

---

[57] Although Nafffine notes that 'P1 is not immune from metaphysical notions of what it is to be a person.' Naffine, above 40, 356.

[58] Naffine, above n 40, 351.

[59] Richard Tur, 'The "Person" in Law' in A. Peacocke and G. Gillett (eds), (1987) *Persons and Personality: A Contemporary Inquiry*,123, 121

[60] Presentation may be by personal attendance at which time the information is provided by a person and/or the ID card is presented. The required information may also be provided by telephone or using the internet.

[61] The ID card is optional and card- not- present verification is clearly contemplated. See *Regulatory Impact Assessment, Identity Cards Bill Introduced to House of Commons on 25 May 2005* (UK)<http//:www.homeoffice.gsi.gov.uk.html.>16 May 2006 cards.gov.uk/ scheme.html >10 May 2006. See paragraphs 58 and 69 and Annex A.

[62] Unlike other notions of the legal person, i.e. P2 and P3, the potentially expansive and inclusive nature of P1 also accords with the enduring nature of identity. Identity, unlike privacy for example, does not necessarily cease on death though of course death affects the enforceability of rights and duties. Neither database identity, nor token identity cease on death and that is reflected in the fact that token identity under the National Identity Scheme includes date of death as well as date of birth.

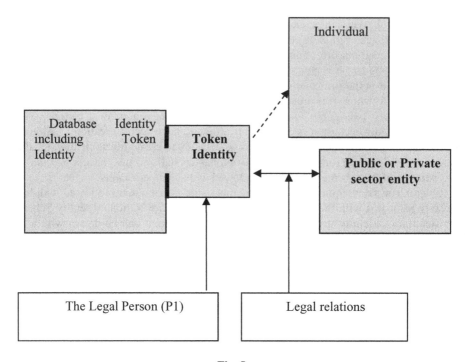

Fig. 5.

Transactional rights and duties, including those arising under contract, attach to the registered identity, through token identity. If, for example, there is subsequent default, the public or private sector entity will, as a matter of practicality, first look to the registered identity.

As a matter of law, this situation raises the line of contract cases on mistaken identity which are still law in both the United Kingdom and Australia.[63] Those cases have been described as impossible to reconcile.[64] However, although reconciliation is difficult, it is not impossible. With one exception (which turned on an unrelated point),[65] all the cases involved face to face, oral contracts and all pre-date the technology which is now a feature of the Scheme and of many, if not most, commercial transactions. The cases turn on the intention of the contracting parties and the particular circumstances, including the nature and seriousness of the mistake, especially whether an innocent third party would be disadvantaged if the contract was

---

[63] The leading cases are *Ingram v Little* (1961) 1 QB 31, *Lewis v Avery* (1972) 1 QB 198 and *Cundy v Lindsay* (1878) 3 App Cas 459. See also *Phillips v Brooks Ltd* (1919) 2 KB 243 and *Shogun Finance Ltd v Hudson* (2004) 1 AC 919 and in Australia, *Porter v Latec Finance (Qld) Pty Ltd* (1964) 111CLR 177, *Papas v Bianca Investments Pty Ltd* (2002) 82 SASR 581.

[64] See JW Carter, Elisabeth Peden, GJ Tolhurst, *Contract Law in Australia*, 5th Ed (2007), 459.

[65] *Shogun Finance Ltd v Hudson* (2004) 1 AC 919. In this case a written hire purchase contract was signed by a rogue in the name of Patel. The House of Lords held that the contract purported to be with Patel but because he did not sign it, nor did he authorise anyone else to sign it on his behalf, the contract was a nullity.

considered void. While that is the general justification for the courts' approach in finding the contract voidable, there is a strong theme in the decisions that the law will presume that in face to face dealings each party intends to deal with the person who is physically present. That presumption can, however, be rebutted by clear, admissible [66] evidence to the contrary – which can be presented in relation to transactions using token identity.

Unlike the parties in the line of mistaken identity cases, the public or private sector entity actually deals with token identity, not the individual.[67] This is so for all transactions which use token identity, but it is most clearly illustrated in remote transactions where the required token identity information is presented by telephone or using the internet. The token identity information is automatically compared to the information as recorded in the National Identity Register. If it matches, the system deals with the registered identity. Information and advice is provided to that registered identity. Invitations to treat and contracts are made with that identity – an identity which is composed of digitally stored information, which is accorded authenticity and given legal personality by the Scheme. There is no doubt that the transaction is with the registered identity.

6 Conclusion

It is a major departure from the familiar to assert that there is an emergent legal concept which is comprised of a set of information, let alone to assert that it is endowed with legal personality. To many, P1 is controversial because of its abstract, artificial nature and any assertion that token identity is invested with legal personality of this sort is also likely to be controversial. However, when viewed from the perspective of other disciplines such as computer science, the notion that information has function, as well as meaning, is well established.

No doubt a court will strive to find a human being behind the registered identity who can be considered the legal person in the transaction and in many ways it is appealing to follow the P2 theorists because it is the more conventional approach. It is the approach adopted in the mistaken identity contract cases, for example, but much has changed about how transactions are conducted since those cases were decided. Most significantly, it is not the way the National Identity Scheme actually works. Face to face dealings are now not the norm and computer technology, and in particular digital technology, is an integral part of commerce and of transactions, even those of a routine nature.

---

[66] I include the requirement of admissibility, primarily because of the parol evidence rule.

[67] In this regard it is important to distinguish the information which constitutes token identity from associated information such as a PIN or answers to additional designated questions which are used to provide additional security at the time of a transaction. Under the Scheme, a PIN and answers to designed questions are used to check that the identity is in the right hands. That information is part of an individual's database identity but it is not part of token identity. The same comment can be applied to the additional security measures including automatic messaging used by banks, for example. That information is generally not part of the individual's token identity in the context of the particular proprietary scheme, although it depends on the particular circumstances.

Under the Scheme, the system recognizes token identity and transacts with the registered identity, not the individual who is notionally associated with that identity. Even when aspects are discussed and clarified with a human being in person, by telephone or using the internet, the details are entered in the system against the registered identity. Of course, there is nothing new in this method. It is widely used for transactions. What sets the Scheme apart is that it is the official, national identity scheme of the United Kingdom. Its size and particularly, its nature mean that there is, and must necessarily be, less discretion given to human operators to ensure system security.

Information plays the critical role, not human beings. Although courts have traditionally resisted recognition of machine intelligence,[68] usually to prevent an obvious miscarriage of justice, this approach ignores that fact that computers are performing intelligent functions and making decisions which often cannot be readily overridden by human operators.

Under the Scheme, token identity determines a person's right to be recognised and transact as an individual. If the Scheme is sufficiently robust to ensure the integrity of identity authentication at the time of registration, and the unfailing accuracy of identity verification at the time of each transaction, then it is of little practical significance whether a Court would accept the argument that token identity is the legal person or whether the P2 approach would be followed. A human being must still be involved, albeit as the administrator of the rights and duties attaching to P1. The individual to whom the identity is attributed in the National Identity Register is the most obvious administrator. That individual is presumed to present the token identity at the time of a transaction, and is identified by his/her signature, photograph and /or biometrics.

However, if there is a possibility of human or system error or malfunction or fraud, which affects that accuracy and integrity of authentication, and/or verification of identity, then the practical and legal issues become much more complex and problematic. If there is error, malfunction, or manipulation, or even a possibility of it (as there must be, because no system is infallible), a registered identity may be incorrectly attributed, or not attributed, to an individual.

References

1. Australian Broadcasting Corporation, Govt Stands by Smart Card Despite Senate Concerns, Brookes, Richard R.W Incorporating Race. Columbia Law Review 2023, 106 (2006),
   http://www.abc.net.au/newsitems/200703s1873093.html (March 16, 2007)
2. Carter, J.W., Peden, E., Tolhurst, G.J.: Contract Law in Australia, 5th edn. (2007)
3. Cockfield, A., Pridmore, J.: A Synthetic Theory of Law and Technology, Minnesota Journal of Law, Science and Technology 491, 8 (2007)
4. Concise Oxford Dictionary
5. Davies, M., Naffine, N.: Are Persons Property? Legal Debates Debates About Property and Personality, 54 (2001)

---

[68] See for example, *Davies v Flackett* (1972) Crim L R 708 and *Kennison v Daire* (1985) 38 SASR 404, 416 per O'Loughlin J. See also *Kennison v Daire* (1986) 160 CLR 129.

6. Derham, D.: Theories of Legal Personality. In: Webb, L.C. (ed.) Legal Personality and Political Pluralism, vol. 1 (1958)

7. Ducor, P.: The Legal Status of Human Materials. Drake Law Review 195, 44 (1996)

8. Feenberg, A.: Critical Theory of Technology (1991)

9. Home Secretary, The National Identity Scheme – Delivery Plan 2008. Speech by the Right Honourable Jacqui Smith, MP on March 6 (2008)

10. Identity and Passport Service, Corporate and Business Plans 2006 – 2016 (September 1, 2008),
    http://www.ips.gov.uk/identity/publications-corporate.asp

11. Identity and Passport Service, FrameworkAgreement, 14 (September 1, 2008),
    http://www.gov.uk/idenity/publications-general.asp

12. Identity and Passport Service, What are the Benefits of the National Identity Scheme? Using the Scheme in Daily Life (May 10, 2006),
    http://www.identity.cards.gov.uk/scheme.html

13. Identity and Passport Service, What Kind of Organizations will use the Scheme? (May 10, 2006), http://www.identity.cards.gov.uk/scheme.html

14. Identity and Passport Service, Using the Scheme in Daily Life (September 1, 2008),
    http://www.ips.gov.uk/identity/how-idcard-daily-providing.asp

15. Jones, K.: Meesiah the Cat gets Credit Card with $4000 Limit, The Courier Mail (Brisbane) (January 4, 2007)

16. Lawson, F.H.: The Creative Use of Legal Concepts, New York University Law Review 909, 32 (1957)

17. Mohr, R.: Identity Crisis: Judgment and the Hollow legal Subject. Passages – Law, Aesthetics, Politics 106, 11 (2007)

18. Naffine, N.: Who are Law's Persons? From Cheshire Cats to Responsible Subjects. The Modern Law Review 346 (May 2003)

19. Nekam, A.: The Personality Conception of the Legal Entity (1938)

20. Regulatory Impact Assessment, Identity Cards Bill Introduced to House of Commons on (May 25, 2005) (UK), http://www.homeoffice.gsi.gov.uk.html (May 16, 2006), http://cards.gov.uk/scheme.html (May 10, 2006)

21. Solove, D.: Identity Theft, Privacy and the Architecture of Vulnerability (Enforcing Privacy Rights Symposium). Hastings Law Journal 1227, 54 (2003)

22. Sullivan, C.: The United Kingdom Identity Cards Act, – Proving Identity? Macquarie Journal of Business Law 259, 3 (2006)

23. Sullivan, C.: The United Kingdom Identity Cards Act, – Proving Identity? Macquarie Journal of Business Law 259, 3 (2006)

24. Sullivan, C.: Identity or Privacy? International Journal of Intellectual Property Management 2(3), 289 (2008)

25. Richard, T.: The "Person" in Law. In: Peacocke, A., Gillett, G. (eds.) Persons and Personality: A Contemporary Inquiry, vol. 123 (1987)

26. United Kingdom Information Commissioner, The Identity Cards Bill–The Information Commissioner's Concerns (June 2005),
    http://www.ico.gov.uk/eventual.html (May 10, 2006)

27. Wadham, J.: Gallagher, Coailfhionn and Chrolavicius, Nicol The Identity Cards Act 2006, 127 (2006)

Surveillance and Datenschutz in Virtual Environments

Sabine Cikic[1], Fritz Lehmann-Grube[1], and Jan Sablatnig[2]

[1] Technische Universität Berlin, Center for Multimedia in Education and Research (MuLF), Sekr. MA 7-2, Str. des 17. Juni 136, 10623 Berlin, Germany
{cikic,lehmannf}@math.tu-berlin.de
[2] Technische Universität Berlin, Institute of Mathematics, Sekr. MA 7-2, Str. des 17. Juni 136, 10623 Berlin, Germany
jon@math.tu-berlin.de

Abstract. Virtual environments are becoming more and more accepted, and part of the everyday online experience for many users. This offers new potential for both surveillance and data mining. Some of the techniques used are discussed in this paper.

However, such activities may in many countries conflict with the legal framework in place, for example with the German Federal Data Protection Act (Datenschutzgesetz). This point is illustrated by means of comparisons with real-world collection of personal data scenarios such as telephone tapping or video surveillance.

Keywords: virtual surveillance, virtual environment, privacy.

1 Introduction

With the widespread success and increased user numbers of virtual environments such as *World of Warcraft* and *Second Life* come new challenges and opportunities for law enforcement and intelligence services of all kinds. There are many reasons why one would want to observe and monitor users and their avatars (their digital representations while active in the virtual world).

Firstly, virtual environments may be used as a hitherto unmonitored base for inconspicuous meetings between real criminals [1]. Secondly, real crimes are commited that are related to virtual environments, either because the people involved met in a virtual environment, or because of actions taken by these people within the virtual environment [2]. Finally, observation of an individual's virtual actions may be part of a real-life observation of the individual, perhaps because of a real-life crime investigation or because private individuals (such as employer or spouse) have an interest in finding out about the person's whereabouts and contacts.

The collection of such data may, however, be at odds both with the TOS (Terms of Service) of the virtual environment and with the privacy laws of the country the subject is operating in (or that the virtual environment is operating in). This subject is still under debate, but possible conflicts will be illustrated and discussed, using the example of *Datenschutz* – the very strict privacy concept in force in Germany.

M. Sorell (Ed.): e-Forensics 2009, LNICST 8, pp. 212–219, 2009.

2   Surveillance

As virtual worlds consist entirely of data, it is possible to compile a very complete picture of the user's activities in these virtual worlds – if one has access to the data. Different means of gaining such access are available according to the privileges of the monitoring party.

2.1   Surveillance by ISPs

If you have access to the entire datastream going to and from the monitored user's computer, it is possible to record all data going to and from the virtual environment client. This record can later be used to reconstruct the user's entire virtual environment experience on a different computer. This then represents full surveillance of a single user within the virtual world.

There are several drawbacks to this approach. First of all, analysing the data and creating a log of events demands a large amount of PC processing time (for visualising the data), and a human expert would be required as well to interpret the on-screen data. This operator would have to watch the playback video and translate the images into a condensed description (such as "The suspect enters the house at 9:12pm").

Hence this approach is extremely inefficient, and unfeasible for mass surveillance of a large number of users. Similarly, this approach cannot be used to automatically find users that are engaging in any of a selection of activities on a watch list.

Additionally, the co-operation of the ISP (Internet service provider) must be obtained or the user's computer must otherwise be tampered with, which is an invasive technique liable to be regulated as tightly as telephone tapping.

Finally, it is theoretically possible to encrypt the transmitted data and thus make it difficult or even impossible to allow reproduction just by observing the data sent on the Internet. As yet, however, no virtual environment that offers encryption is freely available.

Surveillance by Internet tap can be neither detected nor avoided by the targeted user.

2.2   Surveillance by Administrators

A more promising point of access for observing a virtual environment is generally the provider's platform. The administrators of the virtual environment are typically able to easily collect and mine the entirety of data in the virtual environment. This also allows for complete surveillance, both of a single user and, in fact, of the entire virtual populace.

The advantage of this scheme is that it can be very efficiently implemented, as the data is there already and only needs to be filtered. It is also possible to, for example, filter for semantic information such as "Avatar enters house", rather than raw data such as "Avatar moves to position (x,y)". This makes mass surveillance easy. In fact, most providers of virtual environments already employ a large number of automatic watchdogs to alert their administrators to actions that the provider is aiming to prohibit in their virtual environment [3,4].

Co-operation with the provider of the virtual environment is necessary in implementing this technique. This can often be difficult to attain as the provider may reside in a different country and therefore lie outside of the jurisdiction of a surveillance order on a particular user or a user group.

It is also worth noting that third-party services such as voice-chat can be used in conjunction with virtual environments (although some offer built-in voice functionality). This information may then be missing from the final surveillance results.

Surveillance by administrators can be neither detected nor avoided by the targeted user. Also, this is the only type of surveillance that might yield answers to questions on *past* occurrences, such as "Was this user logged in last Friday?".

2.3   Surveillance in Programmable Worlds

A vast amount of data about other users can be gathered by simply being logged into the system as a regular user. This is especially the case where there is a programming interface that allows users to run code on the servers, as in *Second Life* or in MUDs (Multi-User Dungeons).

This type of observation requires a standard end-user computer with an account in the virtual environment, along with a good understanding of the programming interface that is used to create the virtual apparatus in question. Alternatively, many of the required virtual objects (such as listening devices) are already freely available from third parties.

Mobile Listening Device. It is easy to create a listening device that simply records all text chat. It is usually not difficult to make this device nearly undetectable – either very small or entirely transparent. The device can either be smuggled into the user's inventory or can be self-propelled and auto-following so that it will continuously watch an avatar while always staying at just the maximum "hearing" range from it.

These devices exist within the virtual world, and this is where they aggregate, filter, and collect their data. The devices available in *Second Life* are able to transmit their data to any computer outside of the *Second Life Grid* for further processing [5].

Where voice-chat is enabled within the world, this voice chat can likewise be captured.

Countermeasures exist for such devices, such as *Second Life*'s skyboxes (special rooms that control access by specific permission), chatbug scanners (that are trying to find listening devices nearby), or encryption tools providing simple in-world chat encryption [6]. As the virtual environments themselves are not meant to provide privacy, however, add-ons such as these are clumsy and not much used.

Stationary Listening Device. Listening devices may also be employed to watch a certain area and transcribe all chat there. Such devices may be deployed covertly or even openly.

These devices can be countered in a number of ways, especially if their presence is known, e. g. by refraining from substantive discussion while observation is in place, by teleporting through the area or moving in an otherwise unexpected way to avoid detection.

Camera. Within a virtual environment, a camera is very similar to a listening device, except that in addition to chat it can also store positions, movements, and the actions of nearby avatars.

The data thus collected can later be analysed and visualised to be displayed as a conventional video of what the camera saw.

Gridscanner. A single robot may not be able to easily travel through the entire virtual environment, as the process may take too long if the environment is very large. If the robot is able to clone itself, however, it is possible to scan the entire world and gather information, e. g. the positions of all avatars seen by any of the clones.

The gathered information may be collected to create online profiles of certain avatars, or may be used to find specific avatars and then use one of the techniques described above (e. g. a listening device) on them.

This scanning approach is a form of mass surveillance, and as such cannot be easily prevented by users. It is possible to avoid detection by staying in private rooms, especially if the scanning schedule is generally known.

2.4   Surveillance in Gameworlds

Even if a user has no special rights and no programming interface to the virtual environment, he can still gather large amounts of data about other users.

All of the following techniques require a computer with an account in the virtual environment, as well as a "bot" – a program that can interface with the client on the computer to act autonomously in the virtual environment. Bots are widely available for most popular virtual environments. Finally, transmission interception is required to record the exchange of data between the virtual environment and the client on the monitoring PC. This datastream can then easily be scanned for the information of interest. Although this requires some understanding of the stream format in question, the relevant information on these formats is generally publicly known. The result of the stream analysis then yields the surveillance data. Some of the most effective surveillance techniques using this set-up are listed below.

Who-Scanning. Many virtual environments allow a `who`-like command which shows all users currently logged in, or sometimes just all users in the current zone. In these cases, it is very easy to build a complete list of all avatars present, the times they are on-line, and optionally their area preferences (if this information is given in the world's `who` command). Similar weaknesses include `finger`-type commands which may reveal additional information such as last login time.

The easiest way to gather this information is to have the bot log in every once in a while and issue the corresponding command. The returning data is easily intercepted and compiled.

If information is given only for the current zone, the bot will have to teleport through all zones for each cycle.

Cityscanning. Another way to find attendance lists in a virtual environment is to simply walk through the main congregation points of the world (the cities). By intercepting and logging all avatar names that come into view-range, it is possible to generate incomplete but still considerable amount of avatar attendance data.

Again, the bot will have to walk through each city, teleporting from one to the next.

Chatlog. Most virtual environments offer a conveniently large area of audibility for chat messages. Thus, an entire city's chat can be heard from maybe two or three positions. In addition, there are often world and trade channels that everybody can talk on and listen to, regardless of position.

Again, chat streams are among the easiest to isolate from incoming data. In conjunction with city-scanning, this can yield chatlogs of many but not all of the conversations going on in-game.

If a user wants to collect complete chatlogs, he needs to employ many bots to stay in specific positions in the cities and thus listen in on all conversations in their local area. On the other hand, he can use just the world- and trade-channels as an incomplete variation of the `who`-command.

Trailing. You can also attempt to follow an avatar in a virtual environment, just as a real person can be followed in the real world. This will likely be noticed sooner or later, but with intelligent use of hiding places, changes of costume and of avatars, teleporting, flying, and similar techniques undetected pursuit may also be possible for a while. Actual eavesdropping is then often quite easy, as because of the simple, range-based in-game-logic of most virtual environments, there are usually many places where one can be completely visually occluded but still be within audibility range of another avatar, especially when one of the avatars in question is inside a building. The success of such an endeavour depends both on the chat-audibility range in the virtual environment and the aptitude of the follower. The downside of this is that in general bots cannot be employed for this problem, instead a human controller is required, which makes such surveillance expensive.

It should be noted that many of the techniques described in the last two sections may violate the TOS of the virtual environment in question. In general though, the administration of the virtual world would not specifically scan for such occurences and so they will usually go undetected, with the possible exception of the massive botting involved in cityscanning.

3   Datenschutz

3.1   Origin and Application of Privacy Laws

The precedent for every modern regulation on the collection and flow of personal data is the concept of privacy formulated by the US lawyers Warren and Brandeis over a hundred years ago in 1890 [7]. With the rise of mass media and new technologies, new possibilities had come up to harm individuals by exposing them to the public eye. So Warren and Brandeis introduced the term "privacy", stating "That the individual shall have full protection in person and in property (...)".

In the 1970s, West Germany experienced a surge of terrorism, kidnapping and an principle ideological challenge to the democratic system, which was generally agreed to be the major crisis in the history of the state. Against this backdrop, attempts were made to strengthen democracy wherever possible, which lead to the first German privacy laws. The reasoning behind these laws was that since an atmosphere of surveillance tends to boost conformity of behaviour, the diversity of opinions is lessened by this surveillance. This effect is well-known and used in many totalitarian states (a literary example of this would be Orwell's *1984*), but to a democracy, it is harmful.

Datenschutz (pronounce "dartenshoots") literally translates as data protection, and not to data privacy. The reason for this diction was that these laws were intended to deal with the first forms of mass data collection and analysis that became possible in the 1970s with early computing systems. As such, the German law has very explicit rules as to when, by who and how any amount of data may be collected, if that data can in any way be linked back to individuals. Note that it is not specified what kind of data is targeted by the law, but the law was already applied to personal data (such as name, address, birthday), speech data (such as telephone conversations), and location data (such as gathered by video cameras on public spaces). Alongside a focus on violations of the privacy of an individual by *usage* of personal data, it also regulates *acquisition* and *processing* of the data itself. The law is based on the assumption that it can be harmful to the general democratic ethos if people feel intimidated by the recording of their behaviour.

The German law of Datenschutz is renowned as one of the strictest privacy laws in the world, and is often seen as a major barrier to information flow. To allow the gathering and processing of a collection of data, either a specific law, regulation or court order must be acquired, or each person whose data is to be collected has to state their consent, knowing also the exact type of data and by whom and how it is to be handled. If this is impossible, the data either may not be gathered at all or must be made anonymous before collation.

3.2 Application to Virtual Environments

The fundamental question on the legality of collecting data as detailed in section 2 is whether avatar-linked data should be regarded as user-linked. The provider of a virtual environment can usually access information on this connection, or can at least find it out by applying an IP trace. Yet the information is not common knowledge and so one could take the position that data collected within a virtual environment is not personal data and therefore need not be protected at all. On the other hand, the directive 95/46/EC of the European Parliament applies, which explicitly states, that "account should be taken of all the means likely reasonably to be used either by the controller or by any other person to identify the said person" [8]. Following this, in-game behaviour must be regarded as user-linked.

Another question is whether the data that accrues within the virtual environment can even violate a user's privacy even if everybody knows who the user is. This may depend on the virtual environment in question. Blizzard, maker of the popular *World of Warcraft* game, for instance, has a privacy statement on their website [9] that discloses very specifically how personal data such as the user's address, age and payment history are handled, but this statement does not mention in-world data such as avatar level, log-on times or alliances. Such data is regarded as actively published, impersonal artefact and in no way concerning the player behind. Linden Lab on the other hand claims, that a *Second Life* avatar should be an extension of the personality of a real person, and encourage users to express themselves as easy as in reality. So here the user's privacy can be harmed by surveilling his avatar.

Either way, some of the above practices have very close real-world analogs which can be used to decide whether the practices are probably legal.

ISP Surveillance. This is very much akin to telephone tapping and can in fact be used for that purpose in the case of VoIP. Well-known rules and regulations apply to this practise.

Virtual Cameras. In real life, there are strict rules in Germany as to how long data from a surveillance camera may be retained. This allows this data to be used in case of a criminal incident, but no general analysis and aggregation of the data is allowed.

Gridscanning, Cityscanning. In the real world, the current position of most of the population can be analysed from the cellphone-cells where they are currently registered. In Germany, this kind of data on a specific individual can only be collected with the individual's consent or on a court order.

Listening to Voice-chat. This is a direct analog to telephone tapping and as such is illegal without an explicit court order.

Chatlog. Both real-world mail and telephone conversations are specially protected by law in Germany and, by common extension, so is e-mail and other types of private exchanges of opinion such as instant messenger logs, IRC logs, or chatlogs.

4   Conclusion

Users in virtual environments are generally not highly aware that they may be observed within these environments. This may have to do with the fact that they are regularly monitored by administrators and thus are used to a certain level of surveillance. On the other hand, users usually have a high feeling of security from surveillance. There may be several reasons for this, such as the belief that it is either too expensive or too uninteresting to continually monitor them, as long as they don't do anything conspicuous. Also, virtual environments' principal feature of slipping into a made-up avatar character tends to disassociate users from their online-persona and thus the need to protect their privacy, as well.

Finally, the similarities of virtual environments with the real world tempts users to assume that if they cannot see anybody, they cannot be overheard.

However, while a real-world listening device still costs a few dollars, a *Second Life* listening device costs mere cents and it can clone itself to keep watch on thousands of avatars at the same time. We have illustrated a few particularly cost-effective methods for gathering information on avatars from a virtual environment in this paper.

But any organisation collecting such data must consider the legality of its actions. In Germany, most of the methods described above would *probably* be deemed illegal, especially when executed anonymously. Note however, that the situation becomes legally much more involved when several countries are involved, e. g. if an Australian logs onto an US-American gameserver to gather information on an Italian user.

References

1. Toavs, D.: Emerging Media: Its Effect on Organizations. Talk at DNI Open Source Conference (2008), `http://blog.wired.com/defense/files/OSC-TOAVS.ppt`
2. Chinese gamer sentenced to life, `http://news.bbc.co.uk/1/hi/technology/4072704.stm`
3. MDY v. Blizzard, `http://virtuallyblind.com/category/active-lawsuits/mdy-v-blizzard/`
4. Inside Club Penguin and its Child Safety Program (PlayNoEvil Game Security News & Analysis), `http://playnoevil.com/serendipity/index.php?/archives/1461-FEATURE-ARTICLE-Inside-Club-Penguin-and-its-Child-Safety-Program.html`
5. Dodds, C.: Avatars and the Invisible Omniscience: The panoptical model within virtual worlds. RMIT University (2007), `http://iconinc.com.au/christo/C.Dodds_Exegesis.pdf`
6. Chevalier Encryption HUD, `http://www.xstreetsl.com/modules.php?name=Marketplace&file=item&ItemID=385445&affiliate=10824e9e2587b0d00069c4efba3212`
7. Warren, S.D., Brandeis, L.D.: The Right to Privacy (1890), `http://groups.csail.mit.edu/mac/classes/6.805/articles/privacy/Privacy_brand_warr2.html`
8. Directive 95/46/EC of the European Parliament and of the Council of 24 October 1995 on the protection of individuals with regard to the processing of personal data and on the free movement of such data, `http://eur-lex.europa.eu/LexUriServ/LexUriServ.do?uri=CELEX:31995L0046:EN:HTML`
9. Blizzard Privacy Policy, `http://www.worldofwarcraft.com/legal/`

Author Index

.